# 기초를 잡아주는 영작문

정용권 저

형설출판사

# 머리말

Preface

영어작문은 영어공부의 완성단계이다. 간단한 영어문장을 하나 쓰기 위해서는 우리가 잘 깨닫지 못하는 영어문장과 관련된 다량의 정보를 먼저 가지고 있어야 한다. 이 정보를 많이 가지고 있을수록 그만큼 더 좋은 문장을 쓸 수 있다.

이 책은 필자가 대학에서 영어작문 강의를 하면서 학생들로부터 좀 더 기초를 잘 설명해 주는 쉽게 쓰인 책은 없는가 하는 질문을 종종 받고 이들의 욕구를 충족시키기 위해 쓰게 된 것이다. 따라서 이 책은 영어작문을 효과적으로 공부하기 위해 반드시 알아두어야 할 기본적인 사실들을 자세하게 다루고 있다. 뿐만 아니라 영어작문에 상당히 자신감을 가지고 있는 학습자들이 공통적으로 가지고 있는 문제점을 해결하여 작문능력이 완성단계에 이르도록 구성하였다.

영어작문에 관한 책은 종류가 다양하고 나름대로 특징이 있다. 그러나 많은 책들이 지엽적인 문제에 치중하여 단어나 숙어를 문장 내에 적당히 집어넣으면 작문이 되는 것처럼 기술하고 있다. 이러한 방법은 영어문장에 대한 올바른 이해에 이르지 못하여 결국 작문을 효과적으로 할 수 없게 만든다. 이러한 문제점을 극복하기 위해 이 책에서는 문장의 구성 원리에 대한 명확한 이해를 한 후 작문의 요령을 자연스럽게 터득하도록 하였다. 이를 위한 이 책의 구성은 다음과 같다.

매 장마다 작문에 들어가기에 앞서 문장의 구조와 관련된 충분한 사전지식을 습득하도록 하기 위해 〈기본개념〉을 두고 있다. 이어서 〈기본연습〉에서 정문과 비문을 구별할 수 있는 기초적인 능력의 배양에 초점을 맞추고 이를 기초로 〈심화연습〉에서는 좀 더 구별하기 어려운 문장의 문법성을 판단할 수 있는 고차원의 능력의 배양에 중점을 두었다. 기본개념에서 습득한 문장 구조와 관련된 지식과 연습문제를 푸는 동안 생긴 문법성 판단능력이 〈기본영작〉을 하는 동안 자연스럽게 적용되도록 구성하였다. 〈심화영작〉에서는 한국어 원문의 의미를 크게 해치지 않으면서 다양한 영문으로 작문하는 방법을 자연스럽게 터득할 수 있게 하였다.

무엇보다도, 필자는 기존의 다른 영어작문 책에서 쉽게 찾아볼 수 없는 많은 영어예문을 제시함으로써, 독자가 잘못 생각하기 쉬운 하나의 한국어문장은 하나의 영어문장으로 바뀐다는 잘못된 생각을 없애기 위해 특히 노력하였다. 이제 영어작문을 잘하고 못하고는 영어작문에 대한 독자의 끊임없는 관심과 인내심에 의해 결정될 것이다. 노력하지 않고 영어작문을 잘하기를 바란다면 물과 영양분을 주지 않고 꽃이 피기를 바라는 것과 다름없다. 따라서 필자는 이 책으로 공부하는 독자가 모두 아름다운 영작의 꽃을 피우기를 기대한다.

끝으로 이 책의 영문 부분을 꼼꼼하게 살펴보고 교정해 주신 원어민 그리고 항상 많은 관심과 사랑을 보여주신 주위의 여러분들과 이 책이 나오기까지 수고를 아끼지 않으신 형설출판사 관계자 분들께 깊은 감사의 뜻을 전한다.

English Composition for Strong Foundations

# 차 례

Contents

## 해설 및 정답

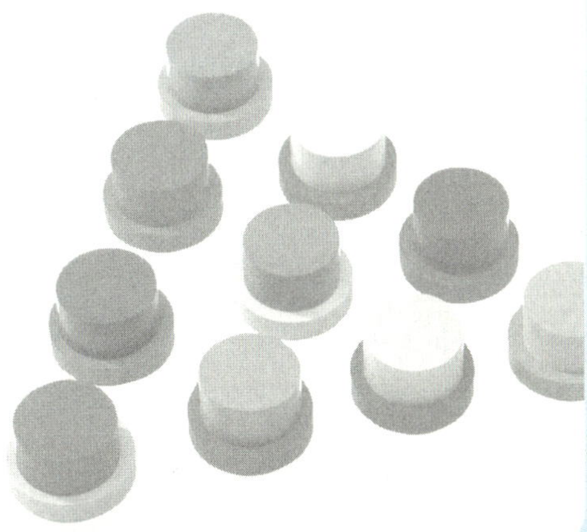

# 제1장 · 단어와 구

## Ⅰ. 기본개념

### 1. 단어와 구란?

단어란 문장을 구성하고 있는 개개의 구성요소로 이것은 더 큰 단위인 구를 만들고 구가 모여서 절을 만든다. 구란 보통 하나의 단어나 하나 이상의 단어로 된 구성요소를 가리킨다.

[The] [evenings] [have] [turned] [very] [cool] [just] [recently].
단어 단어 단어 단어 단어 단어 단어 단어

[The evenings] [have turned] [very cool] [just recently].
명사구 동사구 형용사구 부사구

[I] [have been studying] [English composition] [for two years].
명사구 동사구 명사구 전치사구

### 2. 구의 문장 내 위치

#### A. 명사구

a. [Tom] works hard.

b. [He] is [a student].

c. [He] likes [driving] to [his school].

d. [Mary] gave [him] [a fountain pen].

e. [She] has made [the boy] [a diligent student].

### B. 동사구

a. I [walk] every morning.

b. I [am walking] now.

c. I [have been walking] for an hour.

### C. 형용사구

a. The student is [clever].

b. He is [very clever].

### D. 부사구

a. Da-Bin studies French [hard].

b. She studies English [very hard].

### E. 전치사구

a. Mr. Lee runs [to his school].

b. He goes [to school] [on foot].

## Ⅱ. 기본연습

※ 다음 중 어법이 잘못된 곳을 찾아 고쳐 쓰시오.

1. We are running since two hours ago.

   ________________________________.

2. She usually drives her car very careless.

   ________________________________.

3. I trust you because you and I are friend.

________________________________________.

4. I am glad to hear that you are very happily.

________________________________________.

5. She has just been finished washing her hair.

________________________________________.

6. She is looking forward to receive your e-mail.

________________________________________.

7. Between you and I, he is out of his mind today.

________________________________________.

8. I met foreigner on my way to school and addressed him.

________________________________________.

9. They started very cheerful to see the sunrise near the sea.

________________________________________.

10. He promised his girlfriend that he would make her very happily.

________________________________________.

## 정답 및 해설

### II. 기본연습

1. are running → have been running

두 시간 전부터 지금까지 달리고 있는 중이면 과거와 현재가 연관되어 있을 뿐만 아니라 현재에도 여전히 달리는 행위가 진행 중이므로 현재완료진행시제가 되어야 한다.

2. careless → carelessly

'자동차를 조심스럽게 운전하다'는 동사 drive를 수식하는 부사가 필요하므로 형용사 대신 부사를 써야 한다.

3. friend → friends

be동사 뒤는 형용사구나 명사구가 보어로 와야 한다. 명사 friend는 셀 수 있는 명사로 앞에 한정사도 없고 복수형도 아니어서 명사구가 아니므로 보어가 될 수 없다. 따라서 복수형이 되어야 일반적인 의미의 '친구'가 된다.

4. happily → happy

be동사 뒤는 보어가 와야 하므로 보어인 명사구나 형용사구가 와야 한다. 따라서 부사를 형용사로 바꾸어야 한다.

5. been finished → finished

동사 finish는 '~을 끝내다'는 의미를 가진 타동사이므로 뒤에 목적어인 명사구가 바로 나온다. 목적어가 이 동사의 주어자리로 이동하지 않았으므로 수동태가 될 수 없다.

6. receive → receiving

look forward to의 to는 to-부정사의 to가 아니라 전치사의 to이다. 따라서 전치사 뒤는 전치사의 목적어인 명사구가 와야 하므로 동사는 동명사가 된다.

7. I → me

전치사 between 뒤는 전치사에 의해 목적격이 주어지는 자리이다. 따라서 이 자리에 오는 명사구는 목적격을 가지게 되므로 인칭대명사는 목적격으로 와야 한다. 여기서 you는 주격이 아니라 목적격이다.

8. foreigner → a foreigner

타동사 meet 뒤는 목적어인 명사구가 와야 한다. 셀 수 있는 명사 foreigner는 앞에 한정사가 붙지 않은 단수형으로는 명사구가 될 수 없으므로 앞에 부정관사를 두어야 '한 외국인'을 의미하는 명사구가 된다.

9. cheerful → cheerfully

동사 start는 자동사이며 뒤에 명사구 보어나 형용사구 보어가 반드시 오기를 요구하는 동사도 아니다. 이것을 수식하는 부사는 뒤에 올 수 있다.

10. happily → happy

타동사 make는 '~을 ~하게 하다'는 의미를 전할 때 뒤에 목적어인 명사구와 목적보어인 명사구나 형용사구가 오기를 요구한다. 따라서 make 뒤의 her가 목적어이므로 그 뒤에 목적보어인 형용사구가 와야 한다.

## Ⅲ. 심화연습

※ 다음 영작 중 비문을 고르고 그 이유를 설명하시오.

1. 그 자동차는 승차감이 매우 좋다.

a. The car rides very smoothly.

b. The car has a very smooth ride.

c. You will feel comfortable in the car.

d. You may feel comfortably in the car.

정답 : ________

이유 : ______________________________________________.

2. 날씨가 흐려서 마음이 좀 울적하다.

a. It is cloudy, so I feel a bit depressed.

b. A cloudy weather makes me a bit gloomy.

c. I feel a bit sad because of the cloudy weather.

d. The cloudy weather makes me feel a bit depressed.

정답 : ________

이유 : ______________________________________________.

3. 아직은 매미우는 소리를 들을 수 없다.

a. Cicadas are not singing yet.

b. You cannot hear cicadas sing yet.

c. It's too early to hear cicadas sing.

d. It is impossible for you to hear cicada sing yet.

정답 : ________

이유 : ______________________________________________.

4. 게으르면 너의 목표를 달성할 수 없다.

a. You may not attain your goal if you are lazy.

b. Idleness may prevent you from attain your goal.

c. Your goal may not be attained if you idle about.

d. You should not be lazy if you want to attain your goal.

정답 : ________

이유 : ______________________________________________________________.

5. 적게 먹으면 체중이 좀 줄게 될 것이다.

a. Eat less, and you will lose some weight.

b. If you eat less, you will lose some weight.

c. You can take off some weight by eating less.

d. Light meal will be helpful in reducing your weight more or less.

정답 : ________

이유 : ______________________________________________________________.

6. 아침 일찍 일어나면 하루가 길게 느껴진다.

a. An early riser is apt to feel a day longer.

b. Get up early, and you will feel a day longer.

c. The length of a day tend to be longer to an early riser.

d. When you get up early in the morning, you will feel a day longer.

정답 : ________

이유 : ______________________________________________________________.

7. 비를 맞고 장미가 더 싱싱하고 아름다워졌다.

a. After the rain, the roses became fresher and more beautiful.

b. The roses were exposed to rain, and became fresher and more beautiful.

c. The roses got wet in the rain, and looked fresher and more beautiful.

d. It rained and the roses got wet. It looked fresher and more beautiful.

정답 : ________

이유 : ______________________________________________________________.

8. 토요일은 좀 시간의 여유를 느껴보는 것도 좋다.

a. It is not bad to feel free on Saturdays.

b. You should have leisure hour on Saturdays.

c. You need to have some leisure on Saturdays.

d. It is good to have some leisure time on Saturdays.

정답 : ________

이유 : ________________________________________________.

9. 건강을 유지하려면 식사를 거르지 말아야 한다.

a. Skipping meals may injure your health.

b. One should not skip one's meals to keep in shape.

c. You'd better not to skip your meals if you want to stay healthy.

d. It is important not to skip your meals if you want to keep your health.

정답 : ________

이유 : ________________________________________________.

10. 나는 자두 한 개를 깨물었는데 약간 신맛이 났다.

a. I bit a plum and it tasted a little sour.

b. As soon as I bit a plum, I felt its sour taste.

c. I bit a plum and immediately found a little sour.

d. On biting a plum, I could feel its somewhat sour taste.

정답 : ________

이유 : ________________________________________________.

## Ⅳ. 기본영작

※ 다음을 영작하시오.

1. 꽃은 모두 아름답다. (a flower; beautiful)

______________________________________________.

2. 어제는 공휴일이었지만 오늘은 아니다. (a holiday)

______________________________________________.

3. 그는 추리소설을 읽고 있는 중이다. (a mystery novel)

______________________________________________.

4. 내 친구는 어제 새 컴퓨터를 한 대 샀다. (a computer)

______________________________________________.

5. 그는 저녁 식사 후 산책하러 갔다. (dinner; go for a walk)

______________________________________________.

6. 그녀는 고향에서 막 상경했다. (come up to; one's hometown)

______________________________________________.

7. 나는 수업에 늦지 않으려고 빨리 걸었다. (walk; late for class)

______________________________________________.

8. 그와 나는 같은 고등학교에 다녔다. (the same; go to high school)

______________________________________________.

9. 나는 학생이고 나의 아내는 회사원이다. (a student; an office worker)

______________________________________________.

10. 그는 열일곱 살이고 그의 여동생은 열 세 살이다. (one's younger sister)

______________________________________________.

## V. 심화영작

1. 다음을 영작하시오.

(1) 사흘 동안 계속 비가 내리고 있다. (for; rain)

____________________________________________________.

(2) 그는 부산에 살고 나는 서울에 산다. (live in)

____________________________________________________.

(3) 그는 책을 한 권 들고 학교로 갔다. (with; go to school)

____________________________________________________.

(4) 많이 걸으면 건강에 좋다고 한다. (walk a lot; healthy; hear)

____________________________________________________.

(5) 날씨가 더워 그는 샌들을 신고 외출했다. (hot; wear sandals)

____________________________________________________.

(6) 그녀는 아침 일찍 일어나 조깅하러 갔다. (get up; go jogging)

____________________________________________________.

(7) 내가 역에 도착하자 기차는 이미 떠나고 없었다. (get to; a train)

____________________________________________________.

(8) 커피 한 잔이 생활의 활력소가 되기도 한다. (a cup of coffee; vitality)

____________________________________________________.

(9) 영작을 잘 하면 영어회화도 잘 할 수 있다.
(English composition; good at)

____________________________________________________.

(10) 나는 철수이고 이 사람은 나의 외국인 친구 메리이다.
(one's foreign friend)

____________________________________________________.

2. 다음을 주어진 표현으로 시작하여 영작하시오.

(1) 소나기가 와서 그는 외출하지 않았다. (go out)

a. It ________________________________________.

b. He ________________________________________.

c. The sudden shower ________________________________________.

d. Because ________________________________________.

(2) 그는 자동차를 사고 난 후 걷는 시간이 좀 줄었다. (walk less)

a. After buying ________________________________________.

b. Now that ________________________________________.

c. He ________________________________________.

d. The car ________________________________________.

(3) 규칙적인 운동을 하면 아름다운 몸매를 유지할 수 있다. (stay fit)

a. You ________________________________________.

b. Exercising regularly ________________________________________.

c. Through ________________________________________.

d. Regular exercise ________________________________________.

(4) 자신이 하는 일을 즐겨야 그 분야의 달인이 될 수 있다. (be the best)

a. You ________________________________________.

b. Without ________________________________________.

c. Loving ________________________________________.

d. If ________________________________________.

(5) 칠월 말부터 며칠 동안 여름휴가를 떠나려고 한다. (leave; the end of)

a. My summer vacation ________________________________________.

b. At ________________________________________.

c. It ________________________________________.

d. I ________________________________________.

# 제2장 · 절

## Ⅰ. 기본개념

### 1. 절이란?

절이란 주어와 술부를 포함하고 있는 일단의 단어들을 가리키며 절은 주절과 종속절이라는 두 종류가 있다. 주절은 독립적으로 주장을 하고 문장으로서 홀로 설 수 있는 절을 말하며, 종속절은 문장 내의 어떤 다른 요소에 의존하는 절로 명사·형용사·부사로서의 기능을 하며 홀로 설 수 없다.

#### A. 주 절

a. [The sun shone], and [the birds sang].

b. [The sun rose], and [he got up].

#### B. 종속절

a. [When the sun shone], the birds sang.

b. [After the sun rose], he got up.

## 2. 절의 종류

### A. 명사절

명사로서의 기능을 하며 주어·서술명사·동사나 전치사의 목적어로 쓰인다. 일반적으로 문장에서 명사구가 오는 자리에 온다.

(A) That-절

a. [That she is honest] is doubtful.

b. It is doubtful [that she is honest].

c. His belief is [that she is honest].

d. He believes [that she is honest].

e. He has told me [that she is honest].

f. *He has made [that she is honest] clear. 별표(*)는 비문을 나타낸다.

f.′ He has made it clear [that she is honest].

g. She is honest in [that she has never cheated in the examination].

(B) What-절

a. [What he wants] is a good job.

b. A good job is [what he wants].

c. She knows [what he wants].

d. She has given him [what he wants].

e. *He has made [what he wants] clear.

e.′ He has made it clear [what he wants].

f. I am not interested in [what he wants].

(C) Where-절

a. This is [where he grew up].

b. She knows [where he grew up].

c. He has told her [where he grew up].

d. *He has made [where he grew up] clear.

d.′ He has made it clear [where he grew up].

e. I have no interest in [where he grew up].

### B. 형용사절

명사나 대명사를 수식하는 형용사로서의 역할을 한다. 관계대명사가 이끄는 관계절과 관계부사가 이끄는 관계절이 있으며 문장에서 자신이 수식할 명사나 대명사의 뒤에 온다.

(A) 관계대명사절

a. This is the boy [who broke the window].

b. That is the girl [whose father is very rich].

c. She has a boyfriend [whom she loves very much].

(B) 관계부사절

a. That is the time [when the Korean War broke out].

b. This is the place [where I was born].

c. That is the reason [why I didn't answer the phone].

### C. 부사절

동사·형용사·부사나 문장 전체를 수식하는 부사로서의 기능을 하며 문장에서 이들을 수식하는 부사가 오는 위치에 온다. 종속접속사가 이끄는 that-절, when-절, than-절, while-절, because-절, for-절, as-절, since-절, after-절, before-절, though-절과 같은 것이 있다.

(A) That-절

I am glad [that you have come].

(B) When-절

a. The baby cried [when a stranger appeared].

b. [When a stranger appeared], the baby cried.

(C) Than-절

He reads the book more quickly [than you do].

(D) While-절

a. A burglar broke into her house [while she was away on vacation].

b. [While she was away on vacation], a burglar broke into her house.

(E) Because-절

a. I came here [because I wanted to see you].

b. [Because I wanted to see you], I came here.

## Ⅱ. 기본연습

※ 다음 중 어법이 잘못된 곳을 찾아 고쳐 쓰시오.

1. This is where I was born in.

   ______________________.

2. I am not interested in that he wants.

   ______________________.

3. When you will leave, please close the door.

   ______________________.

4. The U.S.A. is the country we made the treaty.

   ______________________.

5. Mary thinks that she will marry Tom possible.

   ______________________.

6. She has made where she picked up the valuables clear.

   ______________________.

7. The man, that was watching the road, saw the accident.

   ______________________.

8. He invited only the people whom he said were his friends.

   ______________________.

9. Both I wanted to study English hard and I really studied it hard.

   ______________________.

10. She was unwilling to testify, she was afraid of the accused man.

    ______________________.

## 정답 및 해설

### II. 기본연습

1. in → Ø

관계부사 where 뒤는 완전한 절이 나와야 하므로 전치사 in이 없어야 한다.

2. that → what

일반적으로 전치사 뒤에 that-절은 오지 않지만 의문사로 시작되는 간접의문문을 나타내는 명사절은 올 수 있다. 따라서 의문대명사 what으로 시작하는 간접의문문의 형식이 되어야 한다.

3. will leave → leave

때나 조건을 나타내는 부사절에서는 미래시제를 현재시제가 대신한다. 따라서 미래시제 will leave 대신 현재시제 leave를 써야 한다.

4. the treaty → the treaty with

관계대명사 that이 the country와 we 사이에 생략되어 있다. 따라서 we 이하는 '우리가 그 협정을 맺은'이라는 의미로 the country를 수식하는 형용사절이 되어야 하므로 the country를 목적어로 가진 전치사 with가 필요하다.

5. that she will marry Tom possible → it possible that she will marry Tom

동사 think는 '~를 ~하다고 생각하다'는 의미를 전할 때 뒤에 목적어인 명사구가 오고 그 뒤에 목적보어가 온다. 그러나 목적어가 that-절처럼 긴 명사절일 때는 이것을 가목적어 it으로 두고 자신은 목적보어 뒤에 와야 한다.

6. where~clear → it clear where she picked up the valuables

동사 make는 '~를 분명히 하다'는 의미를 전할 때 뒤에 목적어와 목적보어가 나온다. 그러나 목적어가 'where~valuables'처럼 긴 명사절일 때는 이것을 가목적어 it으로 두고 진목적어인 명사절은 목적보어 뒤에 와야 한다.

7. that → who

관계대명사 that은 선행사가 사람인 경우와 사물인 경우 모두 주격과 목적격으로 쓰인다. 그러나 관계대명사 앞에 쉼표가 있는 계속적 용법에는 쓰이지 않는다. 선행사가 사람이고 주격이므로 who가 된다.

8. whom → who

관계대명사의 선행사 the people이 타동사 said의 목적어가 아니라 동사 were의 주어이다. he said는 삽입절이다. 따라서 선행사가 사람이고 동사의 주어이므로 목적격 관계대명사가 아니라 주격 관계대명사가 되어야 한다.

9. Both → Ø

'둘 다 ~하다'는 의미의 상관접속사 both~and는 구와 구를 연결하지만 완전한 두 개의 절을 연결하는 데 쓰지는 않는다.

10. ~testify, she~. → ~testify, for she~. ~testify, she~. → ~testify; she~. She~testify, she~ → She~testify. She was~man, She~testify, she~ → Because she~the accused man, she~testify.

보통 둘 이상의 절이 접속사 없이 콤마에 의해 연결될 수 없다. 뒤의 절은 앞 절에 대한 이유로 이유를 나타내는 접속사 for나 because로 두 절을 연결하거나 세미콜론(;)으로 연결할 수도 있고 각각의 절로 분리할 수도 있다.

## Ⅲ. 심화연습

※ 다음 영작 중 비문을 고르고 그 이유를 설명하시오.

1. 아침식사를 못했더니 벌써 배가 고프다.

a. I skipped breakfast, and I already feel hungry.

b. I didn't have breakfast, so I am already hungry.

c. I already feel hungry because I skipped breakfast.

d. I skipped breakfast; therefore, I already am hungry.

정답 : ________

이유 : ________________________________________________.

2. 일찍 자고 일찍 일어나는 것이 건강에 좋다.

a. Keeping early hours is good for your health.

b. One should keep early hours to preserve one's health.

c. To stay health, you should get up early and go to bed early.

d. It is good for your health to get up early and go to bed early.

정답 : ________

이유 : ________________________________________________.

3. 나도 네가 어제 만난 그 외국인을 알고 있다.

a. I know the foreigner you met yesterday.

b. Yesterday you met a foreigner, whom I know.

c. The foreigner that you met yesterday is the one that I know.

d. The foreigner that you have met yesterday is someone I know.

정답 : ________

이유 : ____________________________________________________________.

4. 노래도 많이 불러봐야 잘 부를 수 있는 것 같다.

a. We may sing well after we practice a lot.

b. You may not sing well until you practice singing a great deal.

c. It seems to me that we can sing well after we have sung a lot.

d. Lots of singing practice seem to be indispensable to a good singer.

정답 : ________

이유 : ____________________________________________________________.

5. 피곤할 때는 빨리 쉬는 것이 너의 건강에 좋다.

a. When you feel tired, it's important to take a healthy rest.

b. You'd better take a rest for your health as soon as you feel tired.

c. Taking a rest at once is the best thing for your health when you feel tired.

d. When you are tired, the best thing you to do immediately is to take a rest.

정답 : ________

이유 : ____________________________________________________________.

6. 나는 나의 여자 친구가 진실하기 때문에 좋아한다.

a. I like my girlfriend because she is true.

b. My girlfriend is true, which is why I like her.

c. It is since she is true that I like my girlfriend.

d. It makes me like my girlfriend that she is true.

정답 : ________

이유 : ____________________________________________________________.

7. 그 소녀는 그가 정직하다는 사실을 높이 평가한다.

a. The girl thinks highly of his honesty.

b. The girl sets a high value on his honesty.

c. His honesty is thought highly of by the girl.

d. He is honest, what is thought highly of by the girl.

정답 : ________

이유 : ________________________________________________________________.

8. 거미는 먹이를 얻기 위해 거미줄을 쳐 놓고 기다린다.

a. Spiders spin webs in advance, waiting for their prey.

b. A spider weaves its web, and then waits for its prey.

c. To catch prey, a spider spins its web first, and then waits for it.

d. After they have finished to weave their webs, spiders wait for prey.

정답 : ________

이유 : ________________________________________________________________.

9. 네가 결혼했는지 아닌지는 나에게 중요한 것이 아니다.

a. I am not interested in whether you are married or not.

b. It doesn't matter to me whether you are married or not.

c. I don't have any interest in whether you are married or not.

d. It's not important thing to me whether you are married or not.

정답 : ________

이유 : ________________________________________________________________.

10. 나는 푸른 치마와 흰 블라우스를 입고 있는 여성을 좋아한다.

a. I like women in blue skirts and white blouses.

b. I like women to wear blue skirts and white blouses.

c. I think blue skirts and white blouses go well with women.

d. It seems to me that a woman looks better in blue skirt and white blouse.

정답 : ________

이유 : ________________________________________________________________.

## Ⅳ. 기본영작

※ 다음을 영작하시오.

1. 그의 방은 멀리 산이 바라다 보인다. (look out to)

______________________________________________________________.

2. 이 비 그치면 나뭇잎이 더 생기를 띠겠지. (after this rain; vivid)

______________________________________________________________.

3. 일이 끝나고 생맥주 한 잔 하는 게 어때? (after work; draft beer)

______________________________________________________________.

4. 나는 그가 언제 거짓말을 그만 할지 모르겠다. (stop lying; know)

______________________________________________________________.

5. 노력하면 누구나 영작을 잘 할 수 있다. (make efforts; be good at)

______________________________________________________________.

6. 그는 몸이 녹초가 될 때까지 열심히 일한다. (become exhausted; hard)

______________________________________________________________.

7. 그는 반에서 가장 열심히 공부하는 학생이다. (in the class; the hardest)

______________________________________________________________.

8. 너는 긴 머리 짧은 치마의 그 여성을 알고 있느냐? (a short skirt; with)

______________________________________________________________.

9. 그는 그녀의 마음을 얻기 위해 장미 백 송이를 주었다. (win one's heart)

______________________________________________________________.

10. 네가 옳은지 그른지는 시간을 두고 기다려 보아야 안다.
(right or not; time)

______________________________________________________________.

## V. 심화영작

1. 다음을 영작하시오.

(1) 그는 8 킬로미터를 달리자 약간 땀이 났다. (run; sweat)

____________________________________________.

(2) 그녀는 여러 가지 장신구를 착용하기를 좋아하는 여성이다.
(an accessory; wear)

____________________________________________.

(3) 여름에는 낮에는 덮지만 밤에는 서늘한 바람이 불어 시원하다.
(during the daytime; a breeze; cool)

____________________________________________.

(4) 그녀는 그 전화를 언제 끊어야 할지 몰랐다. (hang up a phone)

____________________________________________.

(5) 그는 공부를 하는 동안에도 음악을 즐겨 듣는다. (while; listen to)

____________________________________________.

(6) 그녀는 머리를 감고 물기가 마르기도 전에 서둘러 전철을 타러 갔다.
(wash one's hair; dry; get on the subway)

____________________________________________.

(7) 나와 내 친구는 버스를 어디에서 내려야 할 지 몰랐다. (get off a bus)

____________________________________________.

(8) 그는 아침 일찍부터 밤늦게까지 길에서 과일을 판다. (from～to～; fruit)

____________________________________________.

(9) 작은 열매가 달려있는 저 나무가 무슨 나무인지 아니? (small fruit; with)

____________________________________________.

(10) 그는 창가로 들어오는 햇살을 받으며 잠자리에서 일어났다.

(with; wake up)

_______________________________________________.

2. 다음을 주어진 표현으로 시작하여 영작하시오.

(1) 그녀는 영어를 배우기 위해 한 시간 반 동안 전철을 타고 온다.

(spend; on the subway)

a. She _______________________________________________.

b. To learn _______________________________________________.

c. Her learning English _______________________________________________.

d. It _______________________________________________.

(2) 많은 한국인들이 사업을 하러 중국으로 가고 있다. (do business)

a. Many Koreans _______________________________________________.

b. To do _______________________________________________.

c. Business _______________________________________________.

d. China _______________________________________________.

(3) 그와 그의 아내는 인터넷 채팅을 하다가 만났다. (Internet chatting)

a. He and his wife _______________________________________________.

b. He _______________________________________________.

c. Chatting _______________________________________________.

d. It _______________________________________________.

(4) 요즘은 남자나 여자 모두 날씬한 몸매를 가지고 싶어 한다.

(a slim body)

a. Nowadays, _______________________________________________.

b. Both _______________________________________________.

c. Generally, _______________________________________________.

d. Whether _______________________________________________.

(5) 그녀는 일요일마다 두 마리의 애완견을 데리고 학교에 나타난다.

(a pet dog)

a. She brings ______________________________.

b. Every Sunday, ______________________________.

c. She shows up ______________________________.

d. You ______________________________.

# 제3장 · 격

## Ⅰ. 기본개념

### 1. 격이란?

격이란 명사와 대명사가 문장에서 하는 기능을 보여주는 형태를 말하며 She gave me a week's vacation에서 주격 She는 그 대명사가 주어로 쓰이고 있다는 것을, 목적격 me는 그 대명사가 목적어라는 것을, 소유격 week's는 그 명사가 소유격이라는 것을 가리킨다.

### 2. 격의 종류

#### A. 주 격

주격이란 동사의 주어 자리에 주어지는 격으로 주절이건 종속절이건 관계 없이 시제가 있는 문장의 주어자리의 명사구에 주어지는 격이다.

(A) 문장 내 위치

a. [I] know that [he] is a very intelligent man.

b. [Tom] knows that [Mary] is very cute.

c. [They], [he and Mary], came to Korea to study Korean studies.

(B) 제약 위반

a. *Mi-Ra and [him] went to the movies.

b. *I know that [her] and he love each other.

c. *I know that they, Mira and [him], love each other.

## B. 소유격

소유격이란 명사와 대명사의 소유관계를 가리키는 것으로, 두 명사구 중 한 명사구가 다른 명사구에 속해있을 때 이 두 명사구 간에 소유격이 주어진다. 예를 들어, 나 I와 한 권의 책 a book이 있을 때 이 책이 나에게 속해 있다는 것을 가리킬 때 소유격이 주어져 my book이 된다. 대개 [the teacher's] pencil처럼 생물은 '어포스트로피 에스('s) 소유격'을 쓰고 the name [of the book]처럼 무생물은 'of-소유격'을 쓴다.

(A) 문장 내 위치

a. [Jane's] hair is blond.

a.′ I know the name [of the man who lent us the money].

b. You should follow [the government's] decision.

b.′ You should follow the decision [of the government].

c. A new newspaper appeared on [the city's] newsstands.

d. I didn't read [yesterday's] newspaper.

e. She needs [eight hours'] sleep a night.

f. The wheels [of the bicycle] are turning fast.

(B) 제약 위반

a. *The hair [of Jane] is blond.

b. *I know [the man who lent us the money's] name.

c. *She needs [eight hours's] sleep a night.

d. *This is [a my] eraser.

e. *She gave me [this my] eraser.

f. *I like [her] hairpin [of mine].

## C. 목적격

목적격이란 타동사의 뒷자리와 전치사의 뒷자리에 주어지는 격으로, 이 자리에 오는 명사구는 자동적으로 목적격을 가지게 된다.

(A) 문장 내 위치

■ 타동사의 목적어 위치

a. Laura likes [a boy] very much.

b. She likes [John] very much.

c. She meets [him] very often.

■ 전치사의 목적어 위치

a. John gave a ring to [a girl].

b. He gave a ring to [Laura].

c. He gave a ring to [her].

(B) 제약 위반

■ 타동사의 목적어 위치

a. *She likes [he] very much.

b. *She likes [their] very much.

c. *She likes [be] a student.

■ 전치사의 목적어 위치

a. *She bought an electric shaver for [he].

b. *She gave [his] an electric shaver.

c. *She is afraid of [go] abroad.

## Ⅱ. 기본연습

※ 다음 중 어법이 잘못된 곳을 찾아 고쳐 쓰시오.

1. It is said that we need an eight hours' sleep a day.

   ______________________________.

2. My friend and I decided to borrow each others' books.

   ______________________________.

3. Do you remember the man who addressed me's name?

   ______________________________.

4. They, him and Mary, came to Korea to study Korean studies.

_______________________________________________.

5. I got up late yesterday, and didn't read the newspaper of yesterday.

_______________________________________________.

6. Sun-Mi has met he, a friend of mine, and wants to go out with him.

_______________________________________________.

7. These her earrings are so cute that I feel like buying the same earrings.

_______________________________________________.

8. Young-Su forgot to bring his eraser, so he asked me to lend a my eraser.

_______________________________________________.

9. The foreigner brought some presents for her Korean friends, especially for Sun-Ah and I.

_______________________________________________.

10. She has been studying French for five years, but she's still afraid of go to France because of her poor French.

_______________________________________________.

## 정답 및 해설

### II. 기본연습

1. an → ∅

부정관사와 소유격은 모두 한정사이며 함께 나란히 나올 수 없다. 부정관사 an과 소유격 eight hours'가 나란히 나와 비문이다. '여덟 시간의 잠'은 명사 hours가 복수의 -s로 끝나고 있어 어포스트로피만 붙인다.

2. each others' → each other's

상호대명사 each other의 소유격은 each other's로 나타낸다.

3. the man who~name → the name of the man who addressed me

사람이나 동물은 원칙적으로 어포스트로피 에스('s) 소유격을 쓰지만 그 명사 자체에 딸린 수식구가 있을 때는 of-소유격을 쓴다.

4. him → he

주어와 동격관계에 있는 어구는 주어와 같은 격을 가진다. 따라서 주어 they와 동격인 him and Mary는 주격이 되어야 하므로 목적격 him은 주격이 되어야 한다. 고유명사 Mary는 여기서 주격으로 쓰인 것이다.

5. the newspaper of yesterday → yesterday's newspaper

today, yesterday와 같은 시간표현은 어포스트로피 에스('s) 소유격을 쓴다.

6. he → him

타동사 뒤는 타동사에 의해 목적격이 주어지는 자리이므로 타동사 meet 뒤의 인칭대명사의 주격 he는 목적격이 되어야 한다.

7. These her earrings → These earrings of hers

한정사인 지시사와 소유격이 나란히 나와 명사를 수식하는 구조로는 쓰일 수 없다. 따라서 지시사 these와 소유격 her가 나란히 나와 명사 earrings를 수식할 수 없기 때문에 of-소유격으로 나타낸다.

8. a my eraser → my eraser

한정사인 관사와 소유격이 나란히 나와 명사를 수식하는 구조로는 쓰일 수 없다. 따라서 부정관사 a를 빼야 한다.

9. I → me

전치사 뒤는 전치사에 의해 목적격이 주어지는 자리이다. 따라서 전치사 for 뒤의 Sun-Ah와 I는 목적격이 되어야 한다. 고유명사 Sun-Ah는 목적격으로 쓰이고 있지만 인칭대명사 I는 주격이므로 목적격이 되어야 한다.

10. go → going

전치사 뒤는 전치사의 목적어 자리이다. 따라서 동사가 올 때는 목적어가 될 수 있는 동명사의 형태로 와야 하므로 전치사 of 뒤의 동사 go는 동명사로 바뀌어야 한다.

## Ⅲ. 심화연습

※ 다음 영작 중 비문을 고르고 그 이유를 설명하시오.

1. 그는 나의 책을 그의 여자 친구에게 빌려주었다.

a. He lent my book to his girlfriend.

b. That he lent his girlfriend was my book.

c. My book was lent to his girlfriend by him.

d. His girlfriend borrowed my book from him.

정답 : ________

이유 : ________________________________________.

2. 그는 그들로부터 아무것도 받은 적이 없다고 했다.

a. He said that he had received nothing from them.

b. He said that nothing he had received from them.

c. He said, "I have never received anything from them."

d. According to him, he hadn't received anything from them.

정답 : ________

이유 : ________________________________________.

3. 그 책상 다리는 쇠가 아니라 나무로 만들어져 있다.

a. The legs of the table are made of not iron, but wood.

b. The table has legs which are made of wood, not iron.

c. The material of the legs of the table is not iron but wood.

d. The table has legs which material is made of not iron but wood.

정답 : ________

이유 : ________________________________________.

4. 내가 그녀로부터 그 책을 받으면 너에게 빌려줄게.

a. I will lend the book to you when I receive it from her.

b. As soon as I receive the book from her, I will lend it to you.

c. I have to receive the book from her before I will lend it to you.

d. First I have to receive the book from her, and then I will lend it to you.

정답 : ________

이유 : ____________________________________________.

5. 나의 한 친구는 그의 친구 한 사람을 나에게 소개했다.

a. A my friend introduced a friend of his to me.

b. One of my friends introduced one of his to me.

c. A friend of mine introduced a friend of his to me.

d. A friend of mine introduced one of his friends to me.

정답 : ________

이유 : ____________________________________________.

6. 그 제비는 자기 새끼들에게 줄 벌레를 잡아 돌아왔다.

a. To feed the young, the swallow came back with worms in the mouth.

b. In order to feed its young, the swallow caught worms and came back.

c. The swallow came back with worms in its mouth, in order to feed its young.

d. The swallow has caught worms, and came back so that it could feed its young.

정답 : ________

이유 : ____________________________________________.

7. 그 시민단체는 그 단체의 보고서를 대통령에게 제출했다.

a. The citizen's group submitted the President its report.

b. The citizen's group handed in its report to the President.

c. The President received the report from the citizen's group.

d. The President received the report handed in by the citizen's group.

정답 : ________

이유 : ____________________________________________.

8. 그녀는 사람들 앞에서 공공연히 그를 자기 남자라고 말했다.

a. She called openly him her own man.

b. She called him her own man openly.

c. The woman publicly said that he was her own man.

d. The woman said in public that he was her own man.

정답 : ________

이유 : ______________________________________________________.

9. 매일 맛있는 반찬을 만들어 먹는다는 것은 쉬운 일이 아니다.

a. It is not easy to cook delicious side dishes every day.

b. It is not easy to cook delicious side dishes all the time.

c. We have difficulty in cooking delicious side dishes to go with rice every day.

d. One may not cook delicious side dishes every day, for they are not easy to do so.

정답 : ________

이유 : ______________________________________________________.

10. 그가 잠자리에서 일어나자 창 밖에는 가랑비가 내리고 있었다.

a. As soon as he got up, he saw drizzle fallen out of the window.

b. On getting out of bed, he saw, out the window, that it was drizzling.

c. He got out of bed and saw through the window that it was drizzling.

d. When he got out of bed, he looked out the window and saw that it was drizzling.

정답 : ________

이유 : ______________________________________________________.

## Ⅳ. 기본영작

※ 다음을 영작하시오.

1. 너의 여자 친구가 너보다 키가 크다는 말이냐? (tall; mean)

______________________________________________.

2. 그와 그의 여자 친구는 주말이면 교외로 드라이브하러 간다.
(on weekends; drive to the suburbs)

______________________________________________.

3. 그녀는 갓난아이를 등에 업고 장바구니를 들고 걷고 있었다.
(with a baby on one's back; a shopping bag; walk)

______________________________________________.

4. 그는 한 회사에 이력서를 보냈지만 아무런 답장을 받지 못했다.
(a résumé; a reply; receive)

______________________________________________.

5. 우리는 우리의 수명을 무한히 연장할 수 있는가? (one's life; lengthen)

______________________________________________.

6. 모든 꽃이 아름다운 향기를 발산하는 것은 아니다. (not all~; smell good)

______________________________________________.

7. 경찰이 그 범인을 뒤쫓았지만 체포하지 못했다. (a criminal; chase; arrest)

______________________________________________.

8. 그가 떠난 후 그녀는 그에게서 어떤 소식도 듣지 못했다.
(leave; hear from)

______________________________________________.

9. 그 소녀는 미국인 친구로부터 예쁜 그림엽서를 받았다.
(a postcard; receive)

________________________________________.

10. 그는 그녀에게 사랑을 원하지만 그녀는 그에게서 돈을 원한다.
(from; while)

________________________________________.

## V. 심화영작

1. 다음을 영작하시오.

(1) 그 여자들은 모두 자신의 빨래를 빨랫줄에 내건다.
(laundry; a clothesline; hang)

________________________________________.

(2) 음식은 먹어봐야 맛을 알 수 있다. (taste food; flavor)

________________________________________.

(3) 핵가족화로 가족 구성원의 결속력이 많이 약화되어 왔다.
(a nuclear family; a family member; unity)

________________________________________.

(4) 나는 걷고 뛰고 그리고 걸으면서 주변의 경치를 구경했다.
(look at the view)

________________________________________.

(5) 높이가 얼마인지 알 수 없는 건물들이 여기저기 솟아 있다.
(with unknowable heights; a building; here and there)

________________________________________.

(6) 비가 오는 날이면 그녀는 그에게 따뜻한 부침개를 부쳐 준다.

(a warm flat cake; make)

____________________________________________________.

(7) 바람이 강한 힘으로 먹구름을 밀어내어 하늘이 다시 맑아졌다.

(dark clouds; move～away; get clear)

____________________________________________________.

(8) 그 나라의 경제는 몇 년 전부터 회복의 기미를 보이지 않고 있다.

(since; a sign of recovery; show)

____________________________________________________.

(9) 그들은 일제히 낚시를 드리웠다. (all at once; drop one's fishing rod)

____________________________________________________.

(10) 국가를 사랑해야 하는 것은 자신의 어머니를 사랑해야 하는 것과 같다.

(one; love; just as)

____________________________________________________.

2. 다음을 주어진 표현으로 시작하여 영작하시오.

(1) 컴퓨터 작업을 장시간 하면 누구나 피곤하기 마련이다.

(work on a computer; get tired)

a. It ______________________________________________.

b. Most people ________________________________________.

c. Long hours ________________________________________.

d. You ______________________________________________.

(2) 그 시위로 많은 사람들이 부상을 당해 병원으로 실려 갔다.

(be injured; be taken to a hospital)

a. Many people _______________________________________.

b. From _____________________________________________.

c. The many people _____________________________________.

d. That demonstration ___________________________________.

(3) 비가 유리창에 떨어져 굴러 내리는 모양이 보기에 재미있다.

(a glass window; fun)

a. Looking ______________________________.

b. The rolling drops of rain ______________________________.

c. It ______________________________.

d. Rain ______________________________.

(4) 그녀는 어딜 가든 항상 핸드백을 가지고 다닌다. (everywhere; take)

a. She ______________________________.

b. Wherever ______________________________.

c. A handbag ______________________________.

d. No matter ______________________________.

(5) 날씨가 더울 때는 상한 음식을 먹지 않도록 주의해야 한다.

(watch out for)

a. You ______________________________.

b. When ______________________________.

c. Spoiled food ______________________________.

d. Hot weather ______________________________.

# 제4장 · 문 장

## Ⅰ. 기본개념

### 1. 문장이란?

주어와 동사로 되어 있는 것을 절이라고 하며 문장은 하나의 절이나 여러 개의 절로 되어 있다. 단 하나의 주절로 되어 있는 문장을 단문, 둘 이상의 주절로 되어 있는 문장을 중문, 하나의 주절과 하나 이상의 종속절로 되어 있는 문장을 복문이라 한다.

#### A. 단 문

a. [It] [snowed].

b. [The boy and the girl] [quarreled].

c. [The boy] [growled and left].

d. [The boy and the girl] [growled and left].

#### B. 중 문

a. [It snowed] and [the road was slippery].

b. [I ran for a long time] and [I took a short rest].

### C. 복 문

a. [Because it snowed], [the road was slippery].

b. [After I ran for a long time], [I took a short rest].

## 2. 문장의 종류

### A. 평서문

a. Teresa usually enjoys parties very much.

b. She has been in the garden all the time since breakfast.

### B. 의문문

(A) 직접의문문

a. Is Tom married?

b. Does he have a wife?

c. What does he do?

(B) 간접의문문

a. Tell me [whether Tom is married].

a.′ *Tell me [is Tom married?]

b. Tell me [whether he has a wife].

b.′ *Tell me [does he have a wife?]

c. Tell me [what he does].

c.′ *Tell me [what does he do?]

### C. 부정문

(A) Be동사가 있는 경우

a. I am [not] a student.

b. I was [not] a teacher last year.

(B) 일반동사가 있는 경우

a. I do[n't] want to go to the party.

b. She does[n't] like to play ping-pong.

c. I did[n't] sleep well last night.

## D. 명령문

(A) 긍정 명령문

a. Put the milk in the refrigerator.

b. [Liz] answer the phone.

c. [Do] drive more carefully.

d. [Get examined] as soon as you can.

e. [Let's] go swimming.

(B) 부정 명령문

a. [Don't] be noisy.

b. [Don't] [anybody] come in.

b.′ *Anybody don't come in.

## E. 감탄문

a. How beautifully you eat!

b. What a kind man he is!

c. What beautiful weather this is!

d. What pretty flowers these are!

e. You're so kind!

f. She's such a cute girl!

f.′ They are such foolish people!

## F. 기원문

(A) 도치구문을 사용하지 않은 기원문

a. God bless you!

b. Heaven help us!

(B) 도치구문을 사용한 기원문

a. May you always be happy!

b. May you break your neck!

## 3. 정문과 비문

문장이 되기 위해서는 필요한 조건을 갖추어야 하며 이 조건을 갖춘 문장을 정문이라 하고 그렇지 않은 문장을 비문이라 한다. 정문이 되려면 다음 조건을 갖추어야 한다.

### A. 주어인 명사구와 동사구가 있어야 한다.

a. [Tom] [sings].

b. [He] [is tall].

c. [The boy] [loves a girl].

d. [He] [gave her a necklace].

e. [He] [made her happy].

### B. 동사에 따라 요구되는 그 동사의 하위요소가 충족되어야 한다.

a. Mary [talks].

a.′ *Mary [enjoys].

a.″ Mary [enjoys good health].

b. *Mary [put].

b.′ *Mary [put a book].

b.″ Mary [put a book on the desk].

### C. 문장을 구성하고 있는 각각의 구가 문법적인 구조를 가져야 한다.

(A) 명사구

a. [Tom] is an actor.

b. [He] is an actor.

c. [The boy] is an actor.

d. [His name] is Tom.

e. [This man] is Tom.

f. [All men] must do their best.

g. [All the women] are as beautiful as you.

(cf. 지시사와 양화사에 관해서는 제5장 〈I. 기본개념〉의 한정사에 관한 설명을 참조하시오.)

(B) 동사구

a. Sophie [walks].

b. She [walks very fast].

c. She [is walking her pet dog].

d. She [is walking her pet dog on the park].

e. She [has been walking her pet dog for five years].

f. She [will have been walking her pet dog for six years this time next year].

(C) 형용사구

a. She was [incredibly young].

b. She was [incredibly young enough].

c. She was [incredibly young enough to be inquisitive].

(D) 부사구

a. He spoke to her [very clearly].

b. He spoke to her [very clearly indeed].

c. He spoke to her [very clearly indeed as he could].

(E) 전치사구

a. Tom met Sophie [for dinner].

b. He met her [on Saturday evening].

c. He met her [at the corner of the street].

d. *He met her [the corner of the street at].

### D. 문장을 구성하고 있는 개개의 구는 각기 정해진 위치에서 순서에 맞게 배열되어야 한다.

a. [명사구The boy] [동사구(동사made)] [명사구his girlfriend] [형용사구 very happy].

b. *[The boy] [his girlfriend] [made] [very happy].

c. *[His girlfriend] [the boy] [made] [very happy].

d. *[Made] [the boy] [his girlfriend] [very happy].

e. *[Very happy] [the boy] [made] [his girlfriend].

## Ⅱ. 기본연습

※ 다음 중 어법이 잘못된 곳을 찾아 고쳐 쓰시오.

1. He sent her some books, and she lent to a friend of hers.

   ______________________________.

2. She said to me, "Is your friend have a wife and children?"

   ______________________________.

3. Let us, my girlfriend and me, to get married sooner or later.

   ______________________________.

4. The teacher asked the student whether did he know the answer.

   ______________________________.

5. The teacher asked the student whether did he know the answer.

   ______________________________.

6. His friend said to him, "You succeed in the entrance examination!"

   ______________________________.

7. The boy kissed the girl when they arrived the corner of the street at.

   ______________________________.

8. His resignation was so abruptly that his wife was at a loss what to do.

   ______________________________.

9. When I met her near the mountain, she said, "What beautiful weather is this!"

   ______________________________.

10. Clean the surfaces of the materials, put some glue on them, and then one presses them for a few minutes.

_______________________________________________.

## 정답 및 해설

### II. 기본연습

1. lent → lent them

동사 lend는 '~을 빌려주다'는 타동사이므로 뒤에 목적어인 명사구가 와야 한다. 따라서 앞에 이미 나온 명사구 some books를 대명사로 받는다.

2. Is → Does

일반동사가 있는 문장은 의문문으로 만들 때 조동사 do가 필요하다. 문장의 동사가 일반동사 have이고 주어가 3인칭 단수 your friend이므로 조동사 does가 주어 앞에 필요하다.

3. to get → get

사역동사 뒤에서는 to-부정사가 원형부정사로 와야 한다. 따라서 사역동사 let 뒤의 to-부정사 to get은 원형부정사 get이 되어야 한다.

4. did he know → he knew

간접의문문의 어순은 의문사가 앞에 오고 그 뒤에 주어와 동사가 와야 한다. 따라서 의문사 whether 뒤에 주어 he가 오고 그 뒤에 동사 knew가 온다.

5. came → came to

자동사 뒤는 목적어인 명사구가 오지 못하므로 명사구 my house가 자동사 come과 연결이 되지 않아 비문이다. 따라서 이 명사구 앞에 전치사를 두어 이 명사구가 전치사의 목적어가 되게 한다.

6. You → May you

기원문은 조동사 may를 주어 앞에 두어 만든다. 따라서 주어 you 앞에 조동사 may를 둔다.

7. the corner of the street at → at the corner of the street

전치사는 뒤에 명사구인 목적어가 오는 전치사구의 형태로 쓰여야 한다. 따라서 전치사 at이 목적어인 명사구 the corner 앞에 와야 한다.

8. abruptly → abrupt

be동사는 불완전 자동사로 그 뒤에 보어인 명사구나 형용사구가 오기를 요구한다. 따라서 부사 abruptly는 형용사구의 형태로 와야 한다.

9. is this → this is

의문사 what으로 시작되는 감탄문은 what 뒤에 오는 명사가 셀 수 없는 명사일 경우 'what + 형용사 + 명사 + 주어 + 동사'의 어순을 가진다. 따라서 주어 this가 동사 is 앞에 와야 한다.

10. one presses → press

긍정 명령문은 동사의 원형으로 나타낸다. 따라서 등위 접속사 and로 연결된 세 개의 절 모두 똑같이 동사원형으로 시작되어야 한다. clean, put, press 모두 동사원형이 되어야 한다.

## Ⅲ. 심화연습

※ 다음 영작 중 비문을 고르고 그 이유를 설명하시오.

1. 너는 너의 아버지와 얼굴이 닮았니?

a. Do you resemble your father?

b. Do you look like your father?

c. Are you much like your father?

d. Are you resembling your father?

정답 : ________

이유 : ________________________________________________________________.

2. 그는 만사를 제쳐두고 미국에 공부하러 갔다.

a. He left for the U.S. to study before anything else.

b. He went to the U.S.A. to study before everything.

c. He went to America to study at his inconvenience.

d. He left for U.S. to study, postponing all other things.

정답 : ________

이유 : ________________________________________________________________.

3. 그 회사는 주문은 많이 받지만 이윤은 별로 없다.

a. The company has many orders, but sells product at a small profit.

b. The company has lots of orders, but it doesn't make a good profit.

c. The company gets a lot of orders, but it sells its products at a small profit.

d. The company receives not a few orders; however, it does not make a good profit.

정답 : ________

이유 : ________________________________________________.

4. 이 일을 마치기 전에는 너는 외출을 해서는 안 된다.

a. First, finish this work, and then go out.

b. You can go out only after you finish this work.

c. This work should be finishing before you go out.

d. You should not go out until you finish this work.

정답 : ________

이유 : ________________________________________________.

5. 그는 팔월 초 가족들과 몇 일간의 여름휴가를 떠나려고 한다.

a. In early August, he is leaving for a summer resort and spend a few days with his family there.

b. He plans to go to a summer resort in early August and spend a few days with his family there.

c. In early August, he is to go to a summer resort with his family and spend a few days there.

d. He is spending a few days in a summer resort with his family in early August.

정답 : ________

이유 : ________________________________________________.

6. 국력이 국민의 단결력에서 나온다는 점은 잘 알려진 사실이다.

a. It is a well-known fact that national strength comes from national solidarity.

b. The strength of a nation depends on whether its people is strongly united or not. This is an undeniable fact.

c. We cannot deny fact that national strength comes out from national solidarity.

d. It is well-known that national strength lies in the solidarity of a people.

정답 : ________

이유 : ________________________________________________________________.

7. 그녀는 얼굴이 햇볕에 타지 않도록 썬크림을 바르고 외출했다.

a. She put sun cream on her face to protect it from the sun, and then went out.

b. To protect her face from the sun, she put sun cream on it and then went out.

c. She put sun cream on her face to keep it from getting sunburnt, and went out.

d. She went out after she put on sun cream on face to protect it from the sun.

정답 : ________

이유 : ________________________________________________________________.

8. 나는 그가 누구인지 모르지만 외국인이라는 것은 알 수 있다.

a. All I know about him is that he is a foreigner.

b. I don't know who is he, but I know that he is a foreigner.

c. I have no idea of who he is, but I can say that he is a foreigner.

d. I am sure that he is a foreigner, even though I don't know who he is.

정답 : ________

이유 : ________________________________________________________________.

9. 그들은 저녁식사 후 맥주 한 잔 마시고 노래방에 노래하러 갔다.

a. They drank a glass of beer after dinner, and then went to a singing room to sing.

b. They had a dinner and then drank a glass of beer. After that, they went to a singing room to sing.

c. They drank a glass of beer after they ate dinner, and then went to a singing room to sing.

d. After finishing dinner, they drank a glass of beer and then went to a singing room to sing.

정답 : ________

이유 : ________________________________________.

10. 그 노인은 언제나 자신이 소유하고 있는 건물 앞에서 서성거린다.

a. The old man habitually walks back and forth in front of his own building.

b. You can easily see the old man walking up and down in front of his own building.

c. That is easy to see the old man walking up and down in front of his own building.

d. The old man usually walks up and down in front of his own building.

정답 : ________

이유 : ________________________________________.

## Ⅳ. 기본영작

※ 다음을 영작하시오.

1. 이 아이들 참 귀엽기도 하다! (a kid; cute)

________________________________________.

2. 네가 그 전투에서 꼭 승리하기를! (a battle; win)

________________________________________.

3. 전등을 끄고 문을 잠근 후 외출해야 한다는 점을 잊지 마라.
(turn off a light; lock; be sure to)

______________________________________________.

4. 그녀는 흰 티셔츠에 분홍색 짧은 치마와 분홍색 모자를 쓰고 있다.
(a T-shirt; a short pink skirt)

______________________________________________.

5. 나는 네가 좋은데 너는 내가 싫은가 보구나. (like; dislike; seem)

______________________________________________.

6. 언제나 약속시간에 늦지 않도록 주의해라. (an appointment; punctual)

______________________________________________.

7. 비 내리는 날은 왜 막걸리를 한 잔 하고 싶은가? (a rainy day; want)

______________________________________________.

8. 그는 키가 크지도 않고 얼굴이 잘 생긴 것도 아니다. (tall; good-looking)

______________________________________________.

9. 너는 그것을 할 수 있고 나는 그것을 할 수 없다고 생각하니? (do; while)

______________________________________________.

10. 북한산에 올라가 서울 시내를 내려다 보아라.
(the whole Seoul downtown)

______________________________________________.

## V. 심화영작

1. 다음을 영작하시오.

(1) 우리가 언제쯤 산 정상에 오를 수 있을지 모르겠다.
(the mountain top; reach)

______________________________________________.

(2) 이 작은 꽃들 정말 예쁘다! (a small flower; pretty)

______________________________________________.

(3) 그녀는 운동하는 것을 좋아하지도 싫어하지도 않는다.
(exercising; neither ~ nor ~)

______________________________________________.

(4) 기어를 P 위치에 두고 브레이크를 밟은 채 시동을 걸어라.
(put ~ in P; step on the brake; start)

______________________________________________.

(5) 계속해서 앞으로 가라. 그러면 틀림없이 그 건물이 보일 것이다.
(keep ~ ing; definitely)

______________________________________________.

(6) 네가 그 입사시험에 성공하기를! (a company entrance exam; pass)

______________________________________________.

(7) 내 친구를 거기에 데리고 오는 데 대해 네가 왜 반대하는지 모르겠다.
(bring; be against)

______________________________________________.

(8) 그녀는 약간 살이 찌긴 했지만 귀여운 편이다. (plump; cute; kind of)

______________________________________________.

(9) 그는 당구를 치러 가서 아직 돌아오지 않았다.
(play billiards; come back)

______________________________________________.

(10) 그는 너의 열쇠를 본 적이 없고 나 역시 본 적이 없다.
(a key; not ~ either)

______________________________________________.

2. 다음을 주어진 표현으로 시작하여 영작하시오.

(1) 무엇 때문에 너는 거기 서 있기만 하니? (stand; just)

a. Why ______________________________________________.

b. What ________________________________________.

c. Are ________________________________________.

d. Is ________________________________________.

(2) 바람이 불어 그 나무의 꽃들이 많이 떨어졌다. (blow; fall off)

a. The tree ________________________________________.

b. The wind ________________________________________.

c. Lots of flowers ________________________________________.

d. Many of ________________________________________.

(3) 그들은 저녁식사를 끝내자마자 일제히 운동장을 돌기 시작한다.

(finish dinner; go around a playground)

a. On ________________________________________.

b. They ________________________________________.

c. The moment ________________________________________.

d. Right after ________________________________________.

(4) 그 나라의 정치적 불안정이 경제발전을 가로막고 있다. (prevent)

a. The unstable politics ________________________________________.

b. That country's development ________________________________________.

c. The country ________________________________________.

d. The country's economic development ________________________________________.

(5) 그는 머리를 너무 자주 깎아 그의 머리는 언제나 짧다.

(get a haircut; short)

a. With ________________________________________.

b. He ________________________________________.

c. Because of ________________________________________.

d. His hair ________________________________________.

# 제5장 · 주 어

## Ⅰ. 기본개념

### 1. 주어란?

주어란 한 문장이나 절의 술부가 주장을 하거나 질문을 하는 사람이나 사물을 말한다.

### 2. 주어가 될 수 있는 요소

#### A. 명사구

a. [Sun-Mi] is clever.

b. [She] is diligent.

c. [A girl] likes to study English composition.

d. [The girl] studies English composition hard.

e. [Her mother] enjoys cooking various dishes.

f. [This girl] goes a long way to learn English.

g. [All girls] like to buy new clothes.

### B. 부정사

a. [To write] a good book is not easy.

a.′ [It] is not easy [to write] a good book.

b. For my friend [to go] there is nearly impossible.

b.′ [It] is nearly impossible for my friend [to go] there.

### C. 동명사

a. [Singing] popular songs is his hobby.

b. His [singing] popular songs makes his friends glad.

### D. 명사절

a. [That she is ambitious] is not known to her friends.

a.′ [It] is not known to her friends [that she is ambitious].

b. [When they will come], is the question.

c. [Where they went] does not matter.

d. [How you divide up the money] is your business.

e. [Why she married him] remains a mystery.

f. [Whether I can rely on her] is another matter.

g. [What she needs most] is a new car.

## 3. 한정사와 명사

한정사란 명사구의 첫머리에 오지만 형용사는 아닌 관사, 소유격, 지시사, 양화사를 말한다.

| | | | |
|---|---|---|---|
| **[a]/[the]**<br>관사 | [beautiful] | [young] | [woman] |
| **[my]**<br>소유격 | [beautiful] | [young] | [woman] |
| **[this]**<br>지시사 | [beautiful] | [young] | [woman] |
| **[some]**<br>양화사 | [beautiful] | [young] | [women] |
| 한정사 | 형용사 | 형용사 | 명사 = 명사구 |

## 4. 한정사의 종류

### A. 관 사

(A) 부정관사 : a/an

셀 수 있는 명사의 단수형 앞에 놓여 어떤 지시대상의 하나를 가리킨다.

[a] pencil (연필 하나), [a] student (한 학생), [an] apple (사과 한 개), [an] hour (한 시간)

(B) 정관사 : the

화자나 글을 쓰는 사람이 자기가 가리키는 지시대상이 어느 것을 가리키는지 그의 청자나 독자도 알고 있다고 보고 말을 하거나 글을 쓸 때 그 셀 수 있는 명사나 셀 수 없는 명사 앞에 붙인다.

[the] eraser (그 지우개), [the] erasers (그 지우개들), [the] professor (그 교수), [the] professors (그 교수들), [the] sugar (그 설탕), [the] salt (그 소금), [the] wheat (그 밀)

### B. 소유격: Tom's, the scientist's, her, ...

명사나 대명사의 소유를 나타낼 때 명사 앞에 붙인다.

[Sophia's] car (소피아의 자동차), [the teacher's] ball-pen (그 선생의 볼펜), [the teachers'] books (그 선생들의 책들), [my] book (나의 책)

### C. 지시사: this, that, these, those

셀 수 있는 명사와 셀 수 없는 명사 앞에 놓여 그 명사가 어느 것을 가리키는지 나타낸다.

[this] novel (이 소설), [these] novels (이 소설들), [that] teacher (저 선생), [those] teachers (저 선생들), [this] water (이 물), [that] salt (저 소금)

### D. 양화사: some, any, no, little, a little, few, a few, much, many, every, each, other, a lot of, lots of, ...

셀 수 있는 명사 앞에 놓여 그 지시대상의 수를 가리키거나 셀 수 없는 명사 앞에 놓여 그 지시대상의 양을 나타내는 말이다.

[some] foreigners (몇 명의 외국인들), [some] water (약간의 물), [many] nurses (많은 간호사들), [much] salt (많은 소금)

## 5. 명사구의 의미

a. a daughter (한 명의 딸)

b. the daughter [그 딸(한 명)]

c. the daughters (그 딸들)

d. the water (그 물)

e. my daughter [나의 딸(한 명)]

f. my daughters (나의 딸들)

g. this daughter [이 딸(한 명)], that daughter [저 딸(한 명)]

h. these daughters (이 딸들)

i. any daughter [어떤 딸이건 간에 딸(한 명)], no daughter (어떤 딸도 ~ 아니다), each daughter (각각의 딸, 개개의 것에 초점), every daughter (모든 딸, 전체에 초점)

j. some daughters (몇 명의 딸들), any daughters (어느 딸이건 간에 딸들), a lot of daughters (많은 딸들)

k. any water (어떤 물이건 간에 물), no water (어떤 물도 ~아니다), much water (많은 물)

l. daughters (일반적인 의미의 딸, 분류상의 개념으로서의 딸)

m. water (일반적인 의미의 물, 분류상의 개념으로서의 물)

## 6. 주어자리에서의 위반

일반적으로 주어는 명사구가 되어야 하므로 명사구의 자격이 없는 표현이 오면 비문이 된다.

### A. 주어가 셀 수 있는 명사인 경우

a. [A boy] loves a girl.

b. [The boy] loves a girl.

c. [My boy] loves a girl.

d. [This boy] loves a girl.

e. [No boy] loves the girl.

f. [Boys] are apt to fall in love with girls.

g. *[Boy] loves a girl.

### B. 주어가 셀 수 없는 명사인 경우

a. *[A water] is what he needs.

b. [The water] is what he needs.

c. [My water] is what he needs.

d. [This water] is what he needs.

e. [No water] is indispensable to the experiment.

f. *[Waters] are drunk when you feel thirty.

g. [Water] is necessary to the life of living things.

## Ⅱ. 기본연습

※ 다음 중 어법이 잘못된 곳을 찾아 고쳐 쓰시오.

1. I felt very thirsty, and a water was what I wanted most.

   ______________________________________________.

2. They drove for the sea, and every boys had their own girls.

   ______________________________________________.

3. The soup was too salty to eat, so some sugars were needed.

   ______________________________________________.

4. There were lots of people; therefore, many water was needed.

   ______________________________________________.

5. Beautiful this young woman always remained my girl in my heart.

   ______________________________________________.

6. Professors do not always demand that their student submit reports.

   ______________________________________________.

7. That is not easy for all of us to become patriots, but we can try to.

______________________________________________.

8. The woman's singing popular songs make her male friends very glad.

______________________________________________.

9. All kind of music interest him, but he usually have little time to listen to music.

______________________________________________.

10. I saw a boy and a girl on the subway train. It seemed to me that boy loved the girl.

______________________________________________.

## 정답 및 해설

### II. 기본연습

1. a → ∅

셀 수 없는 명사 앞에는 부정관사가 붙을 수 없다. 따라서 물 water는 셀 수 없는 명사이므로 부정관사 a와 함께 쓰일 수 없다.

2. every boys had their own girls→ every boy had his own girl

명사 앞에 놓여 명사의 수를 나타내는 양화사인 every는 뒤에 셀 수 있는 명사가 단수형으로 와야 한다.

또한 이것과 함께 쓰인 셀 수 있는 명사의 단수형은 단수취급을 한다. 따라서 every boy는 대명사 he로 받는다.

3. sugars were → sugar was

셀 수 없는 명사는 수가 아닌 양의 개념으로 쓰인다. 따라서 설탕 sugar는 셀 수 없는 명사이므로 복수를 나타내는 -s를 붙일 수 없다.

4. many → much, a lot of, lots of

물 water는 셀 수 없는 명사로 양을 나타내는 양화사의 수식을 받을 수 있지만 수를 나타내는 양화사의 수식은 받을 수 없다. 따라서 수를 나타내는 many와 함께 쓸 수 없다. a lot of나 lots of는 수와 양에 모두 쓰인다.

5. Beautiful this → This beautiful

명사구에서 한정사의 하나인 지시사는 다른 형용사보다 앞쪽에 온다. 따라서 지시사 this가 형용사 beautiful보다 앞에 와야 한다.

6. student → students

전체 문장의 주어인 Professors는 일반적인 의미의 교수를 가리키며 제자는 한 사람이 아니므로 복수형이 되어야 한다.

7. That → It

To-부정사를 주어로 하려고 할 때 이것을 가주어 it으로 놓는다. 따라서 to-부정사 to become을 진주어로 하는 가주어 it이 필요하다.

8. make → makes

동사는 주어의 수와 일치해야 한다. 따라서 주어인 동명사 singing이 단수이므로 동사 make는 단수형이 와야 한다. 명사구 popular songs는 동명사 singing의 목적어이고 the woman's는 동명사의 주어이다.

9. kind → kinds

명사 kind는 셀 수 있는 명사이므로 양화사 all 뒤에서 복수형이 되어야 한다.

10. boy → the boy 또는 he

명사 boy는 셀 수 있는 명사로 보통 수의 개념으로 쓰이므로 한정사가 앞에 붙지 않은 단수형으로는 쓰이지 않는다. 여기서는 '그 소년'의 의미로 쓰여야 하므로 정관사를 앞에 붙여 쓰거나 대명사로 나타낸다.

## Ⅲ. 심화연습

※ 다음 영작 중 비문을 고르고 그 이유를 설명하시오.

1. 비행기는 자동차보다 빠르다.

a. Airplanes are faster than cars.

b. An airplane is faster than a car.

c. You can travel faster by a plane than by a car.

d. One can reach one's destination faster by plane than by car.

정답 : ________

이유 : ________________________________________.

2. 이 아이들이 저 아이들보다 키가 작다.

a. This children are shorter than that children.

b. These children are shorter than those children.

c. The children here are shorter than the children there.

d. The children over here are shorter than the children over there.

정답 : _______

이유 : ________________________________________.

3. 그녀는 계란, 사과, 감자, 우유, 버터를 샀다.

a. She bought eggs, apples, potatoes and butter.

b. She bought eggs, apples, potatoes and a few butter.

c. She bought some eggs, some apples, some potatoes and some butter.

d. She bought some eggs, a few apples, some potatoes and some butter.

정답 : _______

이유 : ________________________________________.

4. 우리는 점심으로 치즈와 참외와 수박을 먹었다.

a. We ate cheese, melons and watermelon for lunch.

b. We all ate cheese, melon and watermelon for lunch.

c. We had some cheese, melons and watermelon for lunch.

d. All of us had some cheese, a few melon and watermelon for lunch.

정답 : _______

이유 : ________________________________________.

5. 그는 아침식사로 약간의 우유와 삶은 고구마를 먹었다.

a. He had some milk and steamed sweet potatoes for breakfast.

b. He drank some milk and ate some steamed sweet potatoes for breakfast.

c. He had some milk and few steamed sweet potatoes for breakfast.

d. He had some milk and some steamed sweet potatoes for breakfast.

정답 : _______

이유 : ________________________________________.

6. 나는 음악을 좋아하지만 어떤 음악은 좋아하지 않는다.

a. Music I like, but some music I don't.

b. I like music, but I don't like some music.

c. Music interests myself, but some music doesn't.

d. In general, I like music; however, I don't like some music.

정답 : ________

이유 : ________________________________________________.

7. 물은 섭씨 100도에서 끓지만 이 물은 섭씨 90도에서 끓는다.

a. Water boils at 100℃, but this water boils at 90℃.

b. Water boils at 100℃, while this water boils at 90℃.

c. This water boils at 90℃, even though the water boils at 100℃.

d. In general, water boils at 100℃; however, this water boils at 90℃.

정답 : ________

이유 : ________________________________________________.

8. 나는 선생을 좋아하지만 특정한 한 선생을 좋아하는 것은 아니다.

a. I like teachers, but not a particular teacher.

b. It is not particular teacher but teachers that I like.

c. I like teachers but I don't like a particular teacher.

d. I like teachers; however, I don't like a particular teacher.

정답 : ________

이유 : ________________________________________________.

9. 그는 처음에 미국으로 유학가려고 했으나 마음을 바꿔 영국으로 갔다.

a. The U.S. was the country to which he intended to go for study; however, he changed it to England and went there.

b. His first thought was to go to the U.S.A. for study, and later he decided going to England and went there.

c. At first, America was the country that he wanted to go to for study, and later he decided to go to England and went there.

d. At first, he intended to go to America for study, and then changed his mind and went to England.

정답 : ________

이유 : ________________________________________.

10. 네가 그 대학에 입학하려면 그 대학에 관한 많은 정보를 입수해야 한다.

a. If you want to enter the university, you should get lots of information about it.

b. You would better collect much information about the university before you enter it.

c. You should get as much information about the university as possible if you want to enter it.

d. To enter the university, you should obtain a lot of information about it.

정답 : ________

이유 : ________________________________________.

## Ⅳ. 기본영작

※ 다음을 영작하시오.

1. 물고기를 얼마나 많이 잡았니? (fish; catch)

________________________________________.

2. 나의 이 책들은 너의 저 책들보다 비싸다. (expensive)

________________________________________.

3. 잠이 오지 않는 밤이 여러 번 있었다. (sleepless; have)

________________________________________.

4. 외국어를 배운다는 것은 쉽지 않으며 인내심이 필요하다.
(a foreign language; patience)

________________________________________.

5. 이 옷이 저 옷보다 더 더럽다. (this piece of clothing; dirty)

______________________________________________.

6. 길에는 사람들이 많았지만 나는 왜 그들이 모였는지 알지 못했다.
(on the street; get together)

______________________________________________.

7. 많은 사람들이 돈을 많이 벌기 위해 열심히 일한다. (earn money)

______________________________________________.

8. 이 볼펜 중 몇 개는 잉크가 다 닳았다. (a ball-point pen; out of ink)

______________________________________________.

9. 어떤 사람들은 집이 몇 채 되지만 나는 한 채도 없다. (a house; none)

______________________________________________.

10. 너의 그 만년필을 나의 이 만년필과 바꿀래? (a fountain pen; exchange)

______________________________________________.

## V. 심화영작

1. 다음을 영작하시오.

(1) 우리는 맥주 안주로 오징어와 땅콩을 주문했다.
(a side dish; squid; a peanut)

______________________________________________.

(2) 나는 친구 몇 명과 교외의 호수에 낚시하러 갔다.
(the suburbs; a lake; go fishing)

______________________________________________.

(3) 밤이 깊어지자 가로등만이 더욱 빛을 발하고 있었다.

(get deeper; a street light; get brighter)

________________________________________.

(4) 그 마을 사람들 대부분은 그 마을을 떠나고 몇 명만 남아 있었다.

(a villager; leave; remain)

________________________________________.

(5) 그는 담배를 하루에 두 갑 정도 피지만 술은 거의 마시지 않는다.

(a pack of cigarettes; smoke; rarely; drink)

________________________________________.

(6) 돈 약간 빌려 줄 수 있겠니? 이틀 후에 갚을게. (lend; pay~back)

________________________________________.

(7) 많은 연기가 새어나와 숨을 쉴 수가 없다. (smoke; leak out; breathe)

________________________________________.

(8) 부채 두 개, 선풍기 그리고 에어컨이 더위를 물리칠 준비를 하고 있었다.

(a fan; an electric fan; an air conditioner; fight off; ready)

________________________________________.

(9) 그는 그 책을 약 50쪽 읽고 공을 차러 나갔다.

(about; a page; kick a ball)

________________________________________.

(10) 그는 여행을 많이 하지는 않지만 싫어하는 것은 아니다.

(travel a lot; hate)

________________________________________.

2. 다음을 주어진 표현으로 시작하여 영작하시오.

(1) 영작이 문법지식을 기초로 한다는 것은 잘 알려진 사실이다.

(be the basis of; well-known)

a. Many people ______________________________.

b. It __________________________________.

c. A knowledge of grammar ______________________________.

d. We ______________________________.

(2) 그는 외국에 전혀 가 본 적이 없는데 외국어를 아주 잘 한다.

(be abroad; well; speak)

a. With ______________________________.

b. His foreign languages ______________________________.

c. Although ______________________________.

d. He ______________________________.

(3) 네가 말하는 것은 우리의 공통의 관심사와 거리가 멀다. (far from)

a. What ______________________________.

b. Our common interest ______________________________.

c. You ______________________________.

d. The subject ______________________________.

(4) 그가 책을 쓰고 있는 동안 모기가 그의 다리를 물었다. (write; bite)

a. While ______________________________.

b. A mosquito ______________________________.

c. His leg ______________________________.

d. He ______________________________.

(5) 이 책들을 이삼일 내에 다 읽는다는 것은 불가능하다.

(within; impossible)

a. Two or three days ______________________________.

b. You ______________________________.

c. It ______________________________.

d. Reading ______________________________.

# 제6장 · 동 사

## Ⅰ. 기본개념

### 1. 동사란?

어떤 사람이나 사물이 무엇을 하는지 그리고 그들에게 무슨 일이 일어나는지 말하거나 그들에 관해 정보를 제공하기 위해 주어와 함께 쓰이는 말이다.

### 2. 동사의 종류

동사에 따라 그 뒤에 오는 요소의 유형이 달라지며 같은 동사라 하더라도 전하려는 의미가 다르면 그 뒤 요소가 달라질 수 있다. 따라서 정문과 비문을 구분하기 위해서는 동사와 그 뒤에 올 수 있는 요소의 유형에 관해 항상 주의를 기울여야 한다.

#### A. 완전자동사

문장의 주요 구성요소인 보어나 목적어가 뒤에 나오기를 요구하지 않는 동사이다. walk, arrive, fall, sleep, laugh, smile, rain과 같은 동사가 여기에 속한다.

a. The student [walked] (fast).
b. He [arrived] (late).
c. The snow [fell] (everywhere).

### B. 불완전자동사

보어가 뒤에 나오기를 요구하지만 목적어가 나오기를 요구하지는 않는 동사이다. look, feel, taste, smell, sound, grow, become과 같은 동사이다.

a. My friend [is] a politician.
b. He [looks] intelligent.
c. He may [become] a very important person.

### C. 완전타동사

목적어가 뒤에 나오기를 요구하지만 보어가 나오기를 요구하지는 않는 동사이다. like, insult, marry, eat, repair, love, study와 같은 동사가 여기에 속한다.

a. The woman [liked] bananas.
b. She [insulted] her classmate.
c. She [married] him.

### D. 수여동사

간접목적어와 직접목적어가 뒤에 나오기를 요구하는 동사이다. give, find, teach, ask, tell, bring, sell, buy와 같은 동사가 여기에 속한다.

a. The woman [bought] her son a storybook.
b. He [asked] his mother some questions.
c. She found him a teacher.

### E. 불완전타동사

목적어와 목적보어가 뒤에 나오기를 요구하는 동사이다. call, make, appoint, choose, elect, judge, consider와 같은 동사가 여기에 속한다.

a. The woman [called] the man a genius.
b. She [appointed] him president of the company.
c. She [made] him happy.

### 3. 동사의 기능

동사가 어떤 의미를 가지고 있느냐에 따라 동사 뒤에 올 요소를 결정할 뿐만 아니라 동사 앞에 나타날 주어를 선택한다.

#### A. 주어선택 기능

a. *A car [collided].

a.′ A car and a truck [collided].

a.″ A car [collided] with a truck.

b. *The boy dispersed.

b.′ The boy and the girl dispersed.

#### B. 동사 뒤에 나타날 요소에 대한 예측기능

a. They [ate].

b. They [ate] [a watermelon].

c. They [ate] [a watermelon] [deliciously].

d. They [ate] [a watermelon] [deliciously] [on a mountain].

## Ⅱ. 기본연습

※ 다음 중 어법이 잘못된 곳을 찾아 고쳐 쓰시오.

1. Young though he was, he looked very brightly and cleverly.

______________________________________________.

2. He sometimes used to walk the park with his young nieces.

______________________________________________.

3. The boy's mother bought for him some interesting storybooks.

______________________________________________.

4. They left for a sightseeing tour, and their car collided another car.

______________________________________________.

5. Put the book immediately on your desk, close it, and close your eyes.

______________________________________________.

6. The woman called his son genius when she talked to his acquaintances.

______________________________________________.

7. He suffered from a severe illness as a boy, and later became famous politician.

______________________________________________.

8. My girlfriend and I went fishing, and we ate deliciously our lunch near the lake.

______________________________________________.

9. I went up Mt. Bukhan with some friends of mine, and we ate some melons delicious.

______________________________________________.

10. It rained heavily, and we reached at our destination a little later than the appointed time.

______________________________________________.

## 정답 및 해설

### II. 기본연습

1. brightly and cleverly → bright and clever

동사 look은 '~하게 보이다'는 의미를 전할 때 뒤에 형용사구인 보어가 오기를 요구한다. 따라서 부사를 형용사로 바꾸어야 한다.

2. walk → walk in

동사 walk는 '걷다'는 의미를 전할 때 자동사로 뒤에 목적어인 명사구가 올 수 없다. 따라서 명사구 the park이 앞의 동사 walk와 연결이 되지 않아 비문이다. 따라서 전치사를 넣어 이것이 전치사의 목적어가 되게 한다.

3. for → ∅

동사 buy는 '~에게 ~을 사주다'는 의미를 전할 때 뒤에 간접목적어인 명사구와 직접목적어인 명사구가 나오기를 요구한다. 그리고 간접목적어가 직접목적어 앞에 올 때 전치사 없이 와야 한다.

4. collided → collided with, collided against

동사 collide는 '충돌하다'는 자동사이다. 따라서 이 동사와 뒤에 나오는 명사구 another car가 서로 관련을 맺지 못해 비문이다. 이 명사구를 전치사의 목적어가 되게 하면 정문이 된다.

5. immediately on the desk → on the desk immediately

동사 put은 '~을 ~에 두다'는 타동사로 목적어인 명사구 뒤에 장소를 나타내는 부사구가 반드시 나타나기를 요구한다. 따라서 이 부사구는 다른 부사보다 동사 가까이 와야 한다.

6. genius → a genius

동사 call은 '~을 ~라고 부르다'는 의미를 전할 때 목적어 뒤에 목적보어인 명사구가 나오기를 요구한다. 따라서 셀 수 있는 명사 genius는 한정사가 앞에 붙지 않은 단수형으로는 명사구가 아니므로 부정관사를 앞에 둔다.

7. politician → a politician

동사 become은 '~가 되다'는 의미로 뒤에 보어인 형용사구나 명사구가 반드시 오기를 요구한다. 따라서 뒤의 요소가 명사구가 되어야 하는데 famous politician이 명사구가 아니어서 비문이다.

8. deliciously our lunch → our lunch deliciously

일반적으로 타동사와 짧은 목적어 사이에는 부사가 들어와 둘의 관계를 방해해서는 안 되므로 타동사 eat과 목적어 our lunch 사이의 부사 deliciously를 목적어 뒤로 이동시켜야 한다.

9. delicious → deliciously

동사 eat은 타동사 중에서도 완전타동사이다. 따라서 목적어 뒤에 목적보어가 나오기를 요구하지 않으므로 목적어 some melon 뒤에 형용사 delicious가 올 수 없다. 그러나 동사를 수식하는 부사는 올 수 있다.

10. at → ∅

동사 reach는 '~에 도착하다'는 타동사이므로 뒤에 목적어인 명사구가 직접 나와야 한다.

## Ⅲ. 심화연습

※ 다음 영작 중 비문을 고르고 그 이유를 설명하시오.

1. 해가 지자 바람이 살랑살랑 불기 시작했다.

a. A gentle breeze began to follow sunset.

b. After the sun sank, it began to blow gently.

c. Soon after sunset, a breeze began to blow softly.

d. The sun sank, and then gentle wind began to blow.

정답 : ________

이유 : ______________________________________________.

2. 천둥이 치기 시작하면 곧 소나기가 내리는 법이다.

a. Thunder often precedes a shower.

b. After it thunders, it often showers.

c. You are likely to find a shower soon after it thunder.

d. When you see it thunder, you will probably see it shower soon.

정답 : ________

이유 : ______________________________________________.

3. 그는 뛰었지만 그녀가 어디로 갔는지 알 수 없었다.

a. He ran after her, but he couldn't find her.

b. He ran but couldn't know where she went.

c. She was nowhere, even though he ran after her.

d. She was not seen nowhere, though he ran after her.

정답 : ________

이유 : ______________________________________________.

4. 그는 그들에게 껌을 주었고 그들은 그를 즐겁게 했다.

a. He gave them a stick of gum each, and they pleased him.

b. They each received a stick of gum from him, and they made him happily.

c. A stick of gum was handed out to them each, and they made him merry.

d. He handed out a stick of gum to them each, and they made him glad.

정답 : ________

이유 : ________________________________________________.

5. 그는 사색하기 좋아하고 글 쓰는 일을 즐기는 사람이다.

a. He not only likes speculation, but also enjoys writing.

b. He is a person who likes to speculate and enjoy writing.

c. He likes to speculate about something, and enjoys writing.

d. Speculation and writing are what he likes and enjoys respectively.

정답 : ________

이유 : ________________________________________________.

6. 그는 운동 후 샤워를 하고 스킨로션을 바르고 외출했다.

a. He took exercise, took a shower, put on skin lotion and left.

b. He took a shower after exercise, put on skin lotion, and went out.

c. He finished exercise, took a shower, put on skin lotion and went out.

d. He took a shower after finish exercise, put on skin lotion and left his house.

정답 : ________

이유 : ________________________________________________.

7. 그녀는 화가 나서 그의 말에 아무런 대꾸도 하지 않았다.

a. She was angry, so she did not answer him.

b. Her anger made her not to answer his words.

c. She didn't respond to him, because she was angry.

d. She was so angry that she did not respond to his words.

정답 : ________

이유 : ________________________________________________.

8. 그는 빨리 걸었고 그녀는 그가 빨리 걷는 데 대해 투덜거렸다.

a. He walked fast, and this made her complain.

b. He walked so fast that she complained about.

c. He walked fast and she complained about this.

d. He walked so fast, and she complained that he walked fast.

정답 : ________

이유 : ____________________________________________.

9. 그녀는 약속시간보다 늦게 나타났으며 이것이 그를 화나게 했다.

a. He got angry with her, because she showed up later than the appointed time.

b. She showed up later than the appointed time, so he got angry with her.

c. This made him get angry with her that she appeared later than the appointed time.

d. She appeared later than the appointed time, which made him get angry with her.

정답 : ________

이유 : ____________________________________________.

10. 우리는 고속도로 휴게소에서 차를 멈추고 커피를 한 잔 마신 후 떠났다.

a. We stopped our car at a service plaza by an express highway, had a cup of coffee, and left.

b. We dropped by at a service plaza by an express highway, had a cup of coffee, and then continued our motor trip again.

c. We stopped our car at a service plaza by express highway, had a cup of coffee, and left for our destination.

d. We parked our car at a service plaza by the express highway, drank a up of coffee, and started.

정답 : ________

이유 : ____________________________________________.

## Ⅳ. 기본영작

※ 다음을 영작하시오.

1. 집에서 학교까지 차로 한 시간 반이 걸렸다.
   (by car; an hour and a half; take)
   ______________________________.

2. 강한 바람이 불어 우리는 낚시를 포기해야만 했다.
   (a strong wind; fishing; give up)
   ______________________________.

3. 그는 영리하지만 현명하지는 않다. (clever; wise)
   ______________________________.

4. 우리는 걷고 또 걸어도 산 정상에 다다르지 못했다.
   (walk; the mountain top; get to)
   ______________________________.

5. 그녀는 어려서 결혼하여 벌써 아들이 초등학교에 다닌다.
   (marry young; already; elementary school)
   ______________________________.

6. 그들은 통닭과 과일과 음료수를 사서 산을 향해 출발했다.
   (fried chicken; head for)
   ______________________________.

7. 여름에는 대중목욕탕을 이용하는 사람들의 수가 크게 준다.
   (a public bath; less people)
   ______________________________.

8. 마음이 즐거우면 만사가 아름다워 보인다. (happy; everything; look)
   ______________________________.

9. 주말에는 바람 쐬러 소양호에나 가봐야겠다. (for a change; Lake Soyang)

______________________________________________.

10. 아침식사를 늦게 해서 아직 점심 생각이 없다.
(have breakfast; late; want)

______________________________________________.

## V. 심화영작

1. 다음을 영작하시오.

(1) 그녀는 박사학위 논문을 준비하느라 매우 바쁜 모양이다.
(a doctoral dissertation; prepare; busy)

______________________________________________.

(2) 자동차와 트럭이 충돌했지만 다행히 아무도 다치지 않았다.
(a truck; collide with; get hurt)

______________________________________________.

(3) 한강을 따라 바람을 가르며 인라인스케이트를 타면 즐겁다.
(along the Han River; in-line skate; fun)

______________________________________________.

(4) 그는 종종 탁구를 치곤 했지만 지금은 거의 치러 가지 않는다.
(play ping-pong; used to)

______________________________________________.

(5) 인간은 자연이 주는 혜택을 받기만 하고 보답하는 데 인색하다.
(a human being; a benefit; receive; repay)

______________________________________________.

(6) 그는 장차 외교관이 되기 위해 외국어를 열심히 공부하고 있다.

(in the future; a diplomat; a foreign language)

________________________________________.

(7) 멀리 보이던 산봉우리가 새로 지은 아파트에 가려 보이지 않는다.

(far away; a mountain top; a newly built apartment)

________________________________________.

(8) 그녀는 영어작문과 영문독해와 영어회화 모두 잘하고 싶다고 했다.

(English reading comprehension; be good at)

________________________________________.

(9) 왜 남자 옷은 대개 푸른색을 사용하고 여자 옷은 붉은색을 사용할까?

(why; men's wear; usually)

________________________________________.

(10) 그들은 뿔뿔이 흩어졌지만 곧 다시 모였다. (scatter away; get together)

________________________________________.

2. 다음을 주어진 표현으로 시작하여 영작하시오.

(1) 그들은 서해안에 도착하여 일몰을 지켜보았다.

(the west sea; a sunset; watch)

a. They __________________________________.

b. After __________________________________.

c. When __________________________________.

d. On __________________________________.

(2) 소나기 때문에 시야가 가려 운전하기가 매우 어려웠다.

(blur the field of vision; drive; difficult)

a. It __________________________________.

b. The sudden shower __________________________.

c. The field of vision __________________________.

d. I __________________________________.

(3) 그는 프린터 잉크가 다 떨어져 인쇄를 할 수 없었다. (out of ink)

a. The printer ________________________________________________.

b. He ________________________________________________.

c. The ink ________________________________________________.

d. It ________________________________________________.

(4) 그 교수는 수업시간에 학생들이 휴대폰을 만지작거리면 신경이 쓰인다.

(in class; play with a cell phone; feel bothered)

a. Whenever ________________________________________________.

b. The professor ________________________________________________.

c. Students ________________________________________________.

d. It ________________________________________________.

(5) 점심을 늦게 먹고 나니 식곤증으로 졸리기 시작한다.

(eat; feel sleepy; start)

a. With ________________________________________________.

b. The late lunch ________________________________________________.

c. Because ________________________________________________.

d. I ________________________________________________.

# 제7장 · 보어

## Ⅰ. 기본개념

### 1. 보어란?

보어란 넓은 의미로는 수식어를 제외하고 동사의 의미를 완전하게 해 주는 직접목적어와 간접목적어, 주어의 의미를 완전하게 해 주는 주격보어, 목적어의 의미를 완전하게 해 주는 목적보어를 가리킨다. 그러나 좁은 의미로는 주격보어와 목적보어를 가리킨다.

### 2. 보어가 될 수 있는 것

#### A. 명사구

a. Helen is [a singer].

b. She made her daughter [another singer].

#### B. 명사절

a. The fact is [that she did everything to be good at English].

b. The question is [how she got there without anyone's help].

C. 형용사구

a. Tom is [handsome].

b. He made his son [attractive].

D. 분사

(A) 현재분사

a. The TV program is [boring].

b. I found him [drinking] my whisky.

(B) 과거분사

a. The house looked [abandoned].

b. The scene made him [excited].

## 3. 보어자리에서의 위반

보어자리는 보어가 될 수 있는 명사구나 형용사구가 와야 하며 보어가 될 수 없는 요소가 오면 비문이 된다.

A. 주격 보어자리에서의 위반

a. *Helen is [singer].

b. *She is [attractively].

c. *The game was [excited].

B. 목적보어자리에서의 위반

a. *She made her daughter [singer].

b. *He made his son [attractively].

c. *I saw a small girl [stood] on the table.

## II. 기본연습

※ 다음 중 어법이 잘못된 곳을 찾아 고쳐 쓰시오.

1. They elected Mr. Yang the President of the country.

   ______________________________________.

2. We didn't eat the dishes, for they tasted a bit sourness.

   ______________________________________.

3. It is not always easy to make one's own children famously.

   ______________________________________.

4. As the child grew older, he became more and more prudently.

   ______________________________________.

5. My question is how did the child get there without anyone's help.

   ______________________________________.

6. She was made angrily when her employer scolded her for carelessness.

   ______________________________________.

7. The football game was excited as the same player got successive goals.

   ______________________________________.

8. I found my roommate drunk my beer when I came back home from my workplace.

   ______________________________________.

9. The stewardess does not want to make her daughter an another stewardess.

   ______________________________________.

10. At first the little children hesitated to enter the house, since it seemed to be abandoning.

______________________________________________.

## 정답 및 해설

### II. 기본연습

1. the President → President

유일무이한 지위를 나타내는 말이 보어로 쓰일 때 그 명사 앞에 관사를 쓰지 않는다. '그 나라 대통령'은 유일무이한 지위를 나타내는 말이며 문장에서 동사 elect의 목적보어이다.

2. sourness → sour

동사 taste는 '~한 맛이 나다'는 의미를 전할 때 불완전자동사로 뒤에 형용사구인 보어만이 나타나기를 요구한다. 따라서 sourness는 명사구이므로 비문이다.

3. famously → famous

동사 make는 '~을 ~하게 되게 하다'는 의미를 전할 때 목적어와 목적보어가 뒤에 오기를 요구한다. 따라서 목적보어자리에 부사구가 아닌 형용사구가 온다.

4. prudently → prudent

동사 become은 '~가 되게 하다'는 의미를 전하는 불완전자동사로, 뒤에 보어가 와야 하므로 보어가 될 수 있는 형용사구는 오지만 부사구는 올 수 없다.

5. did the child get → the child got

be동사는 불완전자동사로 뒤에 보어가 와야 한다. 의문사로 시작되는 간접의문문은 보어가 될 수 있으며 동사 is 뒤의 어순은 '의문사 + 주어 + 동사'이다.

6. angrily → angry

동사 make는 '~을 ~하게 되게 하다'는 의미를 전할 때 뒤에 목적어와 목적보어가 오기를 요구한다. 능동문의 make의 목적어가 수동문의 주어 she이므로 목적보어인 형용사구가 필요하다.

7. excited → exciting

be동사 뒤는 보어자리로 현재분사나 과거분사가 보어로 올 수 있다. 그러나 현재분사 exciting은 '흥미진진한'이라는 의미로 이것의 주어로 사물이 오는 데 반해 과거분사 excited는 '흥분된'이라는 의미로 보통 주어 자리에 사람이 온다.

8. drunk → drinking

동사 find는 '~가 ~하고 있는 중인 것을 발견하다'는 의미를 목적어와 목적보어인 현재분사로 전한다. 타동사의 현재분사는 능동의 의미를 전하고 과거분사는 수동의 의미를 전한다.

9. an → ∅

명사 앞의 another는 한정사의 하나인 양화사로 명사와 함께 명사구를 이룬다. another stewardess는 완전한 명사구로 앞에 한정사인 부정관사가 올 수 없다.

10. abandoning → abandoned

동사 abandon은 '~을 버리다'는 타동사이다. 타동사의 현재분사는 능동의 의미를 전하는데 반해 과거분사는 수동의 의미를 전한다. '그 집이 버려져 있다'는 의미이므로 과거분사가 되어야 한다.

## Ⅲ. 심화연습

※ 다음 영작 중 비문을 고르고 그 이유를 설명하시오.

1. 그는 팔짱을 끼고 잠시 사색에 잠겼다.

a. He folded his arms and was lost in thought for a while.

b. He lost himself in thought for some time with folded arms.

c. With his arms folding, he lost himself in thought for a while.

d. Having his arms folded, he was wrapped in thought for a while.

정답 : ________

이유 : ________________________________________.

2. 매일 빠짐없이 일기를 쓴다는 것은 쉬운 일이 아니다.

a. It is hard to write a diary regularly.

b. You may find it hard to write a diary regularly.

c. You may find difficult to keep a diary every day.

d. It is not easy to write something in one's diary every day.

정답 : ________

이유 : ________________________________________.

3. 그가 무사히 귀가하자 가장 기뻐한 것은 그의 아내였다.

a. His wife was most pleased when he came home safely.

b. When he returned home safely, his wife welcomed him most glad.

c. Most of all, his wife was pleased that he came back home in safety.

d. He came back home without accident, so his wife was pleased most of all.

정답 : ________

이유 : ________________________________________________.

4. 그의 어린 딸은 그만 보면 아이스크림을 사달라고 조른다.

a. His little daughter always presses him to buy her an ice cream whenever she sees him.

b. His young daughter tends to ask him to buy an ice cream for her whenever she meets him.

c. His little daughter asks him to buy her an ice cream whenever she meets him.

d. His a young daughter cannot meet him without clamoring for an ice cream.

정답 : ________

이유 : ________________________________________________.

5. 도시에서 참새가 지저귀는 소리를 듣는다는 것은 쉽지 않다.

a. It is not easy to hear sparrows sing in a city.

b. You may find it hardly to hear sparrows sing in cities.

c. It is not always easy to hear sparrows sing in the city.

d. You may have difficulty in hearing sparrows sing in a city.

정답 : ________

이유 : ________________________________________________.

6. 그녀는 가끔 방청소도 하고 어머니가 설거지하는 것을 돕는다.

a. At times, she sweeps up the room and helps her mother wash the dishes.

b. She sometimes cleans the room and helps her mother do the dishes.

c. She occasionally cleans the room; besides, she helps her mother do the dishes.

d. From time to time, she sweeps both the room and helps her mother to do the dishes.

정답 : ________

이유 : ______________________________________________.

7. 그 학자의 지칠 줄 모르는 연구정신이 많은 사람들을 감동시켰다.

a. The scholar's tireless spirit of study moved lots of people.

b. The scholar had tireless spirit of research, and this moved lots of people.

c. The scholar studied so passionate that lots of people were moved.

d. Lots of people were moved by the scholar's tireless spirit of study.

정답 : ________

이유 : ______________________________________________.

8. 가장 중요한 것은 네가 어느 누구도 다치게 하지 않았다는 것이다.

a. You hurt nobody, this is the most important thing.

b. The most important thing is that you did not hurt anybody.

c. Nobody was hurt by you, which is the most important thing.

d. What is the most important is that you did not hurt anybody.

정답 : ________

이유 : ______________________________________________.

9. 날씨가 더울 때는 많은 사람들이 나무그늘 아래서 수박을 즐겨 먹는다.

a. It is not difficult to see lots of people enjoying watermelons in the shade of a tree, especially in hot weather.

b. When weather is hot, most people enjoy eating watermelons in the shade of a tree.

c. People usually enjoy eating watermelons in the shade of a tree when the weather is hot.

d. You may see lots of people enjoying eating watermelons under a tree in hot weather.

정답 : ________

이유 : ________________________________________________________________.

10. 시간이 지남에 따라 물질적으로 더 풍요로워지지만 자연환경은 더 악화된다.

a. As time passes, we become materially more comfortable, while our natural environment becomes worse.

b. Our natural environment becomes worse with time, even though our living conditions become better.

c. Time makes us live better materially. On the contrary, it also makes our natural environment worse.

d. Human beings become materially more comfortable with time; however, his natural environment becomes worse.

정답 : ________

이유 : ________________________________________________________________.

## Ⅳ. 기본영작

※ 다음을 영작하시오.

1. 너의 여자 친구가 걸어가고 있다. (there; go)

________________________________________________________________.

2. 그 책을 책상 위에 올려놓고 덮어라. (put; close)

________________________________________________________________.

3. 그 여학생은 공부를 잘 하지는 못하지만 매우 성실하다.
(a girl student; good at one's studies)

________________________________________________________________.

4. 이 말에 그녀는 깊은 감동을 받았다. (deeply; be moved)

________________________________________________________________.

5. 많은 현대인들의 고민거리 중 하나가 똥배가 나오는 것이다.
(modern people; be troubled with; a potbelly)

______________________________________________.

6. 사실은 그가 선보러 가서 그녀와 밤늦게까지 술을 마셨다는 거야.
(go on a blind date; until late at night; drink)

______________________________________________.

7. 어제 늦게 잠들었더니 계속 하품이 나오네. (late; go to bed; yawn)

______________________________________________.

8. 그는 피로할 때면 멀리 창밖을 내다보곤 한다.
(tired; look out the window)

______________________________________________.

9. 그녀는 키도 크고 얼굴도 예쁜데 아직 미혼이야.
(tall; pretty; remain single)

______________________________________________.

10. 그는 매우 영리하지만 성실성이 좀 부족한 것 같다.
(though; sincerity; lack)

______________________________________________.

## V. 심화영작

1. 다음을 영작하시오.

(1) 그가 박사학위를 취득하자 그의 어머니는 매우 기뻤다.
(a doctor's degree; get)

______________________________________________.

(2) 중요한 시험에서는 반드시 잉크 필기구를 사용해야 한다.
(important; in ink; writing tools)

______________________________________________.

(3) 그는 10층 건물 8층에 사는데 그의 방은 전망이 매우 좋다.

(a ten-story building; a floor; have a great view)

______________________________________________.

(4) 그는 요즘 체중을 줄이기 위해 땀을 흘리며 운동하고 있다.

(lose weight; sweat; exercise)

______________________________________________.

(5) 그녀는 남자친구와 헤어지기로 결심하고 머리를 짧게 깎았다.

(break up with; decide; cut one's hair short)

______________________________________________.

(6) 밀폐된 공간에서 선풍기를 켜 놓고 잠이 들면 매우 위험하다.

(a closed area; an electric fan; with~on)

______________________________________________.

(7) 하늘이 맑게 개어 기분이 한결 좋다. (clear; feel much better)

______________________________________________.

(8) 그는 예순 살이 훨씬 넘었지만 인라인스케이트를 배우고 있었다.

(over sixty; in-line skate; learn)

______________________________________________.

(9) 음악을 들으며 조깅하는 것도 그렇게 나쁘지는 않다. (listen to; jog)

______________________________________________.

(10) 그녀의 목소리는 너무나 매력적이어서 그녀의 이야기를 들으면 즐겁다.

(attractive; listen to; pleasant)

______________________________________________.

2. 다음을 주어진 표현으로 시작하여 영작하시오.

(1) 그의 확신에 찬 이야기가 주위사람들을 더욱 흥미롭게 했다.

(interested; make)

a. His confident story ____________________.
b. People ____________________.
c. He ____________________.
d. The story ____________________.

(2) 빗물이 점점 옷 속으로 스며들고 있었지만 우리는 계속 걸었다.
(gradually; get absorbed into; continue)
a. The rain ____________________.
b. We ____________________.
c. Although ____________________.
d. Despite ____________________.

(3) 이런 색의 옷은 너의 나이가 더 들어 보이게 한다. (look older; make)
a. These colors ____________________.
b. Clothes ____________________.
c. You ____________________.
d. When ____________________.

(4) 그 농촌 총각은 지붕을 푸르게 칠하고 그의 배우자가 생기길 기다렸다.
(paint one's roof blue; take a wife; wait)
a. After ____________________.
b. Having painted ____________________.
c. To ____________________.
d. The young man ____________________.

(5) 시간이 지남에 따라 사람이 더 젊어질 수 있는가? (time; grow younger)
a. With ____________________.
b. Can ____________________.
c. Is ____________________.
d. As ____________________.

# 제8장 · 목적어

## Ⅰ. 기본개념

### 1. 목적어란?

타동사나 전치사의 행위에 영향을 받거나 행위를 받는 단어나 단어집단을 가리킨다. 직접목적어는 동사의 행위를 받는다. 간접목적어는 어떤 것이 누구에게 혹은 무엇을 위해 행해지는가를 가리킨다.

### 2. 목적어가 될 수 있는 것

목적어가 될 수 있는 것은 일반적으로 명사처럼 쓰일 수 있는 말이다. 명사구, 명사절, to-부정사, 동명사 등이 이에 속한다.

#### A. 명사구

a. The child met [his mother].

b. He gave [her] [a present].

c. He gave it to [his mother].

d. He gave it to [her].

### B. 명사절

a. The thief confessed [that he had stolen the money].

b. He didn't know [whether he had to confess further crimes].

### C. to-부정사

a. The boy wanted [to buy] the toy.

b. He hoped [to give] it to his younger sister.

### D. 동명사

a. The student finished [reading] his book.

b. He regrets [having read] his book so fast.

## 3. 목적어 자리에서의 위반

일반적으로 타동사나 전치사의 뒤는 목적어가 될 수 있는 명사구가 와야 한다. 따라서 이 자리에는 명사구의 자격을 가진 말이 와야 한다.

### A. 타동사의 목적어 자리에서의 위반

목적어의 자격과 관련된 위반

a. *The child met [mother].

b. *He gave [mother] a present.

c. *He gave it to [mother].

d. *He wanted [that his mother would be happy].

e. *He postponed [to meet] his girlfriend.

f. *He planned [pleasing] his mother.

### B. 수여동사와 관련된 위반

두 개의 목적어를 취하는 수여동사는 뒤에 간접목적어가 오고 그 뒤에 직접목적어가 나오기를 요구한다.

(A) 간접목적어 자리에서의 위반

a. The girl gave [her father] a present.

a.′*She gave [to him] a present.

a.″ She gave a present [to him].

b. She bought [her father] a present.

b.′*She bought [for him] a present.

b.″ She bought a present [for him].

(B) 직접목적어 자리에서의 위반

a. *The girl gave her father [present].

b. *She gave [present] to him.

(C) 격의 위반

타동사의 뒷자리는 타동사에 의해 목적격이 주어지는 자리로 여기에 나타나는 모든 명사구는 목적격을 가지게 된다.

a. The woman patted [Tom] on the shoulder.

b. She patted [her boyfriend] on the shoulder.

c. She patted [him,] on the shoulder.

d. *She patted [he] on the shoulder.

e. *She patted [his] on the shoulder.

## B. 전치사의 목적어 자리에서의 위반

(A) 목적어의 자격과 관련된 위반

전치사의 뒤는 전치사의 목적어 자리로 명사구가 와야 한다. 따라서 명사구의 자격을 가진 말이 와야 한다.

a. The man bought a book for [Teresa].

b. He sent it to [his daughter].

b.′*He sent it to [daughter].

c. He gave it to [her].

(B) 격의 위반

전치사의 뒤는 전치사에 의해 목적격이 주어지는 자리로 이곳에 오는 명사구는 목적격을 가지게 된다.

a. The man bought the books for [Tom and Teresa].

b. He bought the books for [his son and daughter].

c. He bought the books for [them].

d. *He bought them for [they].

e. *He bought them for [their].

## 4. 가목적어와 진목적어

### A. 가목적어

동사의 목적어가 형용사보어나 명사보어를 가진 부정사나 절일 때, 이 부정사나 절을 대명사 it으로 나타내고 이것이 가리키는 부정사나 절을 보어 뒤에 둔다. 이 때 전자를 가목적어, 후자를 진목적어라 한다.

### B. 진목적어가 될 수 있는 것

(A) to-부정사

a. I find it difficult [to write] a good composition book.

b. My athlete's foot made it a problem [to walk].

(B) that-절

a. She thought it strange [that he had not written].

b. He thought it a problem [that she always wanted him to do everything for her].

(C) 의문사절

a. He made it clear [what he wanted].

b. He thought it a mystery [how the thief had run away].

(D) 동명사구

a. She finds it interesting [talking] to the stranger.

b. She thinks it an important thing [starting] before noon.

### C. 가목적어와 진목적어 위반

가목적어와 진목적어가 나오는 구문은 보통 동사 뒤에 형용사구보어나 명사구보어가 없으면 쓰이지 않는다.

a. He cannot bear to see women crying.

a.′*He cannot bear [it] to see women crying.

b. She remembers that they were very happy.

b.′*She remembers [it] that they were very happy.

## Ⅱ. 기본연습

※ 다음 중 어법이 잘못된 곳을 찾아 고쳐 쓰시오.

1. He always wanted that his parents would be happy.

   ______________________________________.

2. She sometimes finds interesting talking to complete strangers.

   ______________________________________.

3. First of all, you should avoid to quarrel with others unnecessarily.

   ______________________________________.

4. The man bought a pretty bracelet, and gave it to she, his girlfriend.

   ______________________________________.

5. His mother thought strange that he had not phoned her for a long time.

   ______________________________________.

6. His friends thought a mystery how he had earned so much money in so short a time.

   ______________________________________.

7. The scholar often writes books, but he finds this difficult to write a good one.

   ______________________________________.

8. As the new semester began, the student planned studying all the subjects hard.

   ______________________________________.

9. Miss Kim patted boyfriend on the shoulder, and he turned his head toward her.

______________________________________________.

10. The teacher thought a problem that some students came in the classroom late and annoyed all the people around.

______________________________________________.

## 정답 및 해설

### II. 기본연습

1. that his parents would → his parents to

타동사 want는 목적어로 명사구는 취하지만 명사절은 취하지 않는다. 또한 뒤에 목적어인 명사구와 목적보어인 to-부정사가 올 수 있다.

2. finds → finds it

동사 find는 목적어와 목적보어를 취해 '~가 ~하다는 것을 발견하다'는 의미를 전한다. 목적어가 바로 뒤에 없고 목적보어인 형용사 interesting이 나와 있다. 동명사 talking이 목적어이므로 이것을 가목적어 it으로 둔다.

3. to quarrel → quarreling

동사 avoid는 목적어로 동명사는 오지만 to-부정사는 올 수 없다. 따라서 동사 quarrel을 동명사로 바꾼다.

4. she → her

전치사 뒤는 전치사에 의해 목적격이 주어지므로 인칭대명사를 목적격으로 나타내야 한다.

5. thought → thought it

타동사 think는 '~을 ~하게 생각하다'는 의미를 전할 때 목적어와 목적보어가 뒤에 오기를 요구한다. 의미상 that-절이 think의 목적어이고 형용사구 strange가 목적보어이므로 동사 바로 뒤에 가목적어 it을 두어야 한다.

6. thought → thought it

동사 think는 '~을 ~하다고 생각하다'는 의미를 전할 때 뒤에 목적어와 목적보어가 온다. 목적어가 의문사 how가 이끄는 간접의문문이고 목적보어가 명사구 a mystery이므로 동사 thought 바로 뒤에 가목적어가 필요하다.

7. this → it

동사 find는 '~가 ~하다는 것을 발견하다'는 의미를 전할 때 목적어와 목적보어가 뒤에 와야 한다. to-부정사 to write가 목적어이고 형용사구 difficult가 목적보어이므로 동사 find 뒤에 가목적어 it이 와야 한다.

8. studying → to study

동사 plan은 뒤에 목적어로 to-부정사는 오지만 동명사는 올 수 없다.

9. boyfriend → her boyfriend

타동사의 뒤는 목적어가 와야 하고 목적어가 되려면 명사구가 되어야 한다. boyfriend는 명사이지만 명사구가 아니므로 명사구로 바꾸어야 한다.

10. thought → thought it

동사 think의 목적어가 that-절이고 목적보어가 명사구 a problem이다. 따라서 동사 바로 뒤에 가목적어가 필요하다.

## Ⅲ. 심화연습

※ 다음 영작 중 비문을 고르고 그 이유를 설명하시오.

1. 건물 위 여기저기에 휴대폰 송신탑이 세워져 있다.

   a. Lots of buildings here and there have transmitting towers for mobile phones on their tops.

   b. Transmitting towers for cellular phones are erected on the tops of the buildings here and there.

   c. You may find transmitting towers for cellular phones on the tops of the buildings here and there.

   d. We easily can see transmitting towers for mobile phones on the tops of the buildings here and there.

정답 : ________

이유 : ____________________________________________________________.

2. 그는 책을 한 권 옆구리에 낀 채 우산을 쓰고 걸었다.

   a. He walked holding up an umbrella, with a book under his arm.

b. Having a book under his arm, he walked holding up an umbrella.

c. Carrying a book under his arm, he walked having an umbrella up.

d. He walked with an umbrella holding up and a book under his arm.

정답 : ________

이유 : ________________________________________________.

3. 그는 학생들을 인솔하여 캐나다로 영어연수를 떠났다.

a. He went to Canada to take English training, leading a group of students.

b. He led a group of students to Canada to take training in English.

c. He left for Canada to make English study trip, leading a group of students.

d. He and a group of students led by him left for Canada to take English training.

정답 : ________

이유 : ________________________________________________.

4. 장마철이면 비가 천장에서 벽을 따라 흘러내리곤 했다.

a. The rain used to be leaking along the wall through the ceiling in the rainy season.

b. I was not difficult to see the rain leaking along the wall through the ceiling in the rainy season.

c. I too often saw the rain leaking along the wall through the ceiling in the rainy season.

d. In the rainy season, I could not help seeing the rain leaking along the wall through the ceiling.

정답 : ________

이유 : ________________________________________________.

5. 그는 내일 입사를 위한 면접시험이 있어서 이발하러 갔다.

a. He went to a barbershop to have his hair cut, because he has a personal interview for entering a company tomorrow.

b. He went to a barbershop to have his hair cut in preparation for a personal interview for entering a company tomorrow.

c. He has a personal interview for entering a company tomorrow, so he went to a barbershop to get haircut.

d. A personal interview for the entrance of a company tomorrow made him go to a barbershop to have his hair cut.

정답 : ________

이유 : ______________________________________________.

6. 호박넝쿨이 그 집 지붕을 따라 아래로 길게 늘어져 있었다.

a. Long pumpkin vines were hanging down along the roof of the house.

b. There were pumpkin vines hanging down long along the house's roof.

c. We could see the long pumpkin vines hanging down along the roof of the house.

d. The long pumpkin vines were seen hanging down along the roof of the house.

정답 : ________

이유 : ______________________________________________.

7. 누가 나의 어깨를 톡톡 두드렸으며 나는 즉시 고개를 돌렸다.

a. I immediately turned my head because someone patted me on the shoulder.

b. Somebody patted me on the shoulder, and I at once turned my head.

c. Somebody's patting on the shoulder made me turn my head right to him.

d. I felt someone pat me on the shoulder, and I instinctively turn my head to him.

정답 : ________

이유 : ______________________________________________.

8. 나는 이 책을 아직 다 읽지 못해서 너에게 빌려줄 수가 없다.

a. You cannot borrow this book, for I have not read through it yet.

b. I have not finished reading this book yet, so I cannot lend it to you.

c. I cannot lend to you this book because I have not finished with it yet.

d. It is impossible for me to lend this book to you, for I have not finished with it yet.

정답 : ________

이유 : ________________________________________________________________.

9. 그녀는 요리하기 좋아하지만 자신이 한 요리를 즐겨 먹지는 않는다.

a. She often prepares dishes, even though she seldom enjoys eating her own dishes.

b. She likes the cook, but she does not enjoy eating the dishes that she has prepared.

c. She enjoys cooking; however, she does not like to eat the dishes that she has prepared.

d. She likes to cook, even though she is far from enjoying the dishes she has prepared herself.

정답 : ________

이유 : ________________________________________________________________.

10. 그녀는 방의 커튼을 닫고 어디론가 떠난 후 아직 돌아오지 않았다.

a. She has not come back home since she drew the window curtain and left for somewhere.

b. She left for a some place after she dropped the window curtain. She has not come back since then.

c. She left for somewhere after she drew the window curtain, and has not come back home since then.

d. She drew the window curtain, left for somewhere, and has not returned home yet since then.

정답 : ________

이유 : ________________________________________________________________.

## Ⅳ. 기본영작

※ 다음을 영작하시오.

1. 우리는 그 개울의 하류로 내려갔다 다시 상류로 올라왔다.
(go downstream; upstream; return)
______________________________________________________.

2. 나는 여기서 그 물체가 무엇인지 분명히 식별할 수 있었다.
(an object; what; tell)
______________________________________________________.

3. 나는 네가 누구인지는 알지만 나이가 몇 살인지는 알지 못한다.
(a name; age; know)
______________________________________________________.

4. 그 나라는 북한이 핵개발을 포기해야 한다는 것을 분명히 했다.
(a country; nuclear development; give up)
______________________________________________________.

5. 그 소년은 그 소녀를 좋아했으며 이것을 그녀도 잘 알고 있었다.
(like; very well; know)
______________________________________________________.

6. 그는 음악을 즐겨 들으며 운전 중에도 듣는다. (listen to; drive)
______________________________________________________.

7. 우리의 여행을 계속하는 것이 어려울지 모른다. (a trip; continue)
______________________________________________________.

8. 방학이라 도서관을 찾는 학생들이 적다. (vacation time; come to)
______________________________________________________.

9. 그는 외국에 있는 아내와 자식들이 보고 싶었지만 보러 갈 수 없었다.
(overseas; a child; miss; go)

_______________________________________________.

10. 매일 영어로 글을 써 본다는 것은 쉬운 일은 아니다. (in English; easy)

_______________________________________________.

## V. 심화영작

1. 다음을 영작하시오.

(1) 네가 나를 따르는 한 너와 너의 가족을 돌보아 주겠다.
(follow; as long as; look after)

_______________________________________________.

(2) 요즘 갓난아이에게 젖을 물리는 여성을 보기가 쉽지 않다.
(a baby; breast-feed; rarely)

_______________________________________________.

(3) 나는 커다란 참외를 하나 깎아 먹어서 지금은 배가 부르다.
(a Korean melon; peel; be full)

_______________________________________________.

(4) 한 여성이 그에게 차를 사주었으며 그는 가끔 이것을 타고 다닌다.
(buy; sometimes; drive)

_______________________________________________.

(5) 나는 너의 머리가 좋다고 생각하지만 네가 열심히 공부하길 바란다.
(smart; study hard; want)

_______________________________________________.

(6) 그는 도로지도 없이 혼자 그의 목적지에 도착할 수 있다고 생각했다.

(a road map; a destination; arrive at)

______________________________________________.

(7) 그는 그녀가 결백하다는 것을 알고 있었지만 그것을 증명하지 못했다.

(innocent; prove)

______________________________________________.

(8) 장차 무슨 일이 일어날지 아무도 모른다.

(in the future; happen; nobody)

______________________________________________.

(9) 운전 중 졸리면 신나는 음악을 듣거나 껌을 씹어라.

(feel sleepy; chew gum)

______________________________________________.

(10) 그녀는 그가 생일선물로 준 목걸이를 항상 하고 다닌다.

(a necklace; wear)

______________________________________________.

2. 다음을 주어진 표현으로 시작하여 영작하시오.

(1) 칭찬을 들어야 할 사람은 내가 아니라 너다. (get praises)

a. Instead ______________________________________.

b. You ______________________________________.

c. It ______________________________________.

d. The person ______________________________________.

(2) 여름밤이 깊어지자 여기저기서 풀벌레 우는 소리가 들렸다.

(a summer night; get deeper; a grass insect)

a. Sounds ______________________________________.

b. As ______________________________________.

c. With ______________________________________.

d. I ______________________________________.

(3) 이번 여름은 별로 덥지 않아 에어컨에 대한 수요가 감소할 것 같다.

(an air conditioner; decrease; seem)

a. It ________________________________________.

b. Because ________________________________________.

c. I ________________________________________.

d. The demand ________________________________________.

(4) 비가 그치자마자 잠자리 떼가 나타나 상공을 이리저리 날고 있었다.

(stop; appear; in the air; fly about)

a. The rain ________________________________________.

b. A swarm of dragonflies ________________________________________.

c. No sooner ________________________________________.

d. As soon as ________________________________________.

(5) 그는 휴대폰 벨소리를 듣고 전화를 받기 위해 서둘러 교실 밖으로 나갔다.

(hear; answer; hurry out of)

a. As soon as ________________________________________.

b. He ________________________________________.

c. In order to ________________________________________.

d. When ________________________________________.

# 제9장 · 부 사

## Ⅰ. 기본개념

### 1. 부사란?

동사, 형용사, 다른 부사 또는 문장 전체의 의미를 기술하거나 한정하는 데 쓰이는 말이다.

### 2. 부사의 기능

동사, 형용사, 부사를 수식하거나 문장 전체를 수식한다.

a. The scientist studied [persistently].

b. He was [very] happy.

c. He studied [extremely] hard.

d. [Fortunately] he made a new discovery.

## 3. 부사의 위치와 종류

### A. 부사의 일반적 위치

부사의 주요 위치는 문장의 ①첫머리 위치, ②가운데 위치, ③끝 위치이다. 부사의 종류에 따라 이 세 위치 중 올 수 있는 위치에 제약이 따른다.

[ ① ] 주어 [ ② ] 동사 [ ③ ]

특히, 문장 가운데 위치는 (ⅰ) be동사 뒤, (ⅱ) 일반동사 앞, (ⅲ) 조동사가 있으면 조동사 뒤가 되며, 조동사가 여러 개 있으면 첫 번째 조동사 뒤가 되기도 하고 본동사 앞이 되기도 한다.

### B. 부사의 종류와 위치

(A) 연결부사

앞서 언급한 내용과 지금 말하려는 내용을 연결하는 역할을 하는 부사이다. 주로 문장 첫머리에 오며 however, therefore, then, besides, in addition, next, anyway 등이 있다.

a. [However], he did his best to carry out his duties.

b. [Next], we drove home.

(B) 시간부사

시간을 나타내는 부사로 주로 문장 끝 위치에 오며 문장 첫머리 위치에도 올 수 있다. today, yesterday, tomorrow, last year, this morning, last night, in August 등이 있다.

a. I am to meet my girlfriend's parents [tomorrow].

b. [Tomorrow] I am to meet my girlfriend's parents.

(C) 부정부사

부정의 의미를 가진 부사로 보통 문장 가운데 위치에 온다. 부정어를 강조하고자 할 때는 문장 첫머리 위치에 올 수도 있으며 이때는 주어와 조동사의 어순이 의무적으로 도치된다. not, never, scarcely, hardly 등이 있다.

a. I have [never] driven a car.

b. [Never] have I driven a car.

(D) 부정빈도부사

막연한 빈도를 나타내는 부사로 보통 문장 가운데 위치에 오지만 문장 첫머리위치와 문장 끝 위치에 오는 것도 있다. always, usually, often, sometimes, occasionally, ever, normally 등이 있다.

sometimes, usually, normally, often, frequently, occasionally는 세 위치 모두 가능하다.

a. The boy is [always] late for breakfast.

a.′ He [always] gets up late in the morning.

a.″ He can [always] eat some vegetables with rice.

b. He [sometimes] meets many foreigners.

b.′ [Sometimes] he meets many foreigners.

b.″ He meets many foreigners [sometimes].

(E) 확신부사

확신을 나타내는 부사로 문장 가운데 위치에 오지만 maybe, perhaps는 보통 문장 첫머리 위치에 온다. certainly, obviously, probably, definitely, clearly 등이 있다.

a. His girlfriend is [definitely] older than him.

a.′ He [definitely] thinks that age is nothing more than a number.

a.″ He has [definitely] fallen in love with her.

b. [Maybe] I am right.

(F) 장소부사

어떤 것이 일어나는 장소를 나타내는 부사로, 주로 문장 끝 위치에 오지만 문장 첫머리 위치에도 온다. here, in Seoul, upstairs, around 등이 있다.

a. There was a very tall persimmon tree [in the garden].

b. [In the garden] there was a very tall persimmon tree.

(G) 한정빈도부사

명확한 빈도를 나타내는 부사로, 보통 문장 끝 위치에 오지만 문장 첫머리 위치에도 온다. every day, daily, every week, weekly, every month, every year 등이 있다.

a. The woman washes her very long hair [every day].

b. [Every day] the woman washes her very long hair.

(H) 촛점부사

문장의 어느 한 부분에 촛점을 맞추는 부사로, 촛점을 맞추려는 표현 바로 앞에 온다. 따라서 위치이동이 상당히 자유롭다. only, even, mainly, mostly, either, neither 등이 있다.

a. [Only] I loved Miss Kim.

b. I [only] loved Miss Kim.

c. I loved [only] Miss Kim.

(I) 완전부사

어떤 것이 얼마나 완전하게 일어나는지를 나타내는 부사로, 문장 가운데 위치에 온다. 조동사가 여러 개 있으면 이 조동사들을 모두 제치고 본동사 앞에 오기도 한다. completely, almost, nearly, practically 등이 있다.

a. He has [completely] effaced the memory of her from his mind.

b. He will have [completely] finished by the end of the summer vacation.

(J) 논평부사

어떤 행위에 대해 화자의 견해를 밝히는 부사로, 대개 문장 가운데 위치에 오지만 문장 첫머리 위치에도 온다. stupidly, fortunately, unfortunately 등이 있다.

a. He [fortunately] escaped death.

b. [Fortunately] he escaped death.

(K) 양태부사

어떤 것이 어떻게 일어나거나 행해지는지를 나타내는 부사로, 대개 문장 끝 위치에 온다. -ly로 끝나는 양태부사는 문장 가운데 위치에도 올 수 있다. 수동동사가 있으면 문장 가운데 위치에 온다. slowly, quietly, hard, carefully 등이 있다.

a. The driver drove his car [well].

b. He drove it [carefully].

c. He [carefully] drove it.

d. His car is always [well] driven.

d.′ *He always [well] drives his car.

(L) 강조부사

문장의 특정 단어나 표현 바로 앞에 놓여 그 단어나 표현을 수식한다. very, just, right, extremely, terribly, really 등이 있다.

a. The man appeared [just] before the appointed time.

b. He walked [very] fast.

### C. 부사의 위치 위반

a. *He visits [often] his parents who live in the country.

b. *[Always] he goes abroad every summer vacation.

c. *Put the milk [at once] in the refrigerator.

d. *She danced in the auditorium [beautifully] last night.

e. *[Never] I have driven a truck.

f. *His girlfriend [definitely] is taller than him.

## 4. 부사와 형용사의 혼용

### A. 보어인 형용사를 써야 할 곳에 부사를 잘못 쓰는 경우

a. The marathon runner was [patient].

b. *The marathon runner was [patiently].

### B. 양태부사를 써야 할 곳에 형용사를 잘못 쓰는 경우

a. *The marathon runner ran [patient].

b. The marathon runner ran [patiently].

# Ⅱ. 기본연습

※ 다음 중 어법이 잘못된 곳을 찾아 고쳐 쓰시오.

1. The politician knows definitely how to lead the country.

______________________________________________.

2. My junior in school and I go often hiking along the stream.

______________________________________________.

3. I completely will finish studying English composition sooner or later.

______________________________________________.

4. He didn't go abroad to study because he had to support his parents mainly.

_______________________________________________.

5. Never he has really loved any woman, but he is ready to look for his ideal woman.

_______________________________________________.

6. He and his wife sang and danced beautifully last night in the wedding feast.

_______________________________________________.

7. The aerobic dancing team won the contest because they exercised hard extremely.

_______________________________________________.

8. She always hard studies English composition, even though she is not good at it.

_______________________________________________.

9. He read the book so careful that he scarcely missed important information in it.

_______________________________________________.

10. Always he and his girlfriend quarreled, but they continued their meeting.

_______________________________________________.

## 정답 및 해설

### II. 기본연습

1. knows definitely → definitely knows

확신부사 **definitely**는 문장 가운데 위치인 일반동사 **knows** 앞에 와야 한다.

2. go often → often go

부정빈도부사는 문장 가운데 위치에 오므로 often이 일반동사 go 앞에 온다.

3. completely will → will completely

완전부사는 문장 가운데 위치에 온다. 따라서 조동사 will과 본동사 finish가 있으므로 조동사 뒤에 와야 한다.

4. because → mainly because

초점부사 mainly는 초점을 맞추려는 단어, 구, 절의 바로 앞에 오므로 의미상 이유를 나타내는 'because-절'에 초점을 맞추어야 하므로 그 앞에 와야 한다.

5. he has → has he

부정의 부사가 문두에 와서 뒤의 절 전체를 부정할 때는 이 부정어 뒤의 어순이 의무적으로 도치가 되어야 한다. 따라서 조동사 has가 주어 he 앞에 온다.

6. last night in the wedding feast → in the wedding feast last night

동사 뒤에 오는 부사는 보통 양태부사, 장소부사, 시간부사의 순서가 된다. 따라서 양태부사 beautifully가 동사와 가장 가까이 오고 뒤에 장소부사 in the wedding feast가 오고 그 뒤에 시간부사 last night이 온다.

7. hard extremely → extremely hard

강조부사 extremely는 문장의 특정 단어나 표현 앞에 놓여 그것을 강조한다. 따라서 부사 hard를 강조해야 하므로 그 앞에 와야 한다.

8. hard studies English composition → studies English composition hard

양태부사는 보통 자동사가 있으면 자동사 뒤에 오고 타동사가 있으면 타동사의 목적어 뒤에 온다. 따라서 타동사 study의 목적어 뒤에 와야 한다.

9. careful → carefully

동사 read의 목적어 뒤는 이 동사의 행위가 어떠한 모양으로 행해지는지를 나타내는 양태부사가 와야 할 자리이다.

10. Always he and his girlfriend → He and his girlfriend always

부정빈도부사 always는 문장 가운데 위치인 일반동사 quarreled 앞에 온다.

## Ⅲ. 심화연습

※ 다음 영작 중 비문을 고르고 그 이유를 설명하시오.

1. 네가 그 사고에서 무사하다니 매우 기쁘다.

a. It makes me gladly that you are safe from the accident.

b. You did not get hurt in the accident, so I am very glad.

c. I am very glad that you did not get hurt in the accident.

d. I am very glad that you are safe in spite of the accident.

정답 : ________

이유 : ________________________________________________________________.

2. 그는 그 일을 겪은 후 거의 제정신이 아니었다.

a. The accident left him almost out of his mind.

b. He was not almost in his right mind after he undergoes the accident.

c. He suffered from the accident and became practically out of his mind.

d. He was practically out of his mind after he went through the accident.

정답 : ________

이유 : ________________________________________________________________.

3. 그의 집 창틀에는 화분 두 개가 나란히 놓여 있다.

a. Two flowerpots stand next to each other on the window sill of his house.

b. He has two flowerpots laying side by side on the window sill in his house.

c. You can see two flowerpots which stand side by side on the window sill of his house.

d. There are two flowerpots standing side by side on the window sill of his house.

정답 : _______

이유 : ____________________________________________.

4. 그의 딸은 어제 세종문화회관에서 춤을 멋지게 추었다.

a. In the Sejong Center, his daughter danced well last night.

b. Beautifully his daughter danced in the Sejong Center last night.

c. His daughter danced beautifully in the Sejong Center last night.

d. Last night his daughter danced a dance beautifully in the Sejong Center.

정답 : _______

이유 : ____________________________________________.

5. 그 남자는 어리석게도 정 때문에 자신의 성공을 지연시켰다.

a. The man foolishly delayed his success by being overcome by his sympathy.

b. His sympathy for others resulted in the delay of his success, which was a foolish thing.

c. It was foolish for him to delay his success because of his sympathy for others.

d. The man was so sympathetic to others that he succeeded in life late. This was a regrettable thing.

정답 : _______

이유 : ____________________________________________.

6. 다행히도 그 두 남녀는 우여곡절 끝에 행복한 결혼에 이르렀다.

a. The boy and girl had the luck to get married happily with all the difficulties.

b. The boy and girl were enough fortunate to lead to a happy marriage after many twists and turns.

c. The boy and girl underwent many complications and luckily finally got happily married.

d. Fortunately the boy and girl led to a happy marriage after many twists and turns.

정답 : ________

이유 : ______________________________________________________________.

7. 이번 여름방학이 끝날 때까지는 이 원고가 완전히 끝나 있을 것이다.

a. I am to finish completely this manuscript by the time this summer vacation finishes.

b. This manuscript will have been completely finished by the time this summer vacation finishes.

c. This manuscript is to be completely finished by the time this summer vacation finishes.

d. I will have completely finished this manuscript by the time this summer vacation finishes.

정답 : ________

이유 : ______________________________________________________________.

8. 나는 단지 그녀를 사랑했을 뿐이며 그녀를 괴롭히는 일은 하지 않았다.

a. Far from bothering her, I only loved her.

b. I only loved her, and never bothered her.

c. I did not bother her, but merely loved her.

d. Never I bothered her, but I just loved her.

정답 : ________

이유 : ______________________________________________________________.

9. 그는 자전거 페달을 매우 힘차게 밟았지만 앞선 일행을 따라잡지 못했다.

a. He pedaled his bicycle hard vain to catch up with his teammates ahead.

b. He pedaled his bicycle hard, but he was not able to catch up with his teammates ahead.

c. He tried to catch up with his teammates ahead by pedaling his bicycle hard, but he couldn't.

d. No matter how hard he pedaled his bicycle, he was unable to catch up with his teammates ahead.

정답 : ________

이유 : ________________________________________________.

10. 그 노인은 보행신호가 끝났는데도 불구하고 천천히 횡단보도를 건너고 있었다.

a. The old man was crossing the crosswalk slowly, even though the traffic light turned red.

b. The old man was crossing the crosswalk slowly, even though the green traffic light for pedestrian already turned red.

c. The pedestrian light turned red; however, the old man was crossing the crosswalk slowly.

d. The pedestrian light changed from green to red, but the old man was crossing the crosswalk slowly.

정답 : ________

이유 : ________________________________________________.

## Ⅳ. 기본영작

※ 다음을 영작하시오.

1. 그녀는 심야에는 거의 외출하지 않는다. (hardly; go out)

________________________________________________.

2. 내가 너의 나이였을 때는 햄버거란 이름을 들어보지 못했다. (at your age; hear of)

________________________________________________.

3. 그녀는 운동복을 입고 거울을 본 후 남자친구를 만나러 나갔다. (sportswear; look in the mirror)

________________________________________________.

4. 그녀가 매주 산에 오르는 주된 이유는 건강을 유지하기 위해서다.
(go up a mountain; primarily; maintain health)

______________________________________________.

5. 그는 부자가 되고 가난해지고 또 다시 다른 의미의 부자가 되었다.
(rich; again; in a different sense)

______________________________________________.

6. 유감스럽게도 그들은 이미 그곳을 떠나고 없었다. (already; leave)

______________________________________________.

7. 어쨌든 너는 너의 실수를 인정하지 않으면 안 된다. (a mistake; admit)

______________________________________________.

8. 그는 한국을 떠나 외국에 살고 있는 게 분명하다. (live abroad; must be)

______________________________________________.

9. 나는 좀 늦게 일어나 그 기차를 거의 놓칠 뻔 했다. (get up; nearly; miss)

______________________________________________.

10. 그녀는 매주 시골에 있는 그녀의 노부모를 방문한다.
(the countryside; visit)

______________________________________________.

## V. 심화영작

1. 다음을 영작하시오.

(1) 그녀는 뒤도 돌아보지 않고 계속 앞만 보고 걸었다.
(look back; without; walk forward)

______________________________________________.

(2) 네가 좋아하든 그렇지 않든 나는 나의 갈 길을 가겠다.
(go one's own way; will)

______________________________________________.

(3) 어제는 조깅하다 비가 와서 서둘러 일찍 조깅을 끝냈다.
(jog; hurriedly; finish)

______________________________________________.

(4) 그 아이는 너무나 빨리 뛰어서 곧 넘어질 것처럼 보였다.
(a kid; fall down; look as if)

______________________________________________.

(5) 우리가 거리에 나오자 갑자기 서늘한 바람이 불기 시작했다.
(come out; a cool wind; blow)

______________________________________________.

(6) 어둠이 짙어지면서 가로등이 하나 둘 빛을 발하기 시작했다.
(become darker; a streetlight; one by one; shine)

______________________________________________.

(7) 그는 잠에서 깨어나 썰어 놓은 수박 몇 조각을 먹은 후 외출했다.
(wake up; a slice of watermelon)

______________________________________________.

(8) 토요일 오후 세 시에 나와 쇼핑가는 게 어때? (go shopping; shall)

______________________________________________.

(9) 그는 그 아이들을 즐겁게 했으며 그 역시 즐거웠다. (entertain; happy)

______________________________________________.

(10) 교실 안이 추워지기 시작하자 기침하는 학생의 수가 늘어나기 시작했다.
(get cold; cough; the number of)

______________________________________________.

2. 다음을 주어진 표현으로 시작하여 영작하시오.

(1) 그녀는 개를 걸리면서 천천히 인라인스케이트를 타고 있었다.
(walk a dog; skate)

a. Walking ______________________________.

b. While ______________________________.

c. As ______________________________.

d. She ______________________________.

(2) 산들바람이 불어 막 감고 나온 그의 머리가 서서히 마르기 시작했다.
(shampoo; dry)

a. He ______________________________.

b. It ______________________________.

c. The gentle breeze ______________________________.

d. His wet hair ______________________________.

(3) 그가 영작을 열심히 공부한 것이 좋은 일자리를 얻는데 도움이 되었다.
(a good job; get; helpful)

a. The fact ______________________________.

b. His experiences ______________________________.

c. He ______________________________.

d. If ______________________________.

(4) 그들은 그 문제에 관해 오랫동안 토의를 했지만 아무런 결론도 얻지 못했다. (a problem; discuss; reach a conclusion)

a. Although ______________________________.

b. They ______________________________.

c. Despite ______________________________.

d. Their ______________________________.

(5) 그들이 탄 비행기는 천천히 하늘로 높이 치솟고 있었다.

(slowly; soar into)

a. The plane that ______________________________.

b. The plane on ______________________________.

c. They ______________________________.

d. Having taken ______________________________.

# 제10장 · 부정사

## Ⅰ. 기본개념

### 1. 부정사란?

동사의 기본형으로 보통 to와 함께 쓰이며 몇몇 동사의 뒤에서는 to가 생략되기도 한다.

### 2. 부정사의 종류

#### A. 단순부정사

(A) to-부정사

a. I came here [to see] you.

b. I am glad [to meet] you.

(B) 원형부정사

a. He heard her [speak] to a stranger.

b. He made her [go] home.

#### B. 수동부정사

부정사가 타동사인 경우 이 동사 뒤의 목적어가 이 동사의 주어자리로 이동하면 수동부정사가 된다. 'to be + 과거분사'로 나타낸다.

a. You have to wash your car at once.

a.′ Your car has [to be washed] at once.

b. You have to inform your parents of the truth.

b.′ Your parents have [to be informed] of the truth.

### C. 완료부정사

부정사로 나타나 있는 동사의 행위가 이 부정사 앞 주절동사가 나타내는 행위보다 먼저 일어난 것이라는 것을 나타낼 필요가 있을 때 사용한다. 완료부정사의 형태는 'to have + 과거분사'로 나타낸다.

a. You seem [to have lost] weight.

b. I am sorry not [to have finished] this work.

### D. 진행부정사

부정사로 나타나 있는 동사의 행위가 진행 중에 있다는 것을 나타낼 때 사용한다. 'to be + -ing'로 나타낸다.

a. It's nice [to be talking] to you over a cup of coffee.

b. Nowadays he seems [to be reading] lots of books.

## 3. 부정사의 기능

### A. 명사적 기능

a. [To love] one's enemy is not easy.

b. He wants [to love] his enemy.

c. His job is [to teach] love.

### B. 형용사적 기능

a. It is time [to go] to bed.

b. I have nothing [to give] you.

### C. 부사적 기능

a. He came [to see] his girlfriend.

b. He was glad [to meet] her.

c. He was glad enough [to clap] his hands in his heart.

## 4. 부정사의 주어

부정사 바로 앞에 오는 것이 일반적이다.

### A. 일반주어인 경우

부정사의 주어가 일반인일 때는 보통 생략한다.

a. [To borrow] videos from this shop, it is necessary to register as a member of the shop. (=For one to borrow~)

b. [To do] one's best is the most important thing in sports. (=For one to do~)

### B. 전치사 for와 함께 오는 경우

부정사의 주어는 보통 전치사 for와 함께 온다.

a. It is time [for you] to go to bed.

b. My idea is [for you] to make peace with your friend.

### C. 전치사 of와 함께 오는 경우

가주어 it과 진주어인 to-부정사로 표현되는 문장에서, 가주어 뒤에 동사의 보어로 인간행위를 판단하는 silly, kind, foolish와 같은 형용사가 올 때 부정사의 의미상의 주어 앞에 전치사 of가 온다.

a. It was very unwise [of you] to tell lies.

b. It is kind [of you] to tell me the way to the station.

### D. 타동사의 목적어와 동일한 경우

부정사의 주어가 타동사의 목적어와 동일할 때는 부정사의 주어 앞에 전치사 for를 두지 않는다.

a. I want [him] to join us.

b. She wants [her boyfriend] to go abroad with her.

### E. 부정사 바로 앞에 나타나 있지 않은 경우

부정사의 주어가 특별히 표시되어 있지 않으면 주절의 주어와 같은 것을 가리킨다.

a. [I] will be happy to go to your birthday party.

b. [I] want to go up a mountain with you.

## 5. 부정사의 위치

부정사는 보통 문장에서 명사구가 나타나는 위치에 오지만 전치사 뒤는 오지 않는다.

### A. 주어 위치

(A) 문장의 주어 위치

a. [To do] one's best is not easy.

b. [To go] alone is dangerous.

(B) 가주어에 대한 진주어 위치

a. It is not easy [to do] one's best.

b. It is dangerous [to go] alone.

### B. 주격 보어 위치

a. His intention was [to slip] out of the room.

b. His ambition was [to get] his country out of its economic crisis.

### C. 타동사의 목적어 위치

(A) 직접 목적어 위치

a. She likes [to meet] him only on weekends.

b. He wants [to go] in-line skating on weekends.

(B) 가목적어에 대한 진목적어 위치

a. She thought it natural for him [to admire] her.

b. He considered it unnatural for her [to think] so.

### D. 타동사의 목적보어 위치

a. The farmer believed her [to be] his wife.

b. He thought the shoes [to be] hers.

### E. 전치사의 목적어 위치

a. *The politician is fond of [to read] lots of books.

b. *He is afraid of [to meet] his political opponents.

F. 동격 관계로서의 부정사

a. Your ambition, [to become] a politician, requires leadership and patience.

b. Her wish, [to become] a fluent speaker of English, will be realized.

## Ⅱ. 기본연습

※ 다음 중 어법이 잘못된 곳을 찾아 고쳐 쓰시오.

1. The man heard his wife to talk to a foreigner.

   ____________________________________________.

2. It was nice for you to make peace with your friend.

   ____________________________________________.

3. I will be happy for me to go to your wedding feast.

   ____________________________________________.

4. She considered it unfair for her parents putting boys above girls.

   ____________________________________________.

5. Your wish, become a billionaire, will be realized only if you try to.

   ____________________________________________.

6. Your shoes sometimes have to wash, since they are apt to get dirty.

   ____________________________________________.

7. He speaks English very well, but he is afraid of to speak it in public.

   ____________________________________________.

8. He wanted his daughters come back home before ten o'clock at night.

   ____________________________________________.

9. I am sorry not to finish this work; however, I will finish it sooner or later.

_______________________________________________.

10. She was made go back home soon, because he did not want her to stay any longer.

_______________________________________________.

## 정답 및 해설

### II. 기본연습

1. to talk → talk

지각동사 뒤에 부정사가 올 때는 원형부정사로 와야 한다. 따라서 지각동사 hear 뒤의 to talk은 talk이 되어야 한다.

2. for → of

진주어가 to-부정사이고 가주어 it이 있는 문장에서 가주어 뒤의 보어가 인간 행위를 판단하는 형용사일 때 부정사의 주어 앞 전치사는 of를 쓴다.

3. for me → ∅

부정사의 주어가 전체 문장의 주어와 동일할 때는 특별히 부정사의 주어를 명기할 필요가 없다. 부정사 to go의 주어가 전체 문장의 주어 I와 동일하다.

4. putting → to put

동사 consider의 가목적어 it이 나오고 뒤에 목적보어인 형용사구 unfair가 나와 있으므로 진목적어인 to-부정사가 뒤에 와야 한다.

5. become → to become

주어인 your wish 뒤에 삽입된 요소는 주어와 동격 관계가 되어야 한다. 따라서 주어와 같은 것을 가리키는 to-부정사가 되어야 한다.

6. wash → be washed

to-부정사 to wash에서 타동사 wash의 목적어 자리에 있던 your shoes가 이 동사 앞의 주어자리로 이동한 것으로 부정사는 수동부정사가 되어야 한다.

7. to speak → speaking

to-부정사는 전치사의 뒤인 전치사의 목적어 자리에서 목적어가 될 수 없다. 따라서 이것을 동명사로 바꿔야 한다.

8. come → to come

동사 want 뒤에 목적어인 명사구와 목적보어인 to-부정사가 올 수 있다. 동사 want의 목적보어 자리에 원형부정사 come이 와서 비문이다.

9. finish → have finished

일을 끝마치지 않은 데 대해 미안하다고 말할 때 끝마치지 않은 것은 미안한 것보다 순서상 먼저 일어난 사건이므로 단순부정사 to finish 대신 완료부정사 to have finished를 써야 한다.

10. go → to go

능동문의 사역동사 뒤에서 원형부정사가 된 to-부정사는 수동문에서 다시 to-부정사로 바뀐다.

## Ⅲ. 심화연습

※ 다음 영작 중 비문을 고르고 그 이유를 설명하시오.

1. 그 남자는 신문을 읽고 있는 중인 체 했다.

a. The man pretended to be reading a newspaper.

b. The man feigned him to be reading a newspaper.

c. The man feigned that he was reading a newspaper.

d. The man pretended that he was reading a newspaper.

정답 : ________

이유 : ____________________________________________.

2. 내가 돌아올 때까지 이 방을 깨끗이 청소해야 한다.

a. This room must be swept clean before I come back.

b. You have to clean up this room before I come back.

c. You have to finish sweeping this room clean before I come back.

d. It is required that this room must be cleaned up until I come back.

정답 : ________

이유 : ____________________________________________.

3. 내가 그녀를 우리와 함께 등산 가는 데 동참하게 할게.

a. I will press her to join us in the mountain climbing.

b. I will persuade her to join us in going up a mountain.

c. I will try to make her join us in climbing up a mountain.

d. I will let she consent to her going up a mountain with us.

정답 : ________

이유 : ____________________________________________________________.

4. 그녀는 그를 어디선가 만난 적이 있는 것처럼 보인다.

a. I think she has met him somewhere before.

b. She seems to having met him somewhere before.

c. It seems that she has met him some place before.

d. It seems to me that she has met him somewhere before.

정답 : ________

이유 : ____________________________________________________________.

5. 내가 오늘 너의 집에 갈 수는 없지만 내일은 꼭 가겠다.

a. I cannot go to your house today, but I certainly will tomorrow.

b. I certainly will call at your house tomorrow, though I cannot today.

c. It is impossible for me to go to your house today, but I will certainly call on you tomorrow.

d. I will certainly visit your house tomorrow, even though I cannot today.

정답 : ________

이유 : ____________________________________________________________.

6. 그는 거의 두 시간 동안 신문을 읽고 있는 중인 것 같다.

a. He seems to have been reading a newspaper for about two hours.

b. It seems that he has been reading a newspaper for about two hours.

c. It seems to me that he has been reading a newspaper since about two hours ago.

d. It appears that he began to read a newspaper about two hours ago and is still reading.

정답 : _______

이유 : ________________________________________________.

7. 당신이 그렇게 말씀하시다니 당신은 참으로 친절하시군요.

a. It is very kind of you to say so.

b. You must be very kind to say so.

c. That is very kind of you to say so.

d. Since you say so, you are a very kind person.

정답 : _______

이유 : ________________________________________________.

8. 그 여대생은 그 교수를 이전에 결코 만난 적이 없는 체 가장했다.

a. The coed pretended never to have met the professor before.

b. The coed feigned that she has never met the professor before.

c. The coed pretended that she had never met the professor before.

d. The coed pretended never to have met the professor, even though she had done so before.

정답 : _______

이유 : ________________________________________________.

9. 그는 여가시간을 조깅을 하거나 인라인스케이트를 타는 데 보낸다.

a. He spends his leisure jogging or in-line skating.

b. He spends his spare time on jogging or in-line skating.

c. When he is free, he usually goes jogging or does in-line skating.

d. Jogging or in-line skating are what he usually does in his free hours.

정답 : _______

이유 : ________________________________________________.

10. 그 아이의 어머니는 그에게 학교에서 친구들과 싸우지 말라고 당부했다.

a. The child's mother asked him not to fight his friends in school.

b. The child's mother demanded that he not fight with his friends in school.

c. The child's mother told him not to have a fight with his friends in school.

d. The child was asked to have not a fight with his friends in school by his mother.

정답 : ________

이유 : ____________________________________________.

## Ⅳ. 기본영작

※ 다음을 영작하시오.

1. 너의 자동차는 세차를 할 필요가 있다. (wash; need)

____________________________________________.

2. 솔직하게 말하면 우리는 아주 친한 친구라고 할 수는 없다.
(frankly speaking; close)

____________________________________________.

3. 그는 그녀가 차 안으로 들어간 뒤 곧 멀리 떠나는 것을 보았다.
(get into; drive off)

____________________________________________.

4. 나는 그녀가 거기 가길 바랐지만 그녀는 내가 거기 가길 바랐다.
(there; want)

____________________________________________.

5. 외국어를 자신의 모국어보다 더 잘한다는 것은 거의 불가능하다.
(a foreign language; one's native tongue)

____________________________________________.

6. 비가 내리기 시작해서 나는 잠시 몸을 피하자고 친구를 설득했다.
(start to rain; hide; persuade)

____________________________________________.

7. 그는 내일 여자 친구의 부모님을 만나기로 되어 있다. (meet; be to)

8. 그녀 대신 그녀의 친구를 거기 보내는 게 어떨까? (instead of; send)

9. 그는 열 시 정각에 여기 도착하기로 되어 있었지만 아직 오지 않았다.
(get; be supposed to; come)

10. 네가 그녀를 찾고 있다면 내가 곧 그녀를 너에게 보내겠다. (look for)

## V. 심화영작

1. 다음을 영작하시오.

(1) 그 친구는 유학을 가기 위해 열심히 돈을 저축하고 있다.
(go abroad for study; save money)

(2) 그는 생활비를 벌기 위해 다시 학원에서 강의를 시작했다.
(living expenses; earn; lecture at an academy)

(3) 그 아이는 친구들과 방에서 동화책을 읽고 있는 중인 것 같다.
(a fairy tale; seem)

(4) 그 외국인은 누군가에게 전자메일을 보내고 있는 중인 것 같다.
(a foreigner; an e-mail; send)

(5) 그는 자신이 쓸 돈도 모자랐지만 그의 후배에게 돈을 빌려 주었다.
(enough; one's junior; lend)

____________________________________________________.

(6) 정치가는 국민을 위해 무엇을 해야 하는가? (a politician; a citizen)

____________________________________________________.

(7) 매년 너의 차를 정기적으로 점검할 필요가 있다. (regularly; check)

____________________________________________________.

(8) 그는 그의 친구가 와서 기뻤고 그의 친구는 그의 환영을 받아 기뻤다.
(pleased; be welcomed)

____________________________________________________.

(9) 남의 존경을 받기 위해서는 당연히 남에게 도움이 되는 일을 해야 한다.
(be respected; should; be helpful to)

____________________________________________________.

(10) 그는 자신의 마음을 가라앉히지 않고는 안전운전을 할 수 없다고 생각했다. (calm oneself down; drive safely)

____________________________________________________.

2. 다음을 주어진 표현으로 시작하여 영작하시오.

(1) 그는 요즘 돈을 많이 벌 수 있는 방법을 연구 중이다.
(make money; a way; look for)

a. His objective ________________________________________.

b. These days _________________________________________.

c. He ________________________________________________.

d. The topic __________________________________________.

(2) 바람이 파도를 일으켜 그들은 낚시를 포기하고 돌아왔다.
(fishing; give up; come back)

a. The waves _________________________________________.

b. They ______________________________.

c. The wind ______________________________.

d. Because ______________________________.

(3) 그는 비행기를 놓치지 않으려고 서둘러 집을 나와 택시를 탔다.

(catch; hurriedly; get in the taxi)

a. He ______________________________.

b. As ______________________________.

c. It ______________________________.

d. Because ______________________________.

(4) 그녀는 나이는 어리지만 어떤 어른에 못지않을 정도로 이해력이 있다.

(an adult; understand)

a. Young ______________________________.

b. She ______________________________.

c. Although ______________________________.

d. Despite ______________________________.

(5) 그 어른은 키가 너무 작아서 나는 그를 어린아이로 착각했다.

(mistake~for~)

a. That adult ______________________________.

b. The adult's short height ______________________________.

c. Because of ______________________________.

d. I ______________________________.

# 제11장 · 동명사

## Ⅰ. 기본개념

### 1. 동명사란?

-ing로 끝나면서 명사로서 쓰이는 준동사로 문장에서 주어, 보어, 목적어로 쓰이며 보어, 목적어, 수식어를 취할 수도 있다.

### 2. 동명사의 종류

A. 단순동명사

동사 뒤에 -ing가 붙은 것으로 명사적으로 쓰인다.

a. [Collecting] pretty leaves is her hobby.

b. His hobby is [playing] table tennis.

B. 수동동명사

'being + 과거분사'가 명사처럼 쓰이는 경우를 말하며 수동의 의미를 가지고 있다.

a. He is afraid of [being punished].

b. I don't like [being insulted] by others.

### C. 완료동명사

이미 끝난 행위에 관해 이야기할 때 완료동명사를 쓰며 'having + 과거분사'로 나타낸다.

a. The criminals admitted [having taken] the rifles from the soldiers.

b. The professor regrets [having said] such things in public.

## 3. 동명사의 기능

명사로서의 기능을 하며 형용사로서의 기능을 하는 현재분사와 구별된다.

a. [Reading] books makes us keep calm in mind. (동명사)

b. I met a child [beating] a dog with a stick. (현재분사)

## 4. 동명사의 주어

### A. 일반주어인 경우

특별히 나타낼 필요가 없으므로 생략하는 것이 보통이다.

a. [Loving] others is not always difficult.

b. [Respecting] one's parents is so natural.

### B. 일반주어가 아닌 경우

(A) 명사나 대명사의 소유격을 쓰는 경우

a. [Tom's] reading so many novels surprised his friends.

b. [His] finishing homework so fast made his friends embarrassed.

(B) 목적격을 쓰는 경우

a. My girlfriend hates [me] meeting other girls.

b. There is a possibility of [the villagers in the area] breaking into the city hall.

## 5. 동명사의 위치

### A. 주어 위치

a. [Playing] golf is not very popular among the common people.

b. [Studying] English every day is not an easy thing to do.

### B. 주격보어 위치

a. His job is [teaching] English.

b. Her only purpose is [making] as much money as possible.

### C. 타동사의 목적어 위치

a. The nurse enjoys [caring] for her patients.

b. She hates [living] alone.

### D. 전치사의 목적어 위치

a. The clown is fond of [being] laughed at by others.

b. He makes people pleasant by [pretending] to be a fool.

## 6. 동명사 뒤에 올 수 있는 요소

동명사로 쓰인 동사의 특성에 따라 그 뒤에 나타날 요소가 결정된다.

### A. 어떤 요소도 오지 않는 경우

a. What he does every day is just walking.

b. He enjoys walking [here and there]. (부사는 선택적 요소)

### B. 보어가 오는 경우

(A) 명사구 보어가 오는 경우

a. Becoming [a famous scientist] is not an easy matter.

b. He is afraid of remaining [a mere spectator] in his life.

(B) 형용사구 보어가 오는 경우

a. The police are after the stranger for looking [suspicious].

b. The man hates remaining [single].

### C. 목적어가 오는 경우

(A) 목적어가 하나 오는 경우

a. Living [a happy life] is her only purpose.

b. Her job is teaching [English] to children.

(B) 목적어가 둘 오는 경우

a. She makes the children merry by giving [them] [some eatables].

b. She is fond of bringing [them] [eatables and drinkables].

D. 목적어와 목적보어가 오는 경우

a. Making [somebody] [merry] is not my job.

b. The man criticized his friend severely by calling [him] [a betrayer].

## Ⅱ. 기본연습

※ 다음 중 어법이 잘못된 곳을 찾아 고쳐 쓰시오.

1. I am not good at making people merrily.

   ________________________________________.

2. The boy is afraid of punishing by his mother.

   ________________________________________.

3. Doing some work hasty is apt to make it half-done.

   ________________________________________.

4. She is angry about not to have been invited to the party.

   ________________________________________.

5. He sometimes feels tired, but in general, he enjoys to serve at table.

   ________________________________________.

6. Painting pictures sometimes give him some kind of calmness of mind.

   ________________________________________.

7. They expressed their respect for the scientist by call him a true patriot.

   ________________________________________.

8. What she did in the past was teaching to the elementary school students arithmetic.

   ________________________________________.

9. He and his wife hate not only borrowing something from others, but also to lend it.

______________________________________________.

10. He hates not only remaining bachelor so long, but also marrying a woman that is inappropriate for his spouse.

______________________________________________.

## 정답 및 해설

### II. 기본연습

1. merrily → merry

동사 make는 '~을 ~하게 하다'는 의미를 전할 때 자신이 동명사라 하더라도 여전히 뒤에 목적어와 목적보어가 오기를 요구한다. 따라서 목적어 people 뒤에 목적보어인 형용사가 와야 한다.

2. punishing → being punished

동사 punish는 '~을 벌주다'는 타동사로 뒤에 목적어가 와야 한다. 그러나 뒤에 와야 할 목적어가 이 동사의 앞에 있으므로 수동동명사가 되어야 한다.

3. hasty → hastily

동명사 doing은 타동사가 동명사로 바뀐 것이므로 뒤에 목적어가 와야 한다. 따라서 명사구 some work이 목적어이므로 그 뒤는 동명사 doing을 수식하는 부사는 올 수 있지만 형용사는 올 수 없다.

4. to have → having

전치사의 뒤는 전치사의 목적어 자리로 동사가 올 때는 동명사로 와야 한다. to-부정사 to have는 전치사 about의 목적어가 되려면 동명사가 되어야 한다.

5. to serve → serving

동사 enjoy는 동명사를 목적어로 취할 수는 있지만 부정사를 목적어로 취할 수는 없다. 따라서 to-부정사 to serve를 동명사 serving으로 고쳐야 한다.

6. give → gives

동명사 painting이 명사구 pictures를 목적어로 취하고 있다. 따라서 문장의 주어가 동명사 painting이므로 동사는 단수인 주어와 일치해야 한다.

7. call → calling

전치사 뒤는 전치사의 목적어 자리이므로 동사가 올 때는 동명사가 되어야 한다. 전치사 by 뒤의 동사 call을 동명사로 고쳐야 한다.

8. to → ∅

be동사 was의 보어 자리에 있는 동명사 teaching은 '~에게 ~을 가르치다'는 의미를 전할 때 뒤에 목적어가 두 개 온다. 직접목적어 앞에 간접목적어가 올 때는 간접목적어 앞에 전치사를 쓰지 않는다.

9. to lend → lending

상관접속사 not only~but also 구문에서 not only 뒤와 but also 뒤는 같은 구조의 요소가 와야 한다. 전자 뒤에 동명사 borrowing이 와 있으므로 후자 뒤에도 동명사가 와야 한다. 후자 뒤에 부정사가 와서 비문이다.

10. bachelor → a bachelor

타동사 hate의 목적어인 동명사 remaining은 뒤에 보어인 형용사구나 명사구가 오기를 요구하는 동사이다. 따라서 보어 자리의 명사 bachelor를 명사구로 고쳐야 한다.

## Ⅲ. 심화연습

※ 다음 영작 중 비문을 고르고 그 이유를 설명하시오.

1. 말보다는 행동으로 보여 주어야 한다.

a. Actions speak louder than words.

b. You should act instead of only speaking words.

c. You have to take action instead talking about your ideals.

d. You must show your intention in your manner rather than in your words.

정답 : ________

이유 : ________________________________________.

2. 그 소녀는 남의 웃음거리가 되는 것을 두려워한다.

a. The girl is afraid that she may appear foolish.

b. The girl is afraid of being made a fool of by others.

c. The girl is afraid of being laughed at by other people.

d. The girl is afraid that others may make a fool of herself.

정답 : ________

이유 : ______________________________________________.

3. 성공하는 방법 중 하나는 한 분야에 노력을 집중하는 것이다.

a. One way to succeed is to exert oneself only in one field.

b. Exerting oneself in only one field is a good route to your success.

c. If you want to succeed, you have to exert yourself only in one field.

d. One way to success is to concentrate all one's efforts only in one field.

정답 : ________

이유 : ______________________________________________.

4. 그가 아침에 일어나 제일 먼저 하는 일은 이불을 개는 것이다.

a. When he gets up in the morning, he folds up the bedclothes first.

b. As soon as he gets up in the morning, he folds up the bedclothes.

c. What he does first after he gets up in the morning is to fold up the bedclothes.

d. Folding up the bedclothes is first thing he does after he gets up in the morning.

정답 : ________

이유 : ______________________________________________.

5. 그 남자는 그녀를 만난 적이 없다는 것을 판사 앞에서 인정했다.

a. The man admitted having not met her, in the presence of the judge.

b. The man admitted that he had not met her, in the face of the judge.

c. In the judge's presence, the man admitted that he had never met her.

d. In the presence of the judge, the man admitted that never had he met her.

정답 : ______

이유 : ________________________________________.

6. 매일 열심히 일하는 것이 미래에 대한 가장 믿을 만한 대비책이다.

a. If you work hard every day, you don't have to make any additional efforts to provide for the future.

b. If you really want to provide for the future, you naturally have to do your daily work hard. It is the most reliable way.

c. It is the most reliable way for your future that you will do your best in your daily work.

d. The most reliable way to provide for the future is to work hard every day.

정답 : ______

이유 : ________________________________________.

7. 좋은 책을 읽는 것은 영양분이 풍부한 음식을 먹는 것처럼 중요하다.

a. We have to read good books like we eat nutritious food.

b. Reading good books are as important as eating nutritious foods.

c. Good books are needed for your mind, just as nutritious foods are needed for your body.

d. Good books are to your mind what nutritious foods are to your body.

정답 : ______

이유 : ________________________________________.

8. 그 노인은 도시에 사는 것을 좋아하지 않아서 곧 시골로 가려고 한다.

a. The old man does not like to live in the city, so he is going to the country soon.

b. The old man is not satisfied with living in the city. This is why he is going to the country soon.

c. The old man is not accustomed to living in the city; therefore, he is going to the country soon.

d. The old man is going to the country sooner or later, for he does not like city life.

정답 : ________

이유 : ____________________________________________.

9. 그 거지는 자신이 부양할 가족이 많다는 것을 주위 사람들에게 알렸다.

a. The beggar let others know that he had to keep lots of dependants.

b. The beggar informed of others that he had a large family to support.

c. The beggar told people around him that he had lots of dependants to support.

d. The begger made it known to the people around him that he had a big family to feed.

정답 : ________

이유 : ____________________________________________.

10. 그녀가 그의 어깨를 톡톡 두드린 것이 그 둘의 말다툼의 원인이 되었다.

a. She patted him on the shoulder a few time, which sparked their quarrel.

b. She gave him a few pats on his shoulder, which caused a quarrel between them.

c. A few pats on his shoulder by her started a quarrel between him and her.

d. Her pats on his shoulder brought about a quarrel between him and her.

정답 : ________

이유 : ____________________________________________.

## Ⅳ. 기본영작

※ 다음을 영작하시오.

1. 식사량을 줄이는 것도 체중을 줄이는데 도움이 된다.
(food intake; reduce; lose weight)
______________________________________________.

2. 그 아이가 가장 좋아하는 것은 독후감을 쓰는 것이다.
(favorite; write one's impressions)
______________________________________________.

3. 구타하는 것과 구타당하는 것 모두 보기에 아름답지는 않다.
(abuse and being abused; look at; good)
______________________________________________.

4. 성급하게 결론을 내리는 것은 아무런 결과도 가져오지 못한다.
(a hasty decision; lead to)
______________________________________________.

5. 모기나 파리를 죽이는 것은 살생을 하는 것이어서 나쁜 일인가?
(a mosquito; a fly; take life)
______________________________________________.

6. 네가 그 일을 대충 끝내는 것은 우리 모두에게 바람직하지 않다.
(incompletely; end; desirable)
______________________________________________.

7. 그 여학생은 자신이 학생인 것을 좋아하지 않는다. (a girl student)
______________________________________________.

8. 자식에게 너무 많은 돈을 주는 것은 자식의 인생을 그르치는 것이다.
(too much money; spoil)
______________________________________________.

9. 그는 벌 받는 것을 두려워하고 그의 어머니는 벌주는 것을 두려워한다.

(get punished; afraid; while)

______________________________________________.

10. 어두운 데서 독서를 하는 것은 너의 눈에 좋지 않다.

(in the dark; for; bad)

______________________________________________.

## V. 심화영작

1. 다음을 영작하시오.

(1) 한 겨울에 길거리에서 잠을 자면 동사할 수 있다.

(in midwinter; freeze to death)

______________________________________________.

(2) 컴퓨터 자판을 오랫동안 두드리면 피곤해지기 마련이다.

(type on a computer; get tired; be apt to)

______________________________________________.

(3) 하품은 네가 피곤하다는 것을 보여 주는 하나의 증거이다.

(yawning; tired; a sign of)

______________________________________________.

(4) 그 꽃을 꺾으면 다른 사람이 그 꽃을 감상할 기회가 없어진다.

(pick; appreciate; a chance)

______________________________________________.

(5) 많은 사람이 다니는 길에 침을 뱉는 것은 남을 불쾌하게 한다.

(a busy street; spit; disgusted)

______________________________________________.

(6) 그가 밤늦게까지 열심히 일하는 것은 가족을 부양하기 위해서다.

(till late at night; support)

________________________________________.

(7) TV를 너무 많이 보면 피로하여 일할 때 능률이 떨어질 수 있다.

(get tired; decrease work efficiency)

________________________________________.

(8) 그 소녀의 취미는 예쁜 나뭇잎을 따서 책갈피에 끼워두는 것이다.

(a hobby; pick a leaf; put~in a book)

________________________________________.

(9) 너무 많이 울면 눈이 부을 수도 있다. (cry too much; get swollen)

________________________________________.

(10) 매일 같은 시간에 독서를 한다면 정신적인 안정에 도움이 될 것이다.

(at the same time; feel peace of mind)

________________________________________.

2. 다음을 주어진 표현으로 시작하여 영작하시오.

(1) 교실에서는 휴대폰을 무음이나 진동으로 설정해 두어야 한다.

(put~in silent or vibration mode)

a. Cell phones ________________________________.

b. During ________________________________.

c. In ________________________________.

d. You ________________________________.

(2) 식후에 항상 과일을 먹는가의 여부가 빈부의 차이를 드러낸다.

(fruit; rich; tell)

a. Whether ________________________________.

b. Always ________________________________.

c. One ________________________________.

d. The gap ________________________________.

(3) 채식이 육식보다 건강에 좋다고들 한다. (eat vegetables; meat)

a. I ________________________________________.

b. People ________________________________________.

c. They ________________________________________.

d. It ________________________________________.

(4) 하루에 만보이상 걸으면 건강에 매우 좋다. (a step; good for health)

a. A person ________________________________________.

b. Walking ________________________________________.

c. I ________________________________________.

d. It ________________________________________.

(5) 세월은 새것을 만들어 내고 오래된 것을 사라지게 한다.
(create; disappear)

a. Time ________________________________________.

b. With ________________________________________.

c. It ________________________________________.

d. As ________________________________________.

# 제12장 · 분 사

## Ⅰ. 기본개념

### 1. 분사란?

형용사로서 쓰인 준동사로 명사나 대명사를 수식할 수 있으며 동사로부터 파생되어 목적어를 취할 수도 있고 부사의 수식을 받을 수도 있다.

A. 현재분사

동사 뒤에 -ing를 붙인 것으로 형용사처럼 쓰이는 것을 가리킨다.

B. 과거분사

-d, -ed, -t, -n, -en으로 끝나거나 모음을 변화시켜 만든다.

### 2. 분사의 종류

A. 현재분사

a. The boy is [playing] soccer.

b. The girl met a boy [carrying] a ball.

### B. 과거분사

a. The boy has [finished] playing soccer.

b. He seemed [disappointed].

### C. 완료분사

'having + 과거분사'가 분사로 쓰이는 것을 말하며 분사로 표현되어 있는 동사가 나타내는 행위가 주절동사가 나타내는 행위보다 먼저 일어난 것이라는 것을 분명하게 전달할 필요가 있을 때 쓴다.

a. [Having finished] the game, the boy left to take a shower.

b. [Having eaten] the frog, the snake disappeared slowly.

### D. 완료진행분사

'having been -ing' 형태를 말하며 주절동사가 나타내는 때보다 이전에 시작된 행위가 주절동사가 나타내는 시점에도 여전히 진행 중이라는 의미를 전할 때 사용한다.

a. [Having been reading] the novel for hours, she suddenly felt tired.

b. [Having been running] for an hour, the runner felt very thirsty.

## 3. 분사의 기능

a. A baby is [sleeping].

a.′ The [sleeping] baby is my nephew.

a.″ The baby [sleeping] on the bed is my nephew.

b. The book is [written] in Korean and English.

b.′ You should sit for a [written] examination.

b.″ The book [written] in Korean and English is an English composition book.

## 4. 분사의 시제

현재분사는 주절동사가 나타내는 때를 나타내는 것이 일반적이지만 문장 진술의 때를 나타내기도 한다. 이와 달리 과거분사는 주절동사가 나타내는 때보다 이전의 때를 나타낸다.

a. The stewardess spends hours, [looking] after her passengers.

b. She spent hours, [looking] after her passengers.

c. Stewardesses [wearing] low-heeled shoes tomorrow will be cautioned.

d. The stewardess [wearing] the low-heeled shoes used to be cautioned.

## 5. 현재분사 뒤의 요소

현재분사로 쓰인 동사의 성격에 따라 그 뒤의 요소가 결정된다. 그 동사가 보어, 목적어, 목적보어를 필요로 하는 동사인가 아닌가에 따라 달라진다.

### A. 부사가 오는 경우

a. The foreigner [walking] [hastily] is my teacher.

b. The woman [coming] [here] is his wife.

### B. 보어가 오는 경우

(A) 명사구 보어가 오는 경우

a. He often meets people [becoming] [his opponents].

b. He finds few people [remaining] [his faithful friends].

(B) 형용사구 보어가 오는 경우

a. We often see leaves [turning] [yellow and red] in autumn.

b. We sometimes meet people [looking] [too serious].

### C. 목적어가 오는 경우

(A) 목적어가 하나 오는 경우

a. She met some children [watching] [TV] in her room.

b. She spoke to a boy [carrying] [a big bag] on his back.

(B) 목적어가 둘 오는 경우

a. His wife is the woman [teaching] [the children] [English].

b. He is the man [giving] [the poor old men] [meals] for free.

### D. 목적어와 목적보어가 오는 경우

a. He always remained a person [making] [his acquaintances] [happy].

b. He is a good father [making] [all his children] [experts].

## 6. 과거분사 뒤의 요소

### A. 어떤 요소도 오지 않는 경우

a. The book was well [written].

b. I bought the only ticket [left].

### B. 보어가 오는 경우

a. He wants to live in a house [painted] [blue].

b. She is afraid of meeting her boyfriend [made] [angry].

## 7. 현재분사와 동명사

현재분사와 동명사 모두 동사 뒤에 -ing가 붙어 있지만 전자는 형용사처럼 후자는 명사처럼 쓰인다는 점이 다르다.

a. He likes people [making] others happy. (현재분사)

b. [Making] others happy is not an easy matter. (동명사)

# II. 기본연습

※ 다음 중 어법이 잘못된 곳을 찾아 고쳐 쓰시오.

1. The man plans to live in a modern house painting blue.

______________________________.

2. Having surrounded by the enemy, the fortress fell soon.

______________________________.

3. The student seemed disappointing when he got a bad grade.

______________________________.

4. The news of her son's death at war left her acquaintances surprising.

______________________________.

5. Writing in Korean and English, the manuscript was sent to the publisher.

_______________________________________________.

6. The crying child met with a few soldiers carried rifles and stopped crying.

_______________________________________________.

7. Having been walking for five hours without stop, the mountain climber felt tiring.

_______________________________________________.

8. The woman is looking for a rich man giving to her money, affection and reputation.

_______________________________________________.

9. Having been eaten an ice cream in a moment, the child insisted on eating another.

_______________________________________________.

10. I do not know any woman not having removed her pet-dog's droppings from the subway train floor.

_______________________________________________.

## 정답 및 해설

### II. 기본연습

1. painting → painted

타동사 **paint**의 목적어 **a modern house**가 이 동사의 주어 자리에 있다. 따라서 이 동사의 분사는 능동의 의미를 가진 현재분사가 아니라 수동의 의미를 가진 과거분사가 되어야 한다.

2. surrounded → been surrounded

동사 surround는 '~을 포위하다'라는 타동사로 뒤에 목적어인 명사구가 나와야 하는데 없다. 논리적으로 볼 때 주절주어 the fortress가 이 동사의 행위자가 아니라 행위를 받는 대상이므로 이 동사는 수동형이 되어야 한다.

3. disappointing → disappointed

동사 disappoint의 앞에 있는 주어 the student가 이 동사의 능동적인 행위자가 아니라 행위를 받는 대상이다. 따라서 이 동사는 현재분사가 아니라 과거분사가 되어야 한다.

4. surprising → surprised

타동사 leave의 목적어인 명사구 her acquaintances가 타동사 surprise의 행위자가 아니라 행위를 받는 대상이므로 현재분사가 아닌 과거분사가 되어야 한다.

5. Writing → Written

타동사 write는 뒤에 목적어가 있어야 하는데 없다. 논리적으로 볼 때 주절주어 the manuscript가 동사 write의 목적어인데 주어 자리에 있으므로 이 동사는 수동의 의미를 가진 과거분사가 되어야 한다.

6. carried → carrying

전치사 with의 목적어인 명사구 a few soldiers가 타동사 carry의 행위자가 되어야 하므로 이 동사는 수동의 의미를 가진 과거분사가 아니라 능동의 의미를 가진 현재분사가 되어야 한다.

7. tiring → tired

주절주어 the mountain climber가 타동사 tire의 행위자가 아니라 행위에 영향을 받는다. 따라서 동사 tire는 과거분사가 되어야 한다.

8. to → ∅

동사 give는 수여동사로 이 동사가 현재분사로 바뀌어도 여전히 직접목적어 앞에 간접목적어가 올 때 이 간접목적어 앞에 전치사는 쓰지 않는다.

9. been → ∅

타동사 eat의 행위자가 주절주어 the child이다. 이 동사 뒤에 목적어인 명사구 an ice cream이 그대로 있으므로 동사가 수동형 been eaten이 될 수 없다.

10. not having → who has not

완료분사는 제한관계절처럼 쓰이지 않는다. 완료분사 not having removed가 제한관계절처럼 앞에 있는 명사구 any woman을 수식하고 있어서 비문이다. 따라서 이것을 관계대명사를 이용하여 관계절로 바꾼다.

# Ⅲ. 심화연습

※ 다음 영작 중 비문을 고르고 그 이유를 설명하시오.

1. 밥을 급히 먹으면 속이 불편해질 수 있다.

   a. A hasty meal may upset your stomach.

   b. Don't be hasty while you eat or your stomach may be upset.

   c. When you have your meal hasty, you may have something wrong with your insides.

   d. You'd better take time to eat your meals; otherwise, your stomach may be upset.

정답 : ________

이유 : ______________________________________________________________________.

2. 너는 내가 돌아올 때까지 그 일을 마쳐야 한다.

   a. You must finish the work before I come back.

   b. The work must be done by you before I return.

   c. You have to get the work finished by the time I return.

   d. You have to get through with the work until I come back.

정답 : ________

이유 : ______________________________________________________________________.

3. 곤히 자고 있는 아내 모습이 왠지 측은해 보인다.

   a. I feel sorry for my wife when she is fast asleep, though I don't understand why.

   b. When my wife is fast asleep, I feel sorry for her, but I don't know why.

   c. I feel sorry for my wife when she is fast asleep, for reasons that I cannot understand.

d. I feel pity for my wife when I see her fast asleep, though don't know why.

정답 : _______

이유 : ________________________________________.

4. 그는 내가 어디로 가는 중인지 묻고 그의 길을 갔다.

a. He asked me where I was going, and he went his way.

b. He asked me where was I going, and went on his way.

c. He asked me about my destination, and proceeded on his way.

d. He said to me, "Where are you going?" and made his way along the road.

정답 : _______

이유 : ________________________________________.

5. 가을 단풍은 머지않아 겨울이 올 것이라는 것을 예고한다.

a. Fall foliage tells us that winter will come soon.

b. Winter will begin before long, that the fall foliage tells us.

c. The fall foliage informs us in advance that the winter will be here soon.

d. We can sense, from the fall foliage, that winter is not very far away.

정답 : _______

이유 : ________________________________________.

6. 문법책은 부주의해서 읽으면 오히려 혼동을 야기할 수 있다.

a. A grammar book read carelessly may cause reader's confusion.

b. A grammar book, if it is read carelessly, may bring about your confusion.

c. You may be confused by a grammar book if it is read carelessly.

d. If you read a grammar book carelessly, you are apt to be confused.

정답 : _______

이유 : ________________________________________.

7. 그녀는 등에 아이를 업고 머리에 물동이를 이고 걷고 있었다.

a. She was walking with a baby on her back and a water jar on her head.

b. She was carrying both a baby on her back and a water jar on her head.

c. Having a baby on back and a water jar on head, she was walking.

d. She was carrying not only a baby on the back, but also a water jar on the head.

정답 : ________

이유 : ________________________________________________.

8. 빠르게 스쳐가는 바람이 지난날에 대한 향수를 불러일으킨다.

a. Wind swiftly goes by excites nostalgia.

b. The sudden wind that goes by makes me homesick.

c. I feel homesick at the sudden wind that goes by swiftly.

d. All of a sudden, I feel homesick by the wind swiftly going by.

정답 : ________

이유 : ________________________________________________.

9. 축구가 인기 있을 때는 축구공을 가지고 다니는 아이들을 종종 본다.

a. It is very frequent to meet a child carrying a soccer ball when a soccer enjoys popularity.

b. We often meet children carrying soccer balls when soccer is popular among people.

c. It is not difficult to meet children who are carrying soccer balls when soccer is popular.

d. You are apt to come across children carrying soccer balls while soccer is popular among people.

정답 : ________

이유 : ________________________________________________.

10. 그 처녀는 아주 천천히 걷고 있는 노인을 보자 다가가 부축을 했다.

a. When she saw an old man walking very slowly, the girl neared him and helped him by holding his arms.

b. As soon as she saw an old man walking very slowly, the girl neared him and helped him by holding his arms.

c. On seeing an old man who is walking very slowly, the girl walked up him and helped him.

d. Seeing an old man walking very slowly, the girl walked up to him and helped him by holding his arms.

정답 : ________

이유 : ______________________________________________________________.

## Ⅳ. 기본영작

※ 다음을 영작하시오.

1. 그는 외국에 전혀 가본 적이 없지만 몇 개 국어를 잘 한다.
(have been to; fluent)

______________________________________________________________.

2. 너를 즐겁게 하고 있는 그 남자는 누구냐? (entertain; a man)

______________________________________________________________.

3. 길에서 혼자 울고 있는 어린아이를 만나면 부모를 찾아 주어야 한다.
(on the street; alone; find)

______________________________________________________________.

4. 그 선생이 들어왔을 때 그 학생은 두 시간 동안 공부를 하고 있었다.
(come in; for two hours; study)

______________________________________________________________.

5. 그의 여자 친구에게 실망해서 그는 다른 여자 친구를 찾기로 결심했다.
(disappointed; look for; decide)

______________________________________________.

6. 세 시간 동안 원고를 써 오고 있는 중이어서 그 교수는 매우 피곤했다.
(a manuscript; be tired)

______________________________________________.

7. 큰소리로 책을 읽고 있는 그 아이는 나의 아들이다. (read out a book)

______________________________________________.

8. 매우 행복해 보이는 저 여자는 내가 어제 만났던 여자이다. (happy; look)

______________________________________________.

9. 혼자 커피를 마시고 있는 저 여자를 아니? (alone; have a cup of coffee)

______________________________________________.

10. 그녀는 아이들에게 뭔가를 건네주며 그곳에 서 있었다. (hand out; stand)

______________________________________________.

## V. 심화영작

1. 다음을 영작하시오.

(1) 매우 행복해 보이는 저 두 남녀가 막 결혼한 사람들이다.
(a couple; newlyweds)

______________________________________________.

(2) 감자를 캐고 있는 저 두 사람은 형제이다. (dig a potato)

______________________________________________.

(3) 떠오르는 해를 보고 기분이 좋지 않은 사람은 별로 없을 것이다.
(a sunrise; feel unpleasant; few people)

______________________________________________.

(4) 나는 모두를 즐겁게 하고 있는 그 여자를 얼마 전 만난 적이 있다.
(entertain; not long ago; meet with)

______________________________________________.

(5) 하늘 높이 날고 있는 저 새를 보면 무슨 생각이 드니? (fly up; feel)

______________________________________________.

(6) 빨리 걷고 있는 남자는 남편이고 그 뒤에 가는 여자는 그의 아내이다.
(walk fast; follow)

______________________________________________.

(7) 큰 소리로 노래를 부르고 있는 저 남자가 네 남편이냐? (sing loudly)

______________________________________________.

(8) 그는 머지않아 저 파란색 집에서 살게 될 것이다. (soon; a blue house)

______________________________________________.

(9) 나에게 미소 짓는 저 여자는 내가 잘 알지 못하는 여자이다. (smile at)

______________________________________________.

(10) 인형을 업고 있는 이 아이는 내 딸이고 공을 차고 있는 저 아이는 아들이다. (a doll; on one's back; kick a ball)

______________________________________________.

2. 다음을 주어진 표현으로 시작하여 영작하시오.

(1) 그들은 뜨거운 여름 햇살을 받으면서 열심히 일하고 있었다.
(hot; hard; work)

a. Under ______________________________________________.

b. Over them ______________________________________________.

c. They ______________________________.

d. With ______________________________.

(2) 네가 너의 숙제를 끝마칠 때 나도 내 숙제를 끝마칠 것이다.

(finish; by the time)

a. I ______________________________.

b. At ______________________________.

c. By ______________________________.

d. My homework ______________________________.

(3) 그 외국인이 보낸 편지는 알아보기 힘든 영어로 쓰여 있었다.

(send; difficult-to-understand English)

a. That foreigner ______________________________.

b. The letter ______________________________.

c. It ______________________________.

d. The English letter ______________________________.

(4) 외국어는 꾸준히 공부해야 잘할 수 있다는 것은 잘 알려진 사실이다.

(well-known; a fact)

a. Continuous study ______________________________.

b. A foreign language ______________________________.

c. Everyone ______________________________.

d. It ______________________________.

(5) 그 여성들은 제각기 다른 색으로 머리를 염색한 채 거리를 거닐고 있었다. (dye one's hair; along the street)

a. After ______________________________.

b. With ______________________________.

c. The women ______________________________.

d. Having ______________________________.

# 제13장 · 시 제

## Ⅰ. 기본개념

### 1. 시제란?

동사에 의해 표현된 행위가 일어나는 때를 말한다. 보통 동사에 의해 나타나지만 조동사와 본동사가 함께 나타내기도 한다.

### 2. 시제의 종류

A. 단순시제

(A) 현재시제

현재의 습관적인 행위나 영속적인 상황에 관해 이야기할 때 단순현재시제를 쓴다.

a. My parents [live] in the country.

b. Water [freezes] at zero degree Celsius.

c. First I [take] a bowl and [break] two eggs into it, and then [mix] them with some flour.

d. There [goes] your bus.

e. I will go wherever my wife [goes].

f. I [swear] that I will tell the truth.

g. His plane [arrives] at 11:00.

h. I [open] the door, and I [walk] toward the elevator, and I suddenly [see] an alien.

i. In Chapter 1, Frankenstein [tells] his friend about his Genevese origins. In Chapter 2, he [describes] the perfect serenity of his childhood with his family. In Chapter 3, he [leaves] for Ingolstadt for college. In Chapter 4, he ...

(B) 과거시제

빨리 끝난 행위나 우발사건, 과거의 규칙적이거나 습관적인 행위, 어떤 것을 단지 과거에 일어난 것으로 볼 때 사용한다.

a. My friend [called] on me last night.

b. He [rang] the doorbell more than three times.

c. He [visited] my house while I was sleeping.

d. The New Community Movement [began] in 1970.

e. His girlfriend is not as beautiful as I [expected].

(C) 미래시제

미래에 관해 정보를 제공하거나 미래사건을 예언 또는 예측할 때 사용한다.

a. I think she [will go] abroad to study after graduation.

b. If it rains, the hiking [will be cancelled].

c. [Shall] I [turn] on the heater?

d. The pot is boiling. I [will put] some noodles into it.

e. This car [won't start].

f. You [shall have] this car of mine.

g. All records of the conference [shall] not [be revealed].

## B. 진행시제

화자가 어떤 행위를 완료된 것이나 영속적인 것으로 보지 않고 진행 중인 일시적인 행위로 볼 때 사용한다.

(A) 현재진행시제

a. I [am teaching] English composition.

b. My girlfriend [is studying] English conversation.

(B) 과거진행시제

a. Teresa [was talking] with her friend at ten last night.

b. Her boyfriend [was drinking] beer in a restaurant.

(C) 미래진행시제

a. I [will be writing] a letter this time tomorrow.

b. My roommate [will be reading] a detective novel.

## C. 완료시제

(A) 현재완료시제

과거의 행위나 사건이 현재와 연관이 있을 때 사용하며 기준시점은 현재이다. have / has + 과거분사로 나타낸다.

a. He [has been] to lots of foreign countries.

b. He [has broken] his leg, so he cannot go in-line skating.

(B) 과거완료시제

과거 이전부터 기준시점인 과거까지 일어난 행위나 사건에 관해 이야기할 때 사용한다. had + 과거분사로 나타낸다.

a. When he got to the station, the subway train [had] already [left].

b. He [had finished] his homework when his friend called on him.

(C) 미래완료시제

어떤 행위나 사건이 미래의 기준시점까지 완료되어 있을 것으로 추정할 때 사용한다. will / shall + have + 과거분사로 나타낸다.

a. She [will have finished] eating dinner by then.

b. He [will have got] there this time tomorrow.

## D. 완료진행시제

(A) 현재완료진행시제

어떤 행위나 사건이 과거에 시작되어 기준시점인 현재에도 여전히 진행 중에 있다는 것을 나타낼 때 사용한다. have / has + been + -ing로 나타낸다.

a. It [has been raining] for ten days.

b. She [has been teaching] English for five years.

(B) 과거완료진행시제

과거 이전에 시작된 어떤 행위나 사건이 기준시점인 과거에도 여전히 진행 중이었다는 것을 나타낸다. had + been + -ing로 나타낸다.

a. When she arrived, her friend [had been waiting] for an hour.

b. He [had been reading] a newspaper for two hours when she met him.

(C) 미래완료진행시제

미래의 기준시점까지 그 이전에 시작된 동작이나 상태가 계속되는 셈이 되거나 그때까지 여전히 계속 중에 있을 것이라는 예상을 나타낸다. will / shall + have + been + -ing로 나타낸다.

a. By this time next week, I [shall have been writing] this book for seven weeks.

b. I [will have been teaching] English composition for five years this winter.

## 3. 시제와 관련한 위반

### A. 단순시제와 진행시제의 혼동

a. Mary [writes] science fiction.

b. Mary [is writing] science fiction.

### B. 진행형을 잘못 사용하는 경우

a. *The scholar [is liking] to travel.

b. *The daughter [is resembling] her father.

### C. 단순시제와 완료시제의 혼동

a. The singer [travels] a lot.

b. The singer [has traveled] a lot.

### D. 진행시제와 완료진행시제의 혼동

a. The dancer [is singing].

b. The dancer [has been singing].

E. 완료시제와 완료진행시제의 혼동

a. She [has fed] her baby.

b. She [has been feeding] her baby.

F. 주절과 종속절의 시제가 다른 경우

a. He [said] that New York [is] more exciting than Paris.

a.′ He [said] that New York [was] more exciting than Paris.

b. She [said] that she [wants] to go to New York next year.

b.′ She [said] that she [wanted] to go to New York next year.

G. 종속절에서 특이하게 행동하는 구문

(A) 현재 또는 미래의 의미를 가진 과거형

a. Eleven o'clock. It's time you [went] home.

b. I'd rather you [came] next Saturday.

c. I wish I [had] a beautiful wife.

(B) 과거의 충족되지 않은 욕구를 나타내는 구문

주절동사 hope, want, expect의 과거완료시제 뒤에 종속절이 'would + 동사원형'으로 오면 과거의 충족되지 않은 욕구를 나타낸다.

a. I [had wanted] that I [would become] a famous scientist.

b. I [had expected] that I [would meet] a nice woman like Snow White.

## Ⅱ. 기본연습

※ 다음 중 어법이 잘못된 곳을 찾아 고쳐 쓰시오.

1. I'd rather she will come this Saturday.

______________________________.

2. She will go wherever her boyfriend will go.

______________________________.

3. She will have a daughter by the end of this year.

____________________________________________.

4. The actress is not as beautiful as I have expected.

____________________________________________.

5. My friend has called at my house last night while I was sleeping.

____________________________________________.

6. The Korean War has broken out in 1953, and the New Community Movement has begun in 1970.

____________________________________________.

7. He lives in his wife's home for the moment, because he does not have enough money to buy his own house.

____________________________________________.

8. Writers are writing books, but teachers are teaching students at schools.

____________________________________________.

9. I am knowing that you came to Korea to study Koreans and their culture.

____________________________________________.

10. When he came back from the foreign country, his family already left the old house.

____________________________________________.

## 정답 및 해설

### II. 기본연습

1. will come → came

would rather 뒤에 오는 that-절에서는 동사의 과거형이 쓰여야 한다.

2. her boyfriend will go → her boyfriend goes.

때나 조건을 나타내는 부사절에서는 미래의 의미를 현재가 대신한다. wherever-절이 조건을 나타내는 부사절이므로 미래시제 will go를 현재시제 goes로 바꿔야 한다.

3. have → have had

미래의 기준시점까지 어떤 일이 끝나거나 어떤 일을 경험하게 될 것이라는 의미는 미래완료시제로 전한다. 그녀가 올해 말까지는 딸을 가지게 될 것이라는 의미를 전하려면 미래완료시제를 써야 한다.

4. have → ∅

방금 사실이나 거짓으로 드러난 믿음을 가리킬 때 단순과거시제를 쓴다. 현재완료를 쓰지 않는다.

5. has → ∅

명백한 과거를 나타내는 시간 표현이 있을 때는 단순과거시제를 쓴다. 과거를 나타내는 부사 last night이 있으므로 현재완료시제 has called가 아닌 단순과거시제 called를 써야 한다.

6. has broken → broke, has begun → began

역사적 사실은 보통 단순과거시제로 나타낸다. 따라서 현재완료시제를 단순과거시제로 고쳐야 한다.

7. lives → is living

긴 시간에 걸쳐 이루어지는 행위는 단순시제를 쓰지만 일시적인 행위는 진행시제를 쓴다. 부사구 for the moment가 보여주듯이 그가 처가에서 사는 행위는 현재의 일시적인 행위이므로 현재진행시제를 쓴다.

8. are writing → write, are teaching → teach

작가가 글을 쓰는 행위나 교사가 학교에서 가르치는 행위는 일시적이 아닌 긴 시간에 걸쳐 이루어지는 행위이다. 따라서 단순현재시제가 되어야 한다. 여기서 작가와 교사는 일반적인 의미의 작가와 교사를 가리킨다.

9. am knowing → know

동작동사는 진행형으로 쓰일 수 있지만 일반적으로 상태동사는 진행형으로 쓰일 수 없다. know는 상태동사로 진행형으로 쓰이지 않는다.

10. already → had already

그가 외국에서 돌아온 것이 과거의 기준시점인데 이 때 그의 가족은 이미 옛 집을 떠나고 없었으므로 떠난 것은 과거완료시제가 되어야 한다.

## Ⅲ. 심화연습

※ 다음 영작 중 비문을 고르고 그 이유를 설명하시오.

1. 너무 바빠서 어제 너의 집을 방문할 수 없었다.
   a. I was so busy to visit your house yesterday.
   b. I was so busy that I could not visit your house yesterday.
   c. Too much work made me unable to visit your house yesterday.
   d. Because I had so much work, I was not able to visit your house yesterday.

정답 : ________

이유 : ________________________________________________.

2. 나는 숙제를 하고 있어서 너와 수영하러 갈 수 없다.
   a. I am doing my homework now, so I'm unable to join you for swimming.
   b. I do my homework right now, so I cannot go swimming with you.
   c. I am sorry that I cannot go swimming with you, for I am doing my homework.
   d. I have not finished my homework yet; therefore, I cannot join you for swimming.

정답 : ________

이유 : ________________________________________________.

3. 그는 아파트를 살 때까지 당분간 처가에서 살고 있다.
   a. He is going to buy his own apartment, so he is living in his wife's home for the moment.
   b. He is living in his wife's home for the present, for he wants to buy his own apartment.
   c. He is living in his wife's house for the moment until he will buy an apartment.

d. He is living in his wife's home for the time being, because he plans to buy an apartment.

정답 : ________

이유 : ____________________________________________________________.

4. 정부는 경기회복을 위한 가시적인 조치들을 취했어야 했는데.

a. The government should take some visible measures to recover the economy.

b. I wish the government had taken some visible measures to help the economy recover.

c. It is regrettable that the government did not take visible measures to help the economy recover.

d. Regrettably, the government did not take any visible measures to help the economy recover.

정답 : ________

이유 : ____________________________________________________________.

5. 내년 이맘때에는 그녀는 두 아이의 어머니가 되어 있을 것이다.

a. This time next year she will have had her second baby.

b. By this time next year she will have become the mother of two children.

c. I know she is going to be mother of two children by this time next year.

d. She will have given birth to her second baby by this time next year.

정답 : ________

이유 : ____________________________________________________________.

6. 물은 섭씨 100도에서 끓지만 이 물은 섭씨 90도에서 끓고 있다.

a. Water boils at 100 degrees Celsius, but this water is boiling at 90 degrees Celsius.

b. Water, in general, boils at 100 degrees Celsius, whereas this water is boiling at 90 degrees Celsius.

c. In general, water boils at 100 degrees Celsius. However, this water is boiling at 90 degrees Celsius.

d. Water is boiling at 100 degrees Celsius, but this water is boiling at 90 degrees Celsius.

정답 : _______

이유 : ______________________________________________________________.

7. 구름이 이동하고 있지 않은 것을 보니 비가 올 것 같지는 않다.

a. It does not look rain, for the clouds are not moving.

b. The clouds are not moving, so it is not going to rain.

c. Since there are no clouds moving, it seems that there will be no rain.

d. There are no clouds moving, which indicates that there will be no rain.

정답 : _______

이유 : ______________________________________________________________.

8. 그가 고향을 다시 찾았을 때 노인들은 이미 세상을 떠나고 없었다.

a. The old men and women had already died when he called at his hometown again.

b. He visited his native village again and found that the old men and women had already left the world.

c. When he has revisited his hometown, the old men and women had already passed away.

d. His revisit to his native village made him realize that the old men and women already no longer existed.

정답 : _______

이유 : ______________________________________________________________.

9. 그는 해외여행을 해 본적이 없지만 외국의 명승지에 대해 많이 안다.

a. He has never traveled abroad, but knows lots of foreign showplaces.

b. He has never gone to any foreign countries. However, he has a lot of information about foreign tourist attraction sites.

c. He has lots of knowledge about tourist attractions abroad, even though he has never been to any foreign countries.

d. Even though he has never traveled abroad, he is good at noted places in foreign countries.

정답 : _______

이유 : ________________________________________________.

10. 그 젊은 목사는 그 불쌍한 노인들에게 식사를 무료로 제공해 오고 있다.

a. Free meals have been provided to the poor old men by the young clergyman.

b. The poor old men have been being provided with free meals by the young clergyman.

c. The young clergyman has been providing the poor old men with free meals.

d. The young clergyman has been serving meals to the poor old men for free.

정답 : _______

이유 : ________________________________________________.

## Ⅳ. 기본영작

※ 다음을 영작하시오.

1. 어제 내가 너에게 전화했지만 너는 전화를 받지 않았다.
(call; answer the phone)

________________________________________________.

2. 그들의 대화는 곧 끝날 것이다. (a conversation; be over)

________________________________________________.

3. 그는 내일 그의 어린 아들과 함께 매미를 잡으러 가려고 한다.
(a young son; catch a cicada)

________________________________________________.

4. 내년에 한 권 더 쓰게 되면 나는 세 권의 책을 쓰는 셈이 될 것이다.
(next year; another book)

5. 네가 어제 나에게 전화했을 때 나는 외출하고 집에 없었다. (be out)

6. 내가 이 책을 다 읽자마자 너에게 빌려줄 것이다. (as soon as; lend)

7. 그는 아침 여섯 시에 일어나 운동장을 돌고 일곱 시에 아침식사를 한다.
(get up; run around the athletic field)

8. 내일 비가 오면 우리의 모임은 취소될 것이다. (a meeting; be canceled)

9. 그녀는 삼십분 동안 그 편지를 쓰고 있는 중이다.
(for half an hour; write)

10. 네가 나를 도와주면 내가 너에게 시원한 맥주 한 잔 살게.
(help; cool beer)

## V. 심화영작

1. 다음을 영작하시오.

(1) 나는 내일 바다 구경을 가려고 한다. (see the sea)

(2) 그 학생은 다리가 부러져서 시험을 치러 올 수 없다.
(break one's leg; take a test)

________________________________________.

(3) 운전자가 졸고 있었으므로 그 차는 좌우로 흔들렸다.
(a driver; doze off; sway)

________________________________________.

(4) 나는 그녀를 사랑하며 전에 어떤 여자도 사랑한 적이 없다.
(another woman)

________________________________________.

(5) 그가 전철역에 도착했을 때 그 기차는 이미 떠나고 없었다.
(a subway station; already; leave)

________________________________________.

(6) 나는 지금 면도를 하는 중이어서 너의 전화를 받을 수 없다.
(shave; take one's call)

________________________________________.

(7) 내년 이맘때면 그는 이 학교에서 5년 동안 강의를 하는 셈이 된다.
(this time next year; lecture at)

________________________________________.

(8) 지구가 태양 주위를 돈다는 것은 나도 알고 있다. (go around; also)

________________________________________.

(9) 그는 과거에 담배를 피웠고 현재도 피우고 있으며 앞으로도 피울 것이다.
(smoke; in the future)

________________________________________.

(10) 그녀가 책상에서 시험공부를 하고 있었을 때 그녀 집에 도둑이 침입했다. (at one's desk; a thief; break into)

________________________________________.

2. 다음을 주어진 표현으로 시작하여 영작하시오.

(1) 매일 영어로 문장을 써 보면 영작을 잘 하게 될 것이다.

(in English; be able to)

a. Practicing ______________________________.

b. Your ability ______________________________.

c. You ______________________________.

d. With ______________________________.

(2) 좋은 책을 쓴다는 것은 항상 생각대로 잘 되는 것은 아니다.

(as one might have planned; turn out)

a. Your first book ______________________________.

b. Writing ______________________________.

c. It ______________________________.

d. To write ______________________________.

(3) 그는 자신에 관해서 말하기 싫어하지만 남에 관해서는 캐묻기 좋아한다.

(talk about; avoid; question about others)

a. Despite ______________________________.

b. Although ______________________________.

c. While ______________________________.

d. He ______________________________.

(4) 건강은 건강할 때 지켜야 한다는 말은 맞는 말이다. (take care of; right)

a. People ______________________________.

b. The saying ______________________________.

c. It ______________________________.

d. You ______________________________.

(5) 여름에는 음식이 부패하기 쉬우므로 식중독에 걸리지 않도록 조심해야 한다. (get spoiled; get food poisoning; careful)

a. You ______________________________.

b. Food ______________________________.

c. To prevent ______________________________.

d. Since ______________________________.

# 제14장 · 태

## Ⅰ. 기본개념

### 1. 태란?

주어가 행위를 하는지 아니면 영향을 받는지를 보여주는 동사의 형태를 말한다. 주어가 행위를 할 때의 동사의 형태를 능동태라 하고 행위를 받을 때의 형태를 수동태라 한다. 타동사만이 태를 보여 줄 수 있으며 목적어가 뒤에 나와 있는 타동사는 능동태이다. 수동태에서는 목적어가 주어로 된다.

### 2. 태의 종류

A. 능동태

a. The man [bought] flowers.

b. The woman [sold] her car.

B. 수동태

(A) be-수동태

일반적으로 모든 상황에서 널리 사용할 수 있다.

a. The flowers [were bought] by the man.

b. The car [was sold] by the woman.

(B) get-수동태

어떤 것이 어떤 사람이나 사물에 계획된 것이 아니라 예기치 않게 우연히 일어날 때 쓴다. 격식을 따지지 않는 구어체영어에서 쓰며 구어체에서도 be-수동태만큼 자주 쓰이지는 않는다. 주로 생물인 행위자가 표현되어 있지 않은 구문에서 쓰인다.

a. Our dog [got run over] by a truck.

b. There was a fight in the nightclub, but nobody [got hurt].

## 3. 태의 선택

능동태가 수동태보다 더 직접적이며 힘이 있고 경제적이므로 능동태가 의미 전달에 효과적이다. 그러나 주어가 알려져 있지 않거나 행위자보다 행위를 받는 대상이 더 중요할 때는 수동태가 편리하고 자연스럽다.

a. They [completed] the new bridge in May.

a.′ The new bridge [was completed] in May.

b. They [have written] too many books about Shakespeare.

b.′ Too many books [have been written] about Shakespeare.

## 4. 태와 관련한 위반

'존재'나 '소유'를 나타내는 상태동사는 수동태가 없다. 상태동사 have, become, suit, fit, resemble, lack, hold 등은 수동태가 없다. '의지작용'이나 '태도'를 나타내는 상태동사는 수동태가 있다.

a. *The boy [gets liked] by everybody.

a.′ The boy [is liked] by everybody.

b. *A nice blue house [is had] by you.

b.′ You [have] a nice blue house.

## Ⅱ. 기본연습

※ 다음 중 어법이 잘못된 곳을 찾아 고쳐 쓰시오.

1. His car was damaged by falling branch.

   ________________________________.

2. The criminal was made tell the police everything.

   ________________________________.

3. Mr. Kim was elected the chairman of the committee.

   ________________________________.

4. She wanted to buy the blouse, but money was lacked.

   ________________________________.

5. The mystery cannot explain, since there are no clues left.

   ________________________________.

6. The student was arrived immediately after the class began.

   ________________________________.

7. This school building got built when my grandfather was a schoolboy.

   ________________________________.

8. He hates being made a fool, so he responds actively to others' attack.

   ________________________________.

9. He has been born in Seoul in 1980, and has been living there since then.

   ________________________________.

10. This car must repair before tonight, because I have to drive it tomorrow morning.

    ________________________________.

## 정답 및 해설

### II. 기본연습

1. falling branch → a falling branch

수동문에서 행위자를 나타내는 전치사 by 뒤는 전치사의 목적어인 명사구가 와야 한다. falling branch는 형용사적인 역할을 하는 현재분사 뒤에 셀 수 있는 명사가 단수형으로 와서 명사구가 아니어서 비문이다.

2. tell → to tell

능동문의 사역동사 뒤의 원형부정사는 수동문에서 to-부정사로 바뀐다.

3. the chairman → chairman

유일무이한 지위를 나타내는 말이 문장에서 보어로 쓰일 때 그 명사 앞에 관사를 쓰지 않는다. 능동문에서 타동사 elect의 목적보어가 the chairman of the committee이므로 이 보어 앞의 정관사 the를 쓰지 않는다.

4. money was lacked → she lacked money

lack, resemble 등과 같은 상태동사는 타동사이지만 수동태로 쓰이지 않는다. 그러나 '의지작용'이나 '태도'를 나타내는 상태동사 like는 수동태로 쓰인다.

5. explain → be explained

타동사 explain은 뒤에 목적어인 명사구가 나와야 한다. 그러나 이것이 나와 있지 않고 이 목적어에 상당하는 명사구 the mystery가 주어 자리에 있다. 따라서 동사가 수동태가 되어야 한다.

6. was → ∅

동사 arrive는 '도착하다'는 자동사로 뒤에 목적어인 명사구가 올 수 없다. 따라서 수동문이 만들어 질 수 없다.

7. got → was

의도적이 아닌 우연히 일어나는 일은 get-수동태를 사용할 수 있다. 학교건물이 지어지는 것은 우연히 일어나는 일이 아니므로 get-수동태로 표현할 수 없다. 따라서 be-수동태를 사용해야 한다.

8. a fool → a fool of

make a fool of는 '~을 바보취급하다'는 의미로 전치사 of의 목적어인 명사구가 주어 자리로 이동하여 주어가 되면 타동사 make가 수동태로 바뀐다.

9. has been → was

'~년에 태어났다'는 의미는 단순한 과거의 사실이므로 단순과거시제를 쓴다.

10. repair → be repaired

타동사 repair의 목적어가 이 동사의 주어 자리로 이동해 있으므로 동사는 수동태가 되어야 한다.

## Ⅲ. 심화연습

※ 다음 영작 중 비문을 고르고 그 이유를 설명하시오.

1. 이 책은 잘 팔리며 구하기가 쉽지 않다.

a. This book sells well and is not easy to get it.

b. This book is a good seller, so it is not easy to buy it.

c. This book is so popular among the readers that it is not easy to get it.

d. You may have difficulty in buying this book, because it is quickly sold out.

정답 : ________

이유 : ______________________________________________.

2. 며칠 전 그녀는 하마터면 버스에 치일 뻔 했다.

a. A bus almost ran her over a few days ago.

b. She almost got run over by a bus a few days ago.

c. A few days ago she was nearly run over by a bus.

d. She narrowly missed running over by a bus a few days ago.

정답 : ________

이유 : ______________________________________________.

3. 그는 그 폭도들에게 구타를 당해 병원으로 실려 갔다.

a. The mobs beat him, and he was taken to the hospital.

b. He was beaten by the mobs and carried to the hospital.

c. He was taken to the hospital after he had beaten by the mobs.

d. The mobs beat him, which resulted in his being taken to the hospital.

정답 : ________

이유 : ______________________________________________.

4. 그의 아들은 월남전에서 전사하여 국립묘지에 안장되었다.

a. His son died in action in the Vietnam War and was buried in the National Cemetery.

b. His son was killed in the Vietnam War and buried in the National Cemetery.

c. His son, who was killed in action in the Vietnam War, was buried in the National Cemetery.

d. His son who had been killed in action in the Vietnam War buried in the National Cemetery.

정답 : ________

이유 : ______________________________________________.

5. 우리는 소나기를 만나 재빨리 큰 나무 아래로 몸을 숨겼다.

a. With a sudden shower, we sheltered under a giant tree.

b. The sudden shower made us shelter under a large tree.

c. We were met with a heavy rain, so we quickly sheltered under a big tree.

d. We were caught in a shower and hid ourselves quickly under a large tree.

정답 : ________

이유 : ______________________________________________.

6. 한 번에 모든 것을 해결하려고 하지 말고 하나씩 풀어나가라.

a. I advise you to take time in solving the problems instead trying to solve all the problems at once.

b. Don't try to settle all the problems at once, and settle them one by one instead.

c. You'd better not try to solve all the things at one attempt. Instead, you'd better solve them one by one.

d. Don't be hasty to solve all the problems at a stroke, and solve them one by one.

정답 : ________

이유 : ________________________________________________.

7. 외국어는 마지못해 공부하지 말고 즐겁게 공부해야 효과적이다.

a. A foreign language should be pleasantly learned if it is to learn effectively.

b. If you want to learn a foreign language effectively, you should enjoy studying it.

c. Foreign languages will be effectively learned when they are pleasantly learned.

d. One should not study foreign languages unwillingly. One should enjoy studying them if one wants one's study to be effective.

정답 : ________

이유 : ________________________________________________.

8. 그 꼬마는 쥐가 어머니 차에 치였다고 자기 어머니를 비난했다.

a. The kid blamed her mother for running over a rat with her car.

b. The kid blamed her mother for a rat's being run over by her mother's car.

c. The child reproached her mother for careless driving, insisted that a rat had been run over by her mother's car.

d. A rat got run over by the kid's mother's car, and this made her blame her mother.

정답 : ________

이유 : ________________________________________________.

9. 그는 얼마 전 트럼펫 연주에 깊은 감동을 받았으며 요즘도 종종 듣는다.

a. Some time ago he was deeply moved by somebody's trumpet performance, and he often listens to a trumpet performance nowadays.

b. Some time ago somebody's trumpet performance moved him very deeply, and he often listens to a trumpet performance nowadays.

c. He was deeply moved by a trumpet performance some time ago, and often listens to the trumpet these days.

d. He sometimes listens to a trumpet performance nowadays after he has been deeply moved by it some time ago.

정답 : ________

이유 : ____________________________________________________________.

10. 그가 탄 자동차는 끝없이 긴 자동차 행렬의 호위를 받으며 시가를 달리고 있었다.

a. The car in which he rode was running along the street under the escort of endlessly long escort cars.

b. His car was running along the street with endlessly long rows of cars escorting it.

c. He rode in his car, running along the street, while endlessly long rows of cars were escorting.

d. The car that he rode in was running along the street under the escort of endless rows of escort cars.

정답 : ________

이유 : ____________________________________________________________.

## Ⅳ. 기본영작

※ 다음을 영작하시오.

1. 직업상 항상 남에게 비난을 받는 사람들이 있다.

(because of one's job; criticize)

____________________________________________________________.

2. 그녀는 전철 객차 안에서 한 남자에게 발이 밟혔다.
(a subway train; step on one's foot)

______________________________________________.

3. 이 자동차는 잘 나가지만 너무 비싸서 나는 살 수 없다.
(drive well; expensive)

______________________________________________.

4. 그 시내를 걸어서 건너면 강한 물살에 휩쓸릴 수도 있다.
(a stream; walk across; strong force of)

______________________________________________.

5. 많은 관중으로 둘러싸여 노래하고 있는 저 사람은 누구냐?
(a big audience; surrounded by)

______________________________________________.

6. 한 어린아이가 갑자기 그 차 앞으로 뛰어나와 치일 뻔 했다.
(suddenly; in front of; run over)

______________________________________________.

7. 이 지역은 매년 장마철 개울이 범람하여 홍수피해를 입는다.
(a rainy season; overflow; be damaged by)

______________________________________________.

8. 아내를 구타하는 것과 아내에게 구타당하는 것 모두 피해야 할 일이다.
(beat; avoid)

______________________________________________.

9. 그는 많은 사람들의 존경을 받았지만 자기 아내의 존경을 받지는 못했다.
(respect)

______________________________________________.

10. 옛날에는 미친개에게 사람들이 물리는 일이 종종 있었다.
(a mad dog; bite)

______________________________________________.

## V. 심화영작

1. 다음을 영작하시오.

(1) 그 아이들은 그 이방인을 쫓아다니며 놀렸다.
(a stranger; follow; make fun of)
______________________________.

(2) 그 두 사람이 그 영화관에서 나오는 것을 나는 보았다.
(a movie theater; walk out of)
______________________________.

(3) 그 거지는 구걸하러 그 집에 들어갔지만 주인에게 쫓겨났다.
(a beggar; go into; an owner; turn away)
______________________________.

(4) 그는 그 회사 입사에 실패했지만 다시 도전하여 입사하였다.
(fail; try again)
______________________________.

(5) 날씨가 더운 데도 불구하고 그 도서관은 학생들로 가득 차 있다.
(hot weather; full of)
______________________________.

(6) 그는 초대장을 받았지만 선약이 있어서 그 파티에 가지 않았다.
(invite; a previous engagement)
______________________________.

(7) BMW는 잘 나가지만 너무 비싸서 나 같은 서민은 살 수가 없다.
(a BMW; a common person; afford)
______________________________.

(8) 그 학생은 친구들로부터 조용히 하라는 요청을 받았다. (quiet; ask)

________________________________________.

(9) 그들은 6개월에 한 번 그 죄인을 면회할 수 있다. (a prisoner; visit)

________________________________________.

(10) 나는 할아버지가 지은 집에서 태어나 거기서 아주 어린 시절을 보냈다.

(be born; one's childhood; spend)

________________________________________.

2. 다음을 주어진 표현으로 시작하여 영작하시오.

(1) 남에게 멸시를 당하지 않도록 특히 주의할 필요가 있다.

(others; look down on; careful)

a. You ________________________________________.

b. Special care ________________________________________.

c. It ________________________________________.

d. If ________________________________________.

(2) 그녀는 그에게 뺨을 맞았으며 곧 그녀도 그의 뺨을 때렸다.

(slap one's face; back)

a. As soon as ________________________________________.

b. He ________________________________________.

c. Right when ________________________________________.

d. She ________________________________________.

(3) 그가 어디에 사는지 그리고 무엇을 하는지 알려져 있지 않다.

(what; not known)

a. His place ________________________________________.

b. Both ________________________________________.

c. It ________________________________________.

d. No one ________________________________________.

(4) 차창 밖으로 보이는 시골풍경은 언제나 마음을 평온하게 한다.

(through a car window; a country view)

a. One ______________________________.

b. Seeing ______________________________.

c. The view ______________________________.

d. I ______________________________.

(5) 그가 외출하는 소리가 들렸지만 그녀는 여전히 침대에 누워 있었다.

(go out; hear; stay in bed)

a. She ______________________________.

b. Even when ______________________________.

c. He ______________________________.

d. Even though ______________________________.

# 제15장 · 법

## Ⅰ. 기본개념

### 1. 법이란?

화자가 그 행위를 어떻게 보고 있는지를 보여주는 데 쓰인 동사의 형태를 말한다. 영어에는 직설법, 명령법, 가정법 세 가지가 있다.

### 2. 법의 종류

#### A. 직설법

사실을 말하거나 질문을 하는 동사의 형태를 가리킨다.

a. I [am] happy.

b. You [were] happy.

c. She [was] happy.

#### B. 명령법

명령이나 요구를 표현하는 동사의 형태를 가리킨다. 동사의 원형을 말한다.

a. [Be] quiet.

b. [Go] away.

c. [Wash] your car.

### C. 가정법

소망이나 권고 등 사실에 반하는 조건을 나타내는 동사의 형태를 가리킨다. 가정법 현재는 동사의 원형을 말하며 가정법 과거는 가상의 비실재적 의미를 가지는 were를 말한다.

(A) 가정법 현재

명령, 요구, 주장, 제안, 소망을 나타내는 demand, require, order, request, insist, propose, suggest, prefer, move, decide 같은 동사나 advisable, desirable, fitting, imperative 같은 형용사 또는 decision, decree, order, requirement, resolution 같은 명사 뒤에 나오는 that-절에서 가정법 현재가 쓰인다.

a. I demand that he [resign] his position.

b. I move that the meeting [be] adjourned.

c. The doctor suggested that she [stop] smoking.

(B) 가정법 과거

가정법 과거는 if, as if, as though, though와 같은 접속사가 이끄는 부사절이나 wish, suppose 같은 동사 뒤의 명사절에서 쓰인다.

a. If I [were] rich, I would buy a BMW.

b. He always speaks quietly on the phone, as though he [were] telling a very important thing.

c. I wish the work [were] over.

d. Just [suppose] everyone [were] to speak English fluently.

## 3. 법과 관련한 위반

a. *Both my friend and I [swum] across the lake.

b. *Put the pen on the desk and you will close your eyes.

c. *The professor demands that the student [stops] making a noise.

## Ⅱ. 기본연습

※ 다음 중 어법이 잘못된 곳을 찾아 고쳐 쓰시오.

1. If I was rich, I would buy you a nice country house.

   ______________________________________________.

2. The requirement that you are over 20 should be kept.

   ______________________________________________.

3. President Park lead the nation through some difficult times.

   ______________________________________________.

4. Had she knew the secret, she would have revealed it to her friends.

   ______________________________________________.

5. The teacher required that the noisy student got out of the classroom.

   ______________________________________________.

6. Whenever he is free, he take a walk along the stream near his house.

   ______________________________________________.

7. We considered it desirable that he does not leave the classroom before finishing his exams.

   ______________________________________________.

8. It is essential that every woman has the same opportunity for jobs as men.

   ______________________________________________.

9. Read the book, clean the room, and you have to lock the door when you go out.

   ______________________________________________.

10. The girl wishes that she studied English instead of mathematics while she was in college.

_______________________________________________.

## 정답 및 해설

### II. 기본연습

1. was → were

가정법 과거의 조건절에서 be동사는 were가 되어야 한다.

2. are → be

요구를 나타내는 명사 requirement가 보문으로 that-절을 가지고 있으므로 이 절 내에서 동사는 가정법으로 와야 한다. 따라서 be동사의 가정법 be가 와야 한다.

3. lead → led

과거의 사실을 나타내는 문장이므로 동사는 직설법 과거가 되어야 한다. 따라서 동사 lead의 직설법 과거가 필요하다.

4. knew → known

가정법과거완료의 조건절은 조건을 나타내는 접속사 if를 사용하지 않는 경우에는 조동사 had를 주어 앞에 두고 주어 뒤에는 동사의 과거분사가 와야 한다. 따라서 동사 know의 과거분사가 필요하다.

5. got → get

요구를 나타내는 주절동사 require가 that-절을 보문으로 가지고 있으므로 이 절 내의 동사는 가정법으로 와야 한다. 따라서 got의 가정법이 필요하다.

6. take → takes

현재의 사실을 나타내는 문장이므로 동사는 직설법 현재형이 쓰여야 한다. 주어가 3인칭 단수 he일 때 동사 take의 직설법 현재는 takes이다.

7. does → ∅

소망을 나타내는 형용사 desirable이 보문으로 that-절을 취하고 있으므로 이 절 내에서 동사는 가정법으로 와야 한다. 동사 leave의 가정법은 leave이다.

8. has → have

necessary, imperative, essential 뒤에 나오는 that-절에서 동사는 가정법으로 와야 한다. 따라서 직설법 현재 has가 아닌 가정법 have가 와야 한다.

9. you have to → ∅

등위접속사 and 앞에 있는 두 절은 동사가 명령법 read, clean으로 되어 있는 명령문의 형식을 취하고 있는데 반해, 이 접속사 뒤의 절은 동사가 직설법 현재 have로 되어 있다. 따라서 세 절 모두 명령법으로 통일한다.

10. studied → had studied

과거의 사실과 반대되는 상황을 한 번 가정해 보는 경우 가정법과거완료를 사용한다. 동사 wish를 사용하여 가정법과거완료를 나타낼 때 이 동사 뒤의 that-절의 동사는 'had + 동사의 과거분사'로 표현한다.

## Ⅲ. 심화연습

※ 다음 영작 중 비문을 고르고 그 이유를 설명하시오.

1. TV를 끄고 네 방으로 돌아가 숙제를 해라.

a. Would you please turn off the TV, return to your room, and do your homework?

b. You'd better turn off the TV, go back to your room, and do your homework.

c. I want you to turn off the TV, go back to your room, and do your homework.

d. Turn off the TV, go back to your room, and will do your homework.

정답 : ________

이유 : ______________________________________________________________.

2. 그 학생이 졸고 있을 때 선생이 그에게 질문을 했다.

a. The student was dozing when his teacher asked him a question.

b. It was while the student was dozing that his teacher asked him a question.

c. The teacher required that the student answered his question while he was dozing.

d. The student was asked a question by his teacher while he was dozing.

정답 : ________

이유 : ______________________________________________________.

3. 그녀는 부엌으로 가서 고무장갑을 끼고 설거지를 했다.

a. She went to the kitchen, put on a pair of rubber gloves, and did the dishes.

b. She reached the kitchen, put on rubber gloves, and washed the dishes.

c. She went to the kitchen and washed the dishes with her rubber gloves on.

d. She made for the kitchen, puts on a pair of rubber gloves, and washed the dishes.

정답 : ________

이유 : ______________________________________________________.

4. 내년 이맘때면 십 년 동안 영어를 공부하는 셈이 된다.

a. This time next year be the time that I shall have been studying English for ten years.

b. My English will have been studied for ten years by this time next year.

c. I shall have been studying English for ten years this time next year.

d. This time next year will be the full ten years after I began to study English.

정답 : ________

이유 : ______________________________________________________.

5. 그 남자는 창문으로 걸어가 창문을 열고 담배를 피웠다.

a. The man went to the window, opened it and smoked.

b. The man walked up to the window, opened it, and smoked cigarette.

c. The man walked up to the window, opened it, and smoked a cigarette.

d. The man made toward the window, opened it, and smoked a cigarette.

정답 : ________

이유 : ______________________________________________.

6. 숙제를 끝낸 후 반드시 전등을 끄고 문을 잠그고 외출해라.

a. When you have done your homework, you are sure to turn off the light, lock the door and go out.

b. Remember to turn the light off, lock the door, and go out after you do your homework.

c. Be sure to turn off the light, lock the door, and go out after you finish your homework.

d. Keep it in mind that you have to turn off the light, lock the door, and go out after you have done your homework.

정답 : ________

이유 : ______________________________________________.

7. 그는 그녀에게 대학을 졸업한 후에도 공부를 계속하라고 했다.

a. It was suggested by him that she should go on studying after her graduation from university.

b. She was recommended by him not to stop her studies even after she graduate from university.

c. He suggested that she go on studying even after her graduation from university.

d. He recommended her to continue her studies even after she graduated from university.

정답 : ________

이유 : ______________________________________________.

8. 장마가 끝나자마자 나무에서 매미들이 요란하게 울기 시작했다.

a. The end of the long rain started the cicadas singing in the trees.

b. As soon as the continuous rainy spell be over, the cicadas began to chirr noisily in the trees.

c. Cicadas began to sing noisily in the trees soon after the spell of rainy weather ended.

d. The long rain was over, which in turn made the cicadas begin to chirr loudly in the trees.

정답 : ________

이유 : ________________________________________________________________.

9. 그 사장은 직원들에게 2주 후까지 보고서를 제출하도록 요구했다.

a. It was required by the President that the employees should submit reports not later than the week after next.

b. The employees were required by the President to present reports by the week after next.

c. The President required the employees to present reports by the week after next.

d. The President required that his employees submitted reports not later than the week after next.

정답 : ________

이유 : ________________________________________________________________.

10. 그의 친구가 도착했을 때 그는 한 시간 동안 기다리고 있던 중이었다.

a. He waited an hour, and his friend arrived.

b. He met his friend after he had waited for him for an hour.

c. He could not have met his friend if he had not been waiting for him for an hour.

d. When his friend had arrived, he had been waiting for him for an hour.

정답 : ________

이유 : ________________________________________________________________.

## Ⅳ. 기본영작

※ 다음을 영작하시오.

1. 나는 철수이고 내 친구는 메리이다. (a name; call)

______________________________________________.

2. 그는 어떤 외국에도 가본 적이 없지만 외국어를 잘한다.
(any foreign country; speak)

______________________________________________.

3. 그녀는 내가 그녀 대신에 그녀의 일을 해 주기를 주장했다.
(for her; insist on)

______________________________________________.

4. 대통령은 장관들에게 반인륜적 범죄를 뿌리 뽑도록 명령했다.
(a minister; an inhumane crime; get rid of)

______________________________________________.

5. 차에서 내릴 때는 시동을 끈 후 열쇠를 빼고 자동차 문을 잠가라.
(get out of; turn off; pull out; lock)

______________________________________________.

6. 네가 내년에 프랑스에서 돌아오면 나는 이미 결혼해 있을 것이다.
(return from; already; marry)

______________________________________________.

7. 그 학자는 5년 동안 같은 연구를 해 오고 있다. (a scholar; research)

______________________________________________.

8. 네가 어제 전화했을 때 나는 샤워를 하고 있었다. (call; take a shower)

______________________________________________.

9. 내일 눈이 오면 삼일 동안 눈이 내리는 셈이 될 것이다. (snow; straight)

________________________________________________________________.

10. 내가 친구의 집에 갔을 때 친구는 이미 외출하고 없었다.
(already; go out)

________________________________________________________________.

## V. 심화영작

1. 다음을 영작하시오.

(1) 야외에 나갈 때는 피부가 햇볕에 타지 않도록 주의해라.
(go outdoors; get sunburned; careful)

________________________________________________________________.

(2) 그는 점심식사를 하고 밖에서 담배를 한 대 피우고 있다.
(have lunch; outside; a cigarette)

________________________________________________________________.

(3) 그 꼬마는 자기 어머니에게 장난감을 사주기를 고집했다.
(a kid; a toy; pester)

________________________________________________________________.

(4) 나는 내일 이맘때는 나의 여자 친구와 해변에 누워있을 것이다.
(about this time; on the beach; lie)

________________________________________________________________.

(5) 여름에는 모기에 물리지 않고 상한 음식을 먹지 않도록 주의해라.
(a mosquito; get bitten by; spoiled food)

________________________________________________________________.

(6) 의사는 그녀에게 뱃속의 아이를 위해 담배와 술을 끊으라고 했다.
(one's unborn child; smoking; quit)

______________________________________________.

(7) 그의 어머니는 그가 그 꾸러미를 그의 친척집에 전해주길 요구했다.
(a package; one's relative's home; deliver)

______________________________________________.

(8) 그가 수영장에 도착하자 많은 사람들이 즐겁게 수영을 하고 있었다.
(a swimming pool; arrive at; happily)

______________________________________________.

(9) 그는 그의 목숨을 살려달라고 청하고 그 은혜는 잊지 않겠다고 했다.
(spare one's life; a favor; remember)

______________________________________________.

(10) 그 지휘관은 부하들에게 총기탈취범들을 빠른 시일 내에 잡도록 명령했다. (a commander; a subordinate; get)

______________________________________________.

2. 다음을 주어진 표현으로 시작하여 영작하시오.

(1) 그는 부지런하므로 반드시 성공할 것이다. (surely; will)

a. His diligence ______________________________.
b. His success ______________________________.
c. He ______________________________.
d. I ______________________________.

(2) 시험시간이 모자라 그는 그 시험에 떨어졌다. (make; fail)

a. Lack of exam time ______________________________.
b. Due to ______________________________.
c. He ______________________________.
d. It ______________________________.

(3) 낮이 길어져 활동시간이 늘어남에 따라 몸이 피로해지기 쉽다.

(because of; get tired; apt to)

a. You ______________________________.

b. The longer daylight ______________________________.

c. Your body ______________________________.

d. The hours of activity ______________________________.

(4) 매일 식사를 하듯이 매일 영작을 공부한다면 반드시 잘할 수 있다.

(have daily meals; just as; excel in)

a. I ______________________________.

b. English composition ______________________________.

c. Your daily practice ______________________________.

d. You ______________________________.

(5) 그는 외국어에 능통하여 외국인들과 의사소통을 하는데 전혀 문제가 없다. (good at; communicate with; have no trouble)

a. His foreign languages ______________________________.

b. Because of ______________________________.

c. He ______________________________.

d. Good foreign language skills ______________________________.

# 해설 및 정답

제1장 단어와 구

제2장 절

제3장 격

제4장 문 장

제5장 주 어

제6장 동 사

제7장 보 어

제8장 목적어

제9장 부 사

제10장 부정사

제11장 동명사

제12장 분 사

제13장 시 제

제14장 태

제15장 법

# 제1장 단어와 구

## III. 심화연습

1. 정답 : d

• 이유 : 동사 feel은 뒤에 오는 형용사보어와 함께 '느낌이 ~하다'는 의미를 전하는 동사이다. 따라서 뒤에 형용사는 올 수 있지만 부사인 comfortably는 올 수 없다.

2. 정답 : b

• 이유 : 날씨 weather는 셀 수 없는 명사로 앞에 부정관사가 올 수 없다.

3. 정답 : d

• 이유 : 매미 cicada는 셀 수 있는 명사로 일반적으로 수의 개념으로 쓰인다. 따라서 앞에 한정사인 부정관사, 정관사, 소유격, 지시사, 양화사가 와서 쓰이거나 뒤에 복수를 나타내는 복수어미 -s가 붙어서 쓰인다.

4. 정답 : b

• 이유 : 전치사 뒤 전치사의 목적어 자리에 오는 동사는 동명사형태로 와야 한다. 따라서 동사 attain은 동명사 attaining이 되어야 한다.

5. 정답 : d

• 이유 : 식사 meal은 셀 수 있는 명사로 일반적으로 수의 개념으로 쓰인다. 따라서 가벼운 식사는 a light meal 또는 light meals가 되어야 한다.

6. 정답 : c

• 이유 : 주어가 3인칭 단수이고 동사가 현재시제일 때 동사 뒤에 -s 또는 -es가 붙는다. 따라서 주어 the length of a day가 3인칭 단수이고 동사 tend가 현재시제이므로 tends가 되어야 한다.

7. 정답 : d

• 이유 : 명사구 the roses를 대명사로 바꾸면 복수를 나타내는 대명사 they가 된다. 따라서 뒷 문장의 주어 it을 they로 바꾼다.

8. 정답 : b

• 이유 : 시간 hour는 셀 수 있는 명사로 일반적으로 수의 개념으로 쓰인다. 따라서 한 시간의 여유시간은 a leisure hour이고 일반적인 의미의 여유시간은 leisure hour가 아닌 leisure hours이다.

9. 정답 : c

• 이유 : had better 뒤에는 to-부정사가 아닌 동사원형이 온다. 따라서 to skip 대신 skip이 온다.

10. 정답 : c

• 이유 : 동사 find는 목적어와 목적보어를 취하여 '~가 ~하다는 것을 알다'는 의미를 전한다. 따라서 found 뒤에 앞서 나온 명사구 a plum을 가리키는 대명사 it을 두고 목적보어인 형용사구 a little sour가 와야 한다.

## Ⅳ. 기본영작

1. All flowers are beautiful.
   Flowers are all beautiful.
   Every flower is beautiful.
   There is no flower that is not beautiful.

• '모든 꽃'은 수를 나타내는 양화사 all을 셀 수 있는 명사의 복수형 flowers 앞에 두어 표현하거나 부사 all을 동사 뒤에 두어 표현할 수도 있고 양화사 every를 셀 수 있는 명사의 단수형 앞에 두어 표현할 수도 있다. every 뒤에는 셀 수 있는 명사의 단수형이 와야 하므로 every flowers처럼 쓸 수 없지만 예외적으로 시간표현과 쓸 때는 every two hours처럼 뒤에 복수형이 올 수 있다. 넷째 예문은 명사구 no flower를 수식하는 관계절로 '모든 꽃'의 의미를 전한다.

2. Unlike yesterday, today is not a holiday.
   Yesterday was a holiday, but today isn't.
   Yesterday was a legal holiday, but not today.
   It was a holiday yesterday, but it is not today.

• 어제가 공휴일이었던 것은 과거의 사실이고 오늘이 공휴일이 아닌 것은 현재의 사실이므로 전자는 과거시제로 후자는 현재시제로 표현한다.

• 첫째 예문의 unlike yesterday는 전치사구로 전치사 unlike의 목적어가 명사구 yesterday이다.

• '공휴일'은 a holiday나 a legal holiday로 표현한다.

3. He is reading a mystery novel.
   He is now reading a mystery story.
   The book he is reading is a mystery.
   He is in the middle of reading a detective story.

• '추리소설'은 a mystery novel, a mystery, a mystery story, a detective story로 표현한다.

• '읽고 있는 중이다'는 현재진행시제 is reading으로 옮기거나 be in the middle of reading으로 옮긴다.

• reading은 첫 세 예문에서 진행형을 만드는 현재분사이고 마지막 예문에서는 전치사 of의 목적어인 동명사이다.

4. My friend bought a new computer yesterday.
   One of my friends got a new computer yesterday.

Yesterday, my friend got himself a brand-new computer.

A friend of mine purchased an up-to-date computer yesterday.

- '내 친구'는 my friend, one of my friends, a friend of mine으로 표현한다.
- '새 컴퓨터'는 a new computer, a brand-new computer, an up-to-date computer로 표현한다.
- '사다'는 동사 buy, get, purchase로 옮기며 purchase는 대개 문어체에서 쓴다.
- 셋째 예문의 동사 get은 '~에게 ~을 사주다'는 의미를 전한다.

5. After dinner, he went out for a walk.

He went for a walk after he had dinner.

He went for a walk after having had dinner.

After he ate dinner, he went out for a walk.

- '저녁 식사 후'는 전치사 after 뒤에 전치사의 목적어인 명사구 dinner가 나오는 전치사구로 표현하거나 after를 접속사로 사용하여 뒤에 절이 나오는 구조로 표현한다.
- 셋째 예문의 after는 전치사이고 having had는 완료동명사로 전치사의 목적어이다.
- '산책하러 가다'는 go out for a walk이나 go for a walk으로 표현한다.

6. She just arrived in Seoul from her hometown.

She just came up to Seoul from her hometown.

She has just come to Seoul from her hometown.

She came up to the capital from her hometown only a short while ago.

- '막'은 부사 just나 only a short time ago로 표현한다.
- '상경하다'는 arrive in Seoul, come up to Seoul, come to Seoul로 표현한다.
- '고향에서'는 출처를 나타내는 전치사 from을 사용하여 표현한다.
- 셋째 예문처럼 동사를 단순과거시제 대신 현재완료시제 has come으로 표현하면 현재 막 도착했다는 느낌이 전달된다.

7. I walked fast not to be late for my class.

I walked fast so as not to be late for class.

In order to get to class on time, I walked quickly.

I walked quickly because I didn't want to be late for class.

- '~에 늦지 않으려고'는 not to be late for~, so as not to be late for~로 표현하거나 '정한 시간에 도착하려고'의 의미이므로 in order to get to~on time으로 표현한다.
- 첫째와 둘째 예문의 fast는 동사 walked를 수식하는 부사로 형용사가 아니다.

8. I went to the same high school as him.

He and I went to the same high school.

He and I attended the same high school.

He and I graduated from the same high school.

- '~와 같은 고등학교'는 the same high school as~로 표현하며 형용사 same은 항상 the와 함께 쓰인다는 점에 유의해야 한다.
- '~에 다니다'는 go to~나 attend~로 표현할 수도 있고 '~을 졸업하다'는 의미이므로 graduate from~으로 표현할 수도 있다.

9. I study and my wife works.

   I study, while my wife works for a company.

   I am a student and my wife is an office worker.

   I am a student and my wife works in a company office.

- '학생'은 명사구 a student나 동사 study로 표현한다.
- '회사원'은 명사구 an office worker나 동사구 work for a company, work in a company office로 표현한다.
- '회사' '학생' '회사원'은 셀 수 있는 명사로 일반적으로 수의 개념으로 쓰이므로 부정관사를 붙여 a company, a student, an office worker로 표현한다.

10. He is seventeen and his younger sister is thirteen.

    He is 17-years-old, and his sister is 13-years-old.

    He is 17-years-old and he has a 13-year-old sister.

    He and his sister are seventeen and thirteen respectively.

- '그의 여동생은 열세 살이다'는 His sister is 13-years-old이지만 '열세 살인 여동생'은 a 13-years-old sister가 아닌 a 13-year-old sister로 표현한다는 점에 유의해야 한다.
- 넷째 예문은 '각각'의 의미를 전하는 부사 respectively를 사용하여 표현한 것이다.

## Ⅴ. 심화영작

1. (1) It has been raining since three days ago.

   For three days straight, it has been raining.

   It has been raining for three consecutive days.

   It has continuously been raining for three days.

- '사흘 동안 비가 내리고 있다'는 3일 전인 과거에 비가 내리기 시작하여 현재에도 진행 중이므로 과거와 현재가 연관이 되어 있고 또한 진행 중이므로 현재완료진행시제 have / has been -ing로 표현한다.
- '계속'은 부사 straight나 continuously로 표현하거나 형용사 consecutive를 사용해 표현한다.
- '사흘 동안'은 전치사구 for three days나 since three days ago로 표현한다.

(2) He lives in Busan, and I live in Seoul.

He lives in Busan, while I live in Seoul.

He is living in Busan, and I'm living in Seoul.

He and I live in Busan and Seoul respectively.

- 그가 부산에 살고 내가 서울에 사는 행위를 긴 시간에 걸쳐 이루어지는 행위로 볼 때는 단순현재시제로 나타내고 현재의 일시적인 행위로 볼 때는 현재진행시제로 나타낸다. 단순시제 live는 과거에도 살았고 현재도 살고 있고 미래에도 어느 기간 동안 살 것이 틀림없다고 보는 경우에 쓰는 데 반해 진행시제 is living이나 am living은 현재 일시적으로 살고 있는 경우에 사용한다.

(3) He went to school with one book.

He went to school carrying a book.

With one book in his hand, he went to school.

He grabbed one book, and he headed for his school.

- '학교로 가다'는 go to school로 옮기거나 '~로 향하다'는 의미의 head for를 써서 head for one's school로 표현한다.
- '책을 한 권 들고'는 전치사구 with one book이나 현재분사를 사용하여 carrying a book으로 옮길 수도 있고 전치사 with 뒤에 목적어와 목적보어가 오는 구조 with(전치사)+one book(전치사의 목적어)+in his hand(전치사의 목적보어)로 옮길 수도 있다.

(4) I hear it is healthy to walk a lot.

Walking a lot is supposed to be healthy.

It's been said that walking often is healthy.

They say walking a lot is good for your health.

- '~라고 하다'는 '~라고 들어서 알고 있다'는 의미로 동사 hear로 표현하거나 They say that~, People say that~, It is said that~으로 표현할 수 있다. 또한 '~라고 이야기되어 왔다'는 의미이므로 It's been said that~이나 be supposed to do로 표현할 수 있다.

(5) Because it was hot, he went out wearing sandals.

He went out wearing sandals because of the hot weather.

Because of the hot weather, he went out with his sandals on.

He went out with his sandals on because the weather was hot.

- '날씨가 나빠서'는 첫째 예문처럼 이유를 나타내는 because-절이나 둘째 예문처럼 because of구로 옮긴다.
- '샌들을 신고'는 현재분사 wearing의 목적어로 sandals를 두어 표현하거나 전치사 with 뒤에 목적어인 명사구 his sandals와 목적보어인 부사 on을 두어 표현할 수 있다. on은 '신고'라는 의미의 부사이며 전치사가 아니다.

(6) She got up early to go jogging.

She got up early and went for a jog.

She got up early in the morning and went jogging.

Early in the morning, she got up and went jogging.

- '일찍'은 부사 early로 표현하며 여기서는 형용사가 아니다.
- '일어나다'는 get up이고 '잠이 깨다'는 wake up이다.
- '조깅하러 가다'는 go jogging이나 go for a jog로 표현한다.
- 한국어 문장은 단순히 과거의 사실을 말하는 것이므로 단순과거시제로 표현한다.

(7) I got to the station only to find that the train had left.

When I arrived at the station, the train had already gone.

By the time I got to the station, the train had already left.

When I got to the station, I found that the train had already left.

- 역에 도착한 것은 과거이고 이 때 기차는 이미 떠나고 없었으므로 기차가 떠난 것은 과거완료시제가 된다. 따라서 역에 도착한 것은 단순과거 got, arrived로 기차가 떠난 것은 과거완료 had left로 표현한다.
- 첫째 예문은 주절동사 got 뒤에 부정사를 써서 역에 도착했지만 기차는 이미 떠나고 없었다는 의미를 전한다.

(8) Sometimes, a cup of coffee provides vitality.

A cup of coffee can sometimes be an energizer.

A cup of coffee can at times be a source of energy.

Sometimes, a cup of coffee is all that's needed to give you a boost.

- '활력소'는 명사구 an energizer, a source of energy로 옮기거나 동사구 provide vitality, give a boost 등으로 옮긴다.
- '~되기도 하다'는 될 수도 있다는 의미로 can be~로 옮긴다.

(9) If you are good at English composition, you'll be good at English conversation too.

If you are good at English writing, you can speak English well too.

Good English composition skills lead to good English conversation skills.

If you have good skills in writing in English, you will also communicate well in oral English.

- '영작'은 English composition, writing in English로 옮기고 '영어회화'는 명사구 English conversation이나 동사구 speak English, communicate in oral English로 옮길 수 있다.
- '~을 잘하다'는 be good at, good~, have good skills in~으로 표현한다.
- be good at의 at과 lead to의 to는 전치사로 뒤는 목적어인 명사구가 온다.

(10) I'm Chul-Su and this is my foreign friend Mary.

I'm Chul-Su and this is a foreign friend of mine, Mary.

My name is Chul-Su and this is my foreign friend Mary.

My name is Chul-Su and this is Mary, my foreign friend.

- '나의 외국인 친구'는 my foreign friend로 표현하거나 '나의 한 외국인 친구'의 의미이므로 a foreign friend of mine으로 옮긴다. 그러나 my foreign friend 대신 a my foreign friend로 표현하지 않는다.

2. (1) a. It suddenly rained, so he didn't go out.

c. He didn't go out because of the sudden rain.

b. The sudden shower kept him from going out.

d. Because it suddenly started to rain, he stayed inside.

- '소나기가 와서'는 it suddenly rained, so~로 옮기거나 because of구로 옮길 수도 있고 소나기 the sudden shower를 주어로 옮기거나 because-절로 옮길 수도 있다.
- '외출하지 않다'는 not go out, keep~from -ing, stay inside로 옮긴다.

(2) a. After buying a car, he walks less often.

b. Now that he bought a car, he walks less.

c. He spends less time walking after buying a car.

d. The car he bought is making him walk less often.

- '~을 사고 난 후'는 전치사 after 뒤에 목적어로 동명사 buying을 두어 옮기거나 '~이므로'를 의미하는 now that~뒤에 절을 두어 옮긴다.
- 셋째 예문의 spend time -ing는 '~하는 데 시간을 보내다'는 뜻이다.
- 넷째 예문의 사역동사 make 뒤의 to-부정사 to walk은 원형부정사 walk으로 바뀐다.

(3) a. You can stay fit with regular exercise.

b. Exercising regularly helps you to stay in shape.

c. Through regular exercise, you can maintain a beautiful body.

d. Regular exercise leads to the maintenance of a beautiful body.

- '규칙적인 운동을 하면'은 전치사구 with regular exercise로 옮기거나 동명사를 사용하여 exercising regularly로 옮길 수도 있고 전치사구 through regular exercise나 명사구 regular exercise로 옮길 수도 있다.
- '아름다운 몸매를 유지하다'는 stay fit, stay in shape, maintain a beautiful body, the maintenance of a beautiful body로 표현한다.

(4) a. You can be the best only if you enjoy your work.

b. Without enjoying your work, becoming the best in your field is impossible.

c. Loving your job is an important key to becoming the best at it.

d. If you do not enjoy the work you do, you can't be the best in your field.

- '~을 즐겨야'는 '~을 즐길 때만'의 의미로 only if~로 표현하거나 '~없이 ~않다'는 의미이므로 without~, ~is impossible처럼 옮길 수도 있고 '~하지 않는다면 ~할 수 없다'는 의미이므로 if~not~, cannot~처럼 옮기거나 '~을 즐기는 것이 가장 ~하다'는 의미로 loving~is an important key to becoming the best~로 옮길 수도 있다.

(5) a. My summer vacation will begin at the end of July for a few days.

b. At the end of July, I am going away for my summer vacation for a short time.

c. It will be the end of July when I leave for a short summer vacation.

d. I'm going on a summer vacation for a few days starting the end of July.

- '칠월 말부터'는 '칠월 말에'의 의미로 at the end of July로 옮긴다.
- '떠나려고 하다'는 예정된 미래를 나타내는 'be동사의 현재형+동사의 -ing형'을 사용하여 am going away로 표현하거나 미래에 대한 예측을 나타내는 단순미래시제 will begin으로 표현한다.

## 제2장 절

### Ⅲ. 심화연습

1. 정답 : d

- 이유 : 부사 already는 일반적으로 be동사가 있는 문장에서는 be동사 뒤에 온다. 따라서 am 뒤에 온다.

2. 정답 : c

- 이유 : 동사 stay는 뒤에 형용사보어를 취하여 '~인 채로 있다'는 의미를 전한다. 따라서 stay 뒤의 명사 health는 형용사 healthy가 되어야 한다.

3. 정답 : d

- 이유 : 명백한 과거를 나타내는 시간 표현이 있는 절의 시제는 일반적으로 단순과거를 쓴다. 어제 yesterday는 명백한 과거를 나타내는 시간 표현이므로 이 절의 시제는 현재완료 have met이 아닌 단순과거 met이 된다.

4. 정답 : d

- 이유 : 주어 lots of singing practice가 3인칭 단수이고 동사의 시제가 현재이다. 따라서 동사 뒤에 -s를 붙여 seems가 된다.

5. 정답 : d

• 이유 : to-부정사의 주어는 일반적으로 전치사 for와 함께 온다. 따라서 you to do는 for you to do가 되어야 한다.

6. 정답 : c

• 이유 : 이유를 나타내는 부사절인 because-절과는 달리 이유를 나타내는 부사절인 since-절은 it~ that~ 강조구문을 사용하여 강조할 수 없다.

7. 정답 : d

• 이유 : 앞의 절(He is honest)을 선행사로 취하면서 주어로 쓰일 수 있는 관계대명사는 which이다. 따라서 what을 which로 바꾸어야 한다.

8. 정답 : d

• 이유 : 동사 finish는 뒤에 동사가 올 때 to-부정사가 아닌 동명사로 오기를 요구한다. 따라서 to weave를 weaving으로 바꾸어야 한다.

9. 정답 : d

• 이유 : '중요한 것'은 important thing이 아닌 an important thing이 되어야 한다. 명사 thing은 셀 수 있는 명사로 일반적으로 수의 개념으로 쓰이기 때문이다. 전자는 수의 개념이 아니므로 명사구가 될 수 없는 데 반해 후자는 수의 개념으로 명사구가 될 수 있어 is의 보어가 될 수 있다.

10. 정답 : d

• 이유 : '푸른 치마'와 '흰 블라우스' 모두 셀 수 있는 명사로 일반적으로 수의 개념으로 쓰여야 한다. 예문의 blue skirt와 white blouse는 수의 개념이 아니어서 명사구가 될 수 없어 전치사 in의 목적어가 될 수 없어서 비문이다. 따라서 blue skirt and white blouse 앞에 부정관사 a를 붙인다.

## Ⅳ. 기본영작

1. His room looks far out to the mountains.
   You can see the faraway mountains from his room.
   From his room, you can see the mountains very far away.
   The mountains can be seen from his room far in the distance.

• '멀리 ~이 바라다 보이다'는 look far out to~, see the faraway~, see~very far away, can be seen from~far in the distance로 옮긴다.

• 주어를 '그의 방' his room, 일반인을 나타내는 you, '그 산들' the mountains로 두어 작문할 수 있다.

• 넷째 예문은 see의 목적어 the mountains가 주어가 되어 수동문이 된 것이다.

2. Leaves will be more vivid after this rain.
   The leaves will become more alive after this rain.
   When this rain stops, the tree leaves will have more life.
   After this rain, the trees will be full of more vivid leaves.

- '이 비 그치면'은 '이 비가 온 후에'의 의미로 전치사구 after this rain이나 부사절 when this rain stops로 옮긴다.
- '나뭇잎'은 일반적인 의미의 나뭇잎을 가리킬 때는 셀 수 있는 명사 leaf의 한정사를 붙이지 않은 복수형 leaves로 나타내고 화자가 그의 청자도 알고 있다고 보는 '그 나뭇잎들'의 의미를 전할 때는 정관사를 붙여 the leaves로 나타낸다.

3. Let's grab some beer after work.
   How about a glass of draft beer after work?
   Would you like a glass of draft beer after work?
   What about having a glass of draft beer after work?

- '일이 끝나고'는 전치사구 after work이나 부사절 after you finish your work으로 표현한다.
- 생맥주 draft beer는 한 잔을 말할 때는 a glass of draft beer로 표현하며 a cup of draft beer라고 하지 않는다.
- '~하는 게 어때?'는 '~하자'의 의미로 Let's~, How about~?, Would you like~?, What about ~?으로 표현한다.

4. I don't know when he will stop lying.
   I am not sure when he will quit telling lies.
   I have no idea when he is going to stop lying.
   I don't know when he will finally stop being dishonest.

- '거짓말을 그만하다'는 stop lying, quit telling lies, stop being dishonest로 옮긴다.
- '~을 모르다'는 do not know~, be not sure~, have no idea~로 옮긴다.
- 미래조동사 will 뒤에 동사원형이 오면 단순미래형으로 미래에 대해 예언을 하거나 정보를 제공할 때 사용한다. 그러나 be going to do는 '~하려고 하다'는 의미를 전한다.

5. With effort, anyone can do well at English composition.
   Everyone can be good at English composition if he tries.
   If you make efforts, you can be good at writing in English.
   Anyone can be good at English composition if he works hard.

- '노력하면'은 전치사구 with effort나 if he tries to be good at English의 뒷부분을 생략한 if he tries로 옮기거나 if you make efforts나 if he works hard로 옮길 수 있다.
- '누구나'는 대명사 anyone, everyone, you로 옮긴다.

- '~을 잘하다'는 do well at, be good at으로 옮긴다.

6. He works hard until his body becomes worn out.
He works hard till he becomes utterly exhausted.
He works up to the point where he exhausts himself.
He works with eagerness until he becomes exhausted.

- '녹초가 되다'는 '~을 지치게 하다'라는 wear out, exhaust, exhaust oneself로 옮긴다.
- '~할 때까지'는 접속사 until, till이나 up to the point where~로 옮긴다.
- become worn out, become exhausted의 과거분사 worn과 exhausted는 become의 보어이다.

7. He is the hardest working student in his class.
He is the one who studies the hardest in the class.
Out of all students in the class, he studies the hardest.
He is the student who studies the hardest in the class.

- '반' class는 셀 수 있는 명사로 '하나의 반'은 a class이지만 원문은 '그가 속해 있는 반'이나 '그의 반'을 의미하므로 his class, the class로 옮긴다.
- '가장 열심히 공부하는'은 the hardest working~이나 who studies the hardest로 옮긴다.

8. Do you know the long-haired woman in a short skirt?
Do you know that girl with the long hair and short skirt?
Do you know the woman with long hair and a short skirt?
Do you know that long-haired woman wearing such a short skirt?

- '긴 머리 짧은 치마의 한 여성'은 a long-haired woman in a short skirt이다. 그러나 '긴 머리 짧은 치마의 그 여성'은 정관사를 붙여 the long-haired woman in a short skirt로 표현한다. in은 착용을 나타내는 전치사이다.
- 넷째 예문의 wearing은 명사구 a short skirt를 목적어로 취하면서 앞의 명사 woman을 수식하는 현재분사이다.

9. He gave her a hundred roses to win her heart.
In order to steal her heart, he gave her a hundred roses.
A hundred roses were given to her by him to win her heart.
What he did to gain her heart was to give her a hundred roses.

- '~의 마음을 얻다'는 win one's heart, steal one's heart, gain one's heart로 옮긴다.
- '장미 백송이'는 a hundred rose가 아니라 a hundred roses이다.
- 넷째 예문은 관계대명사 what이 이끄는 명사절 what~her heart가 전체 문장의 주어이다.

10. Time will tell whether you are right or not.
In time, we will know if you are right or wrong.

We have to wait to know if you are right or not.

We will have to wait some time to find out whether you are right or wrong.

- '~가 ~인지 어떤지는'은 whether~or~나 if~or~not으로 옮긴다.
- '시간을 두고 기다려 보아야 안다'는 Time will tell~이나 In time, ~will know~로 옮길 수도 있고 have to wait to know if~나 will have to wait some time to find out~으로 옮긴다.

## V. 심화영작

1. (1) After running eight kilometers, he sweated a little.

By the time he ran eight kilometers, he sweated a little.

He sweated a little when he ran to the eight kilometer point.

When he had run about eight kilometers, he started to sweat a bit.

- '8킬로미터를 달리자'는 '8킬로미터를 달린 후에'의 의미로 전치사구 after running eight kilometers나 '~때에'를 의미하는 전치사 by를 써서 by the time he ran eight kilometers로 옮기거나 when-절로 옮긴다.
- '약간 땀이 나다'는 sweat a little이나 sweat a bit으로 옮긴다.

(2) She likes wearing various accessories.

She is a woman that enjoys wearing a lot of accessories.

She is a woman who likes putting on a variety of accessories.

She is the kind of a woman who likes to wear many kinds of accessories.

- '여러 가지 장신구'는 various accessories, a lot of accessories, a variety of accessories, many kinds of accessories로 표현한다.
- '착용하다'는 '착용하고 있다'는 의미로 보면 동사 wear로 표현하고 착용하는 동작을 의미하는 것으로 보면 put on으로 표현한다.

(3) In summer, it is hot during the daytime, but it gets cooler at night because of the breeze.

In summer, it is hot during the day, but it is cool during the night because of the breeze.

Summer days are hot, but summer nights are cool because of the breeze.

In summer, it is hot in the day, but cool at night because of the refreshing breeze.

- '여름에는'은 in summer나 in the summer 모두 가능하지만 특정한 여름을 가리킬 때는 정관사 the가 붙은 후자를 쓴다.
- '낮에는'은 전치사구 during the daytime, during the day, in the day로 옮긴다.
- '밤에는'은 전치사구 at night, during the night로 옮긴다.

(4) She did not know when to hang up the phone.

She did not know when she should hang up the phone.

She was at a loss as to when to put down the telephone.

She had no idea at what point she should hang up the phone.

- '전화를 끊다'는 hang up the phone, put down the telephone으로 옮긴다.
- '~할지 모르다'는 do not know~, be at a loss as to~, have no idea~로 옮긴다.
- 셋째 예문에서 as to는 '~에 관하여'의 의미이다.

(5) He usually listens to music, even while he studies.

He enjoys listening to music even while he studies.

Even when he is studying, he likes to listen to music.

He enjoys listening to music even when he is studying.

- '~하는 동안에도'는 even while~, even when~으로 옮긴다.
- '음악을 듣다'는 listen to music으로 listen은 자동사이고 to music은 전치사 to와 전치사의 목적어인 명사구 music으로 이루어진 전치사구이다.

(6) She washed her hair and went out in a hurry to get on the subway before it could even dry.

After she washed her hair, she quickly went to catch the subway train even before her hair was dry.

She washed her hair, and it was still wet when she went out in a hurry to catch the subway train.

She hurried out to catch the subway train before her hair had the chance to dry.

- '머리를 감다'는 wash one's hair로 옮긴다.
- '물기가 마르기도 전에'는 before one's hair can even dry, before one's hair is dry, one's hair is still wet when~, before one's hair has the chance to dry로 옮긴다.
- '전철을 타다'는 get on the subway, catch the subway train으로 옮긴다.

(7) My friend and I did not know where to get off the bus.

My friend and I did not know where our bus stop was.

My friend and I did not know where we should get off the bus.

My friend and I had no idea of where we should get off the bus.

- '버스'는 원문의 의미로 볼 때 화자가 한 버스를 가리키는 것이 아니라 그의 청자도 알고 있다고 보는 특정한 버스를 가리키는 것으로 보아야 하므로 a bus가 아니라 the bus로 옮긴다.
- '어디에서 내려야 할지'는 '의문사+to-부정사'인 where to get off~나 where-절로 옮긴다.

(8) He sells fruit on the road from early morning to late night.

From early morning to late at night, he sells fruit on the street.

Everyday he sells fruit on the road from early morning to late night.

His job is selling fruit on the street from early morning to late at night.

- '그는 ~을 판다'는 he sells~, his job is selling~으로 옮긴다.
- '아침 일찍부터 밤늦게까지'는 from early morning to late night, from early morning to late at night으로 옮긴다.
- '길에서'는 on the road, on the street으로 옮긴다.

(9) Do you know what kind of tree that tree with small fruit is?

Do you know what kind of tree that tree, the one with small fruit is?

Do you know what kind of tree that tree with small fruit hanging on it is?

Do you see the tree with small fruit over there? Do you know what kind of tree that is?

- '작은 열매가 달려있는 저 나무'는 that tree with small fruit이나 동격관계로 that tree, the one with small fruit으로 옮기거나 that tree with small fruit hanging on it으로 옮긴다.
- kind of 뒤에 오는 셀 수 있는 명사의 단수형 앞에는 보통 부정관사 a를 생략하므로 what kind of tree의 tree 앞에 부정관사 a가 생략되어 있다.

(10) When he woke up, the sun was shining through the window.

He woke up in his bed, getting the sunlight through the window.

He woke up with the sunlight shining on him through the window.

He woke up from his sleep as the sunshine came through the window.

- '창가로'는 '창문을 통하여'의 뜻으로 through the window로 옮긴다.
- '햇살을 받으며'는 현재분사를 사용한 getting the sunlight나 전치사구 with the sunlight shining on him으로 옮긴다. 전치사 with가 명사구 the sunlight를 목적어로 현재분사 shining을 목적보어로 가지고 있다. on him은 전치사구로 현재분사 shining을 수식하는 수식어이다.

2. (1) a. She spends an hour and a half on the subway to come to learn English.

b. To learn English, she rides on the subway for an hour and a half.

c. Her learning English requires an hour and a half long subway ride.

d. It takes her an hour and a half-long subway ride to come to learn English.

- '영어를 배우기 위해'는 to-부정사 to learn English나 동명사를 사용하여 one's learning English로 옮긴다.
- '한 시간 반 동안 전철을 타다'는 spend an hour and a half on the subway, ride on the subway for an hour and a half, require an hour and a half long subway ride, take~an hour and a half-long subway ride로 옮긴다.

(2) a. Many Koreans are going to China to do business.

b. To do business, many Koreans are going to China.

c. Business is attracting lots of Korean businessmen to China.

d. China is the country many Korean businessmen are heading for to do business.

- '많은 한국인들'은 many Koreans로 옮기거나 '많은 한국의 사업가들'을 의미하므로 lots of Korean businessmen으로 옮긴다.
- '사업을 하러 중국으로 가다'는 go to China to do business로 옮기거나 '사업이 ~을 중국으로 유인하다'는 의미이므로 business attracts~to China나 businessmen head for China to do business로 표현한다.

(3) a. He and his wife met through Internet chatting.

b. He met his wife while chatting on the Internet.

c. Chatting on the Internet is how he met his wife.

d. It was while he was chatting on the Internet that he met his wife.

- '인터넷 채팅을 하다가 만나다'는 '인터넷 채팅을 통해 만나다'는 의미로 meet through Internet chatting, meet~while chatting on the Internet, chatting on the Internet is how~meet, it is while~is chatting on the Internet that~meet~으로 옮긴다.
- 넷째 예문은 it~that~ 강조구문으로 부사절인 while he was chatting on the Internet을 강조한다.

(4) a. Nowadays, both men and women want a slim body.

b. Both men and women desire a slim body these days.

c. Generally, men and women both want a slim body nowadays.

d. Whether it is a man or a woman, everyone wants a slim body these days.

- '요즘은'은 nowadays, these days로 옮긴다.
- '남자나 여자 모두'는 일반적인 의미의 남자와 여자를 가리키므로 셀 수 있는 명사 man과 woman을 한정사를 붙이지 않은 복수형 men과 women을 써서 both men and women, men and women both로 옮기거나 whether it is a man or a woman으로 옮긴다.
- '날씬한 몸매'는 a slim body로 옮긴다.

(5) a. She brings two pet dogs to school every Sunday.

b. Every Sunday, she shows up at school with two pet dogs.

c. She shows up with her two pet dogs at school on Sundays.

d. You can see her with her two pet dogs at school every Sunday.

- '일요일마다'는 every Sunday, on Sundays로 표현한다.
- '두 마리의 애완견을 데리고 나타나다'는 bring two pet dogs, show up with two pet dogs, see~with two pet dogs at으로 표현한다.
- 한국어 문장은 현재의 반복적이거나 습관적인 행위를 나타내므로 시제는 단순현재시제 brings, shows, can see로 표현한다.

## 제3장 격

### Ⅲ. 심화연습

1. 정답 : b

• 이유 : '그가 그의 여자 친구에게 빌려준 것'은 명사절 That he lent his girlfriend로 표현되지 않는다. 그 자체에 선행사를 포함하고 있는 관계대명사 What을 사용하여 What he lent his girlfriend로 표현해야 한다.

2. 정답 : b

• 이유 : 부정어가 자신이 속해있는 절의 첫머리로 이동하여 절 전체를 부정하는 경우 절의 정상적인 어순이 도치된다. 예문에서 부정어 nothing이 종속절의 첫머리로 이동하여 자신이 속한 절 전체를 부정하므로 어순은 '주어 + 조동사 + 본동사'에서 '조동사 + 주어 + 본동사'로 바뀐다. 따라서 he had received는 had he received가 된다.

3. 정답 : d

• 이유 : '(책상)다리의 재료'는 관계대명사 which의 소유격 whose가 되어야 한다. 예문은 다음 두 문장이 하나로 결합된 것으로 볼 수 있기 때문이다. (a) The table has *legs*. (b) *Their* material is made of not iron, but wood.

4. 정답 : c

• 이유 : 때나 조건을 나타내는 부사절에서는 미래의 의미를 현재시제가 대신한다. 예문의 before I will lend it to you는 때나 조건을 나타내는 부사절이다. 따라서 will lend 대신 lend를 쓴다.

5. 정답 : a

• 이유 : 관사와 소유격이 나란히 나와 동시에 명사를 수식할 수 없다. 부정관사 a와 소유격 my가 나란히 나와 모두 명사 friend를 수식하여 비문이다. 따라서 a my friend를 a friend of mine으로 바꾼다.

6. 정답 : d

• 이유 : 등위접속사 and 앞 절은 현재완료이고 뒤의 절은 단순과거로 되어 있다. 제비가 곤충을 잡은 것은 현재이고 잡아서 돌아온 것은 과거로 되어 있어 논리적으로 맞지 않는다. 따라서 현재완료 has caught을 단순과거 caught로 바꾸면 동사의 시제가 모두 과거로 통일되어 과거의 사실을 전하는 좋은 문장이 된다.

7. 정답 : a

• 이유 : 동사 submit는 제출하다는 의미의 타동사로 뒤에 목적어인 명사구가 하나 올 수 있다. 그러나 간접목적어 뒤에 직접목적어가 나올 수는 없다. 따라서 이 동사 바로 뒤에 목적어가 오고 간접목적어는 그 뒤에 전치사 to와 함께 오는 어순 submitted its report to the President로 나타난다.

8. 정답 : a

• 이유 : 부사 openly가 타동사와 그 목적어 사이에 와서 좋지 않은 문장이다. openly는 양태부사로 대개 일반동사 앞에 온다. 그렇지 않으면 타동사의 목적어와 목적보어가 있는 문장에서는 목적보어 뒤에 온다. 따라서 일반동사 called 앞이나 목적보어인 her own man 뒤에 온다.

9. 정답 : d

• 이유 : 예문은 to cook delicious side dishes every day를 to do so로 바꾼 것으로 이것을 주어로 하는 문장은 일반적으로 가주어 it을 사용한다. 따라서 they are를 it is로 바꾼다.

10. 정답 : a

• 이유 : 동사 see는 목적어와 현재분사인 목적보어를 사용하여 '~가 ~하고 있는 중인 것을 보다'는 의미를 전한다. 따라서 예문에서 동사 saw의 목적어인 drizzle 뒤 목적보어 자리에 fall의 과거분사 fallen이 아니라 현재분사 falling이 온다.

## Ⅳ. 기본영작

1. Do you mean your girlfriend is taller than you?
   Are you saying that your girlfriend is taller than you?
   Does that mean that your girlfriend is taller than you?
   You mean your girlfriend is taller than you, don't you?

• '~보다 큰'은 taller than~으로 표현하며 more taller than으로 쓰지 않도록 주의해야 한다.

• '~하다는 말이냐?'는 '~하다는 것을 의미하느냐?'는 의미로 Do you mean~?이나 Are you saying~?으로 옮기거나 You mean~, don't you?처럼 부가의문문으로 옮길 수도 있다.

2. He and his girlfriend drive to the suburbs every weekend.
   On weekends, he and his girlfriend go for a drive to the suburbs.
   He goes to the suburbs with his girlfriend for a drive on weekends.
   Every weekend, he goes to the suburbs with his girlfriend for a drive.

• '주말이면'은 '매 주말에'의 의미로 every weekend, on weekends로 옮긴다.

• '교외로 드라이브하러 가다'는 drive to the suburbs, go for a drive to the suburbs, go to the suburbs for a drive로 옮긴다.

• '주말이면 ~하러 가다'는 현재의 반복적인 또는 습관적인 행위를 가리키므로 시제는 단순현재시

제로 표현한다.

3. She was walking with a baby on her back, holding a shopping bag.
   She was walking, holding a shopping bag, with her baby on her back.
   She was walking with a baby on her back, and a shopping bag in her hand.
   When she was walking, she was holding a shopping bag, and carrying a baby on her back.

- '갓난아이를 등에 업고'는 '~을 ~한 채'의 의미로 'with(전치사) + 명사구(전치사의 목적어) + 전치사구(목적보어)'인 with a baby on one's back이나 carry a baby on one's back으로 옮긴다.
- '장바구니를 들고'는 현재분사를 써서 holding a shopping bag, with a shopping bag in one's hand로 옮긴다.

4. He sent his résumé to a company, but he didn't get any response.
   He sent a company his résumé, but wasn't able to receive any reply.
   He sent his résumé to a company but didn't get any answers back.
   Although he sent his résumé to a company, he didn't receive any replies.

- 이력서 résumé는 셀 수 있는 명사로 '한 장의 이력서'는 a résumé가 되고 '그의 이력서 한 장'은 his résumé가 된다.
- '아무런 답장을 받지 못하다'는 do not get any response, be not able to receive any reply, do not get any answers back으로 옮긴다.

5. Can we forever lengthen our life?
   Can we extend our life span for eternity?
   Are we able to lengthen our span of life infinitely?
   Is it possible for us to prolong our life expectancy infinitely?

- '우리의 수명'은 our life, our life span, our span of life, our life expectancy로 옮긴다.
- '~을 연장하다'는 lengthen~, extend~, prolong~으로 옮긴다.
- '~할 수 있다'는 can, be able to do, be possible로 표현한다.
- 넷째 예문의 it은 가주어이고 to-부정사 'to prolong'이 진주어이다.
- '무한히'는 forever, for eternity, infinitely로 표현한다.

6. Not all flowers smell good.
   Not all beautiful flowers smell nice.
   Not all flowers exhale a beautiful smell.
   It is not true that all flowers smell good.

- '모든 ~이 ~하는 것은 아니다'는 부분부정을 나타내며 not all~로 옮기거나 가주어 it 뒤에 진주어인 that-절을 써서 옮길 수 있다.
- '아름다운 향기를 발산하다'는 smell good, smell nice, exhale a beautiful smell로 표현한다.

7. The police chased the criminal, but failed to arrest him.
   The police chased after the criminal but couldn't arrest him.
   The police ran after the criminal, but were unable to arrest him.
   Even though the police chased after the criminal, they couldn't arrest him.

- '경찰'은 공공기관으로서의 경찰을 가리킬 때는 정관사를 붙여 the police로 표현하고 복수취급하며 공공기관으로서의 경찰에 몸을 담고 있는 남자와 여자를 의미할 때는 정관사를 빼고 police로 표현하며 역시 복수취급한다.
- '~을 뒤쫓다'는 chase~, chase after~, run after~로 표현한다.
- '~을 체포하지 못하다'는 fail to arrest~, cannot arrest~, be unable to arrest~로 표현한다.

8. After he left, he never contacted her again.
   After he left, she never heard from him again.
   She has never heard from him, since he left her.
   After he left, she couldn't hear anything from him.

- '그가 떠난 후'는 부사절인 after-절로 옮기거나 since-절로 옮긴다.
- '~에게서 어떤 소식도 듣지 못하다'는 ~never contact~, never hear from~, cannot hear anything from~으로 옮긴다.
- 한국어 문장은 단순한 과거의 사실로 보면 단순과거시제로 옮기며 과거에 그가 떠난 후 현재까지 어떤 소식도 듣지 못한 것으로 보면 떠난 것은 단순과거로 소식을 듣지 못한 것은 현재완료로 옮긴다.

9. The girl's American friend sent her a pretty postcard.
   The girl received a pretty postcard from her American friend.
   A pretty postcard was sent to the girl by her American friend.
   The girl received a beautiful picture card from her American friend.

- '예쁜 그림엽서'를 '한 장의 예쁜 그림엽서'로 해석하면 a pretty postcard가 되고 몇 장인지는 고려하지 않고 일반적인 의미의 예쁜 그림엽서를 가리키는 것으로 해석하면 한정사를 앞에 붙이지 않은 복수형 pretty postcards가 된다. 여기서는 전자의 의미로 해석하여 a pretty postcard로 옮긴다.

10. He wants her love; however, she wants his money.
    He wants love from her, but she wants money from him.
    While he wants love from her, she wants money from him.
    It is love that he wants from her, but it is money that she wants from him.

- '~하지만, ~하다'는 ~; however, ~나 ~, but~으로 옮기거나 while~, ~로 옮긴다.
- 넷째 예문처럼 it~that~ 강조구문을 이용하여 love와 money를 강조할 수도 있다. 여기서 that은 목적격 관계대명사로 동사 want의 목적어가 각각 love와 money이다.

## V. 심화영작

1. (1) All those women hang their laundry on clotheslines.

All those women hang out their washing on clotheslines.

Those women all hang their own washing on clotheslines.

All of those women hang their laundry on clotheslines without exception.

- '빨랫줄'은 셀 수 있는 명사로 '빨랫줄 하나'는 a clothesline이고 빨랫줄의 수와 관계없이 일반적인 의미의 빨랫줄을 가리킬 때는 관사, 소유격, 지시사, 양화사와 같은 한정사를 앞에 붙이지 않은 복수형 clotheslines로 표현한다.
- '빨래를 빨랫줄에 내걸다'는 hang one's laundry on clotheslines, hang out one's washing on clotheslines, hang one's own washing on clotheslines로 표현한다.

(2) You have to taste food to know its flavor.

Only after tasting food can you know its flavor.

You can know the taste of food only after you taste it.

You cannot know how food tastes without having tasted it.

- '음식을 먹어보다'는 taste food로 옮긴다.
- '~은 먹어봐야 알다'는 taste food to know~, only after tasting~can you know~, can know the taste of~only after you taste~, cannot know how~taste without having tasted~처럼 옮긴다.
- 둘째 예문의 only after tasting food는 부정어로 문장 첫머리에서 뒤의 절 전체를 부정하므로 주어(you)와 조동사(can)가 어순이 도치된다.

(3) Nuclear families are the cause of the weaker unity between family members.

The nuclearization of families has been weakening the unity between family members.

With nuclear families, the unity between family members has become weaker.

The conspicuous trend toward nuclear families has been weakening the unity between family members.

- '핵가족화'는 nuclear families, the nuclearization of families, the trend toward nuclear families로 옮긴다.
- '가족 구성원의 결속력이 약화되다'는 the weaker unity between family members, weakening the unity between family members, the unity between family members로 옮긴다.

(4) I walked, ran, and walked again while looking at the view.

I walked, ran, and walked again as I looked at the landscape.

I watched the surrounding scenery while walking and running.

I looked around the landscape while I walked, ran and walked again.

- '주변의 경치를 구경하다'는 look at the view, look at the landscape, watch the surrounding scenery, look around the landscape로 옮긴다.
- '~하면서'는 동시의 동작을 나타내는 접속사 as나 while로 옮긴다.

(5) There are buildings here and there with unknowable heights.
Buildings with unknown heights are scattered here and there.
You can see many buildings of unknown heights here and there.
There are buildings with unknown heights that are soaring upwards here and there.

- '높이가 얼마인지 알 수 없는'은 전치사구 with unknowable heights, with unknown heights, of unknown heights로 옮긴다.
- '여기저기'는 here and there로 옮긴다.

(6) On rainy days, she makes him warm flat cakes.
She makes him warm flat cakes whenever it rains.
On rainy days, she always makes warm pancakes for him.
When it rains, he always eats warm pancakes that she makes for him.

- '비가 오는 날이면'은 '비가 오는 날은 언제나'의 의미로 on rainy days, whenever it rains, when it rains로 옮긴다.
- '따뜻한 부침개'는 warm flat cakes, warm pancakes로 옮긴다.
- '부쳐 주다'는 동사 make 뒤에 간접목적어와 직접목적어를 두어 옮기거나 make~for~나 eat~that~makes for~로 옮긴다.

(7) The strong wind moved the dark clouds away, and the sky got clear again.
The wind pushed away the dark clouds with great force, and the sky became clear once again.
The strong power of the wind pushed the dark clouds, so the sky was clear again.
The murky clouds were pushed away by the powerful wind, and the sky became clear again.

- '바람이 강한 힘으로'는 the strong wind, the wind~with great force, the strong power of the wind, the powerful wind로 옮긴다.
- '먹구름'은 the dark clouds, the murky clouds로 옮긴다.
- '밀어내다'는 move~away, push away~, push~로 옮긴다.
- '(하늘이)맑아지다'는 get clear, become clear, be clear로 옮긴다.

(8) That country's economy hasn't shown any sign of recovery since a few years ago.
The economy of that country hasn't been showing any signs of recovery since a few years ago.

That country's economy hasn't been showing any signs of recovery for a few years.

We haven't seen any signs of recovery from that nation's economy since a few years ago.

• '그 나라의 경제'는 that country's economy, the economy of that country, that nation's economy로 옮긴다.

• '몇 년 전부터'는 '몇 년 전인 과거부터 현재까지 계속해서'의 의미로 since a few years ago, for a few years를 현재완료시제와 써서 옮긴다. since 뒤는 특정시간이 오고 for 뒤는 시간의 양이 온다.

(9) They dropped their fishing rods all at once.

They cast a fishing line in the water simultaneously.

They cast their fishing lines in the water all at once.

They all dropped a fishing line in the water at the same time.

• '일제히'는 all at once, simultaneously, at the same time으로 옮긴다.

• '낚시를 드리우다'는 drop one's fishing rod, cast a fishing line in the water, drop a fishing line in the water로 옮긴다.

• '(낚싯줄을)던지다'는 동사 cast는 기본형, 과거형, 과거완료형이 같다.

(10) One must love one's country just as one loves one's mother.

As one should love one's mother, so one should love one's country.

You have to love your country, the way that you love your mother.

Having to love your nation is the same as having to love your mother.

• '~하는 것은 ~하는 것과 같다'는 just as~나 as~, so~로 옮기거나 have to~, the way that~이나 ~is the same as~로 옮긴다.

• 둘째 예문의 should는 당연함이나 의무를 나타내는 조동사이다.

2. (1) a. It is not unusual to get tired after long hours of working with the computer.

b. Most people get tired after doing work on the computer for a long time.

c. Long hours of working with the computer usually makes you tired.

d. You will likely get tired after doing work on the computer for a long time.

• '컴퓨터 작업을 장시간 하면'은 after long hours of working with the computer, after doing work on the computer for a long time, long hours of working with the computer로 옮긴다.

• '피곤하다'는 '피곤해지다'의 의미로 get tired, make~tired로 옮긴다.

• '~하기 마련이다'는 ~is not unusual, most people get~, usually~, will likely get~으로 옮긴다.

(2) a. Many people were taken to the hospital because they were injured from that demonstration.

b. From that demonstration, many people were injured, and they were taken to the hospital.

c. The many people who were injured from that demonstration were taken to the hospital.

d. That demonstration brought about lots of injured people, and they were taken to the hospital.

- '그 시위로'는 '그 시위로부터'의 의미로 from that demonstration으로 옮기거나 '그 시위가 ~하다'는 의미이므로 that demonstration을 주어로 옮긴다.
- '부상을 당하다'는 be injured, bring about injured people로 옮긴다.
- '병원으로 실려 가다'는 be taken to the hospital로 옮긴다.

(3) a. Looking at rain sliding down a glass window is fun.

b. The rolling drops of rain on a glass window are fun to look at.

c. It is fun to see the way that rain is sliding down a glass window.

d. Rain is rolling down a glass window in a way that looks enjoyable.

- '유리창에 떨어져 굴러 내리다'는 slide down a glass window, the rolling drops of rain on a glass window, roll down a glass window로 옮긴다.
- '모양이 보기에 재미있다'는 looking~is fun, ~are fun to look at, it is fun to see the way, in a way that looks enjoyable로 옮긴다.

(4) a. She always takes her handbag everywhere.

b. Wherever she goes, she takes her handbag.

c. A handbag is always with her wherever she goes.

d. No matter where she is, she always has her handbag.

- '어딜 가든'은 부사 everywhere나 부사절 wherever she goes, no matter where she is로 옮긴다. wherever-절은 조건부사절로 이 절에서는 미래의 의미(will go)를 현재시제(goes)가 대신한다.
- '핸드백을 가지고 다니다'는 take one's handbag, a handbag is with her, have one's handbag으로 옮긴다.

(5) a. You need to watch out for spoiled food on hot days.

b. When the weather is hot, one must be careful about spoiled food.

c. Spoiled food is something that you must be cautious of when the weather is hot.

d. Hot weather is apt to make food spoiled, so you must be cautious of spoiled food.

- '날씨가 더울 때는'은 전치사구 on hot days나 부사절 when the weather is hot으로 옮기거나 명사구 hot weather로 옮긴다.
- '상한 음식'은 spoiled food로 옮긴다.
- '~하지 않도록 주의하다'는 watch out for, be careful about, be cautious of로 옮긴다.

# 제4장 문 장

## Ⅲ. 심화연습

1. 정답 : d

• 이유 : 동사 resemble은 '~을 닮아있다'는 상태를 나타내는 동사이다. 동작동사와는 달리 상태동사는 일반적으로 진행형으로 쓰이지 않는다.

2. 정답 : d

• 이유 : 미국은 America, the United States of America, the U.S., the U.S.A. 등으로 나타낸다. 따라서 U.S. 앞에 정관사 the를 넣는다.

3. 정답 : a

• 이유 : 제품 product는 셀 수 있는 명사로 일반적으로 수의 개념으로 쓰인다. 예문은 이 명사를 마치 셀 수 없는 명사처럼 사용하여 비문이다. 따라서 한정사가 앞에 붙지 않은 복수형 products를 사용하여 특정한 제품이 아닌 일반적인 의미의 제품의 의미를 전한다.

4. 정답 : c

• 이유 : 능동문에서 동사 finish의 목적어 자리에서 목적어였던 this work이 이 동사의 앞 자리인 주어 자리로 이동했으므로 동사가 수동태가 된다. 따라서 현재분사 finishing은 과거분사 finished가 된다.

5. 정답 : a

• 이유 : 등위접속사 and 앞은 동사가 is leaving으로 예정되어 있는 미래를 나타내는 데 반해 뒤는 동사 spend가 원형으로 나와 있어 이와 같은 의미를 전하지 못한다. 따라서 spend를 현재분사 spending으로 바꿔주면 등위접속사 and 앞처럼 예정되어 있는 미래를 나타내어 전체 문장이 일관성을 유지하게 된다.

6. 정답 : c

• 이유 : 예문에서 that-절인 that~solidarity가 나타내는 내용은 그 앞의 명사구가 나타내는 내용과 동일한 것을 가리킨다. 따라서 그 명사구는 일반적인 의미의 사실이 아니라 '그 사실(the fact)'이라는 특정한 사실을 가리키므로 fact 앞에 정관사 the가 필요하다.

7. 정답 : d

• 이유 : 얼굴 face는 셀 수 있는 명사로 일반적으로 수의 개념으로 쓰인다. 예문에서는 마치 셀 수 없는 명사인 것처럼 쓰여 비문이다. 문장의 내용으로 볼 때 일반적인 의미의 얼굴이 아닌 특정한 얼굴인 '그녀의 얼굴' 또는 '그 얼굴'을 가리켜야 한다. 따라서 her face나 the face

로 나타낸다.

8. 정답 : b

• 이유 : 직접의문문(Who is he?)이 주절의 일부가 될 때는 간접의문문(who he is)으로 바뀐다. 주절동사 know 뒤에 내포되어 있어 간접의문문의 형식이 된다.

9. 정답 : b

• 이유 : 식사이름(breakfast, lunch, dinner, supper)은 일반적으로 셀 수 없는 명사처럼 쓰인다. 따라서 일반적인 의미의 저녁식사는 앞에 한정사를 붙이지 않고 dinner로 표현한다. 그러나 식사이름 앞에 수식어(big, good 등)가 붙어 식사의 한 종류나 유형을 나타낼 때는 a big breakfast처럼 한정사의 하나인 부정관사가 붙는다.

10. 정답 : c

• 이유 : 진주어로 to-부정사(to see)가 나와 있는 문장이므로 가주어 it이 필요하다. 따라서 주어 자리에 있는 That은 가주어 It이 되어야 한다.

## Ⅳ. 기본영작

1. These kids are so cute!
   How cute these kids are!
   What cute children these are!
   These children are very cute!

• '이 아이들'은 these kids, these children으로 옮긴다.

• '참 귀엽기도 하다'는 감탄을 나타내는데 첫째와 넷째 예문처럼 평서문의 문장구조로 표현할 수도 있고 둘째 예문처럼 how로 시작하는 감탄문(how + 형용사 + 주어 + 동사)으로 표현하거나 셋째 예문처럼 what으로 시작하는 감탄문(what + 형용사 + 명사 + 주어 + 동사)으로 표현할 수도 있다.

2. May you win the battle!
   I hope you win the battle!
   I am hoping that you are victorious in the fight!
   I will have my fingers crossed until you win that battle!

• 한국어 문장은 기원문으로 첫째 예문처럼 기원문을 만드는 조동사 may를 주어 앞에 두어 표현할 수도 있고 둘째 셋째 예문처럼 '바라다'는 의미의 동사 hope를 사용하거나 '행운을 빌다'는 의미로 have one's fingers crossed로 표현할 수도 있다.

3. Be sure to turn the light off and lock the door when you go out.
   Don't forget to turn off the light and lock the door before leaving.
   Remember to turn off the light and lock the door before you go out.
   Don't forget that you have to turn off the light and lock the door before going out.

- '전등을 끄다'는 turn off the light, turn the light off로 표현하며 turn off의 목적어가 명사가 아니고 대명사일 때 이 목적어는 반드시 타동사 turn과 부사 off 사이에 와야 한다.
- '~해야 하다'는 be sure to do~, don't forget to do~, remember to do~, don't forget that~으로 옮긴다.

4. She is wearing a white T-shirt, very short pink skirt, and pink cap.
   She has on a white T-shirt, a very short pink skirt, and a pink cap.
   She is wearing a white T-shirt, a very short pink skirt and a pink cap.
   She is dressed in a white T-shirt and a very short pink skirt, and has a pink cap on.

- '흰 티셔츠'는 a white T-shirt, '분홍색 짧은 치마'는 a very short pink skirt, '분홍색 모자'는 a pink cap으로 옮긴다.
- '~을 입고 있다'는 현재진행시제를 써서 is wearing~, has on~, is dressed in~으로 옮긴다.
- 넷째 예문의 on은 전치사가 아니라 '착용하여, 쓰고'라는 의미의 부사이다.

5. I like you, but it seems that you dislike me.
   I like you, but it seems that you don't like me.
   I like you, but it seems that you don't care for me.
   It seems as though you don't like me while I like you.

- '네가 좋은데'는 '너를 좋아하지만'의 의미이므로 I like you, but~이나 while I like you로 옮긴다.
- '~한가 보구나'는 '~인 것 같다'는 의미이므로 it seems that~, it seems as though~로 옮긴다.

6. Try to be punctual all the time.
   Be careful not to be late for every appointment.
   Always be careful not to be late for appointments.
   Be sure to be careful not to be late for your appointments.

- '언제나'는 all the time, always, all~로 옮긴다.
- '약속'은 '만날 약속'을 뜻하므로 promise가 아니라 appointment를 써야 한다.
- '약속시간에 늦지 않다'는 be punctual, be not late for every appointment, be not late for appointments, be not late for one's appointments로 옮긴다.
- '주의해라'는 try to be~, be careful not to be~로 옮긴다.

7. Why do we want makkolli on a rainy day?
   Why do we want to have a glass of makkolli whenever it rains?
   Is there any special reason for our liking for makkolli on a rainy day?
   Why is it that we always want to have a glass of makkolli on rainy days?

- '비 내리는 날은'은 on a rainy day, whenever it rains, on rainy days로 옮긴다.
- '막걸리'는 셀 수 없는 명사로 makkolli로 표현하거나 '막걸리 한 잔'의 의미로 보아 a glass of

makkolli로 옮긴다.

- '왜 ~하는가?'는 Why do we~?, Is there any special reason for~?, Why is it that~?으로 옮긴다.

8. He is not tall or good-looking.
   He is neither tall nor handsome.
   He is not tall, and he is not handsome either.
   His height is not tall, and his appearance is not good.

- '~도 ~도 ~아니다'는 not~or~, neither~nor~나 ~not, and~not either로 옮기거나 not~, and~not~으로 옮긴다.
- '얼굴이 잘생긴'은 good-looking, handsome으로 옮기거나 one's appearance is good으로 옮긴다.

9. Do you think you can do it, but I can't?
   Do you think you can do that, while I can't?
   Do you think that only you can do it but not me?
   Do you think that you are able to do that while I can't?

- '~는 할 수 있고 ~는 할 수 없다'는 ~can do~, but~can't나 ~can do~, while~can't로 옮기거나 only~can do~but not~이나 ~be able to do~while~can't로 옮길 수 있다.
- 첫째 예문의 can't 뒤는 do it이, 둘째 예문의 can't 뒤는 do that이, 넷째 예문의 can't 뒤는 do that이 생략되어 있다.

10. Have a look at the whole Seoul downtown area after you go up Mt. Bukhan.
    Go up to Mt. Bukhan, and look down upon the whole Seoul downtown.
    Look down upon the whole downtown area of Seoul while on top of Mt. Bukhan.
    After climbing up to the top of Mt. Bukhan, have a look at the whole Seoul downtown.

- '북한산'은 Mt. Bukhan이며 the mountains in North Korea가 아니다.
- '~에 올라가다'는 go up~, go up to~, be on top of~, climb up to~로 옮기며 climb up to~는 높고 오르기 험한 산에 올라갈 때 사용한다.
- '서울 시내'는 the whole Seoul downtown area, the whole Seoul downtown, the whole downtown area of Seoul로 옮긴다.

## V. 심화영작

1. (1) I have no idea when we will reach the mountain top.
   I don't know when we will reach the top of the mountain.
   I am uncertain when we will get to the top of the mountain.
   I don't know when we will be able to get to the top of the mountain.

- '~일지 모르다'는 have no idea~, don't know~, ~be uncertain으로 옮긴다.
- '산 정상에 오르다'는 reach the mountain top, reach the top of the mountain, get to the top of the mountain으로 옮긴다.

(2) What pretty small flowers these are!
How pretty these small flowers are!
These small flowers are very pretty!
These small flowers are really pretty!

- 한국어 문장은 감탄을 나타내므로 what으로 시작하는 감탄문(what + 형용사 + 명사 + 주어 + 동사)으로 옮기거나 how로 시작하는 감탄문(how + 형용사 + 주어 + 동사)이나 강조의 의미를 가진 very나 really와 같은 부사를 사용한 평서문의 어순으로 옮길 수도 있다.

(3) She doesn't like or hate exercising.
She neither likes nor hates exercising.
She neither likes exercising nor hates it.
She doesn't like exercising, but, at the same time, she doesn't hate it.

- '운동하는 것'은 동명사 exercising으로 옮긴다.
- '~을 좋아하지도 싫어하지도 않다'는 do not like or hate~, neither like nor hate~, neither like~nor hate~로 옮기거나 do not like~, but, at the same time, ~do not hate~로 옮긴다.
- 셋째와 넷째 예문의 it은 앞의 동명사 exercising을 가리키는 대명사이다.

(4) Put the gear in P, step on the brake, and start the engine.
Start the car after you step on the brakes with the gear in P.
Start the engine with the gear in P and your foot on the brake.
Start the car while stepping on the brakes and having the gear in P.

- '한국어 문장은 동사를 명령법인 동사원형 put, step, start로 옮긴다.
- '기어를 P에 두고'는 '기어를 P에 두어라'의 의미로 put the gear in P나 전치사구 with the gear in P로 옮기거나 having the gear in P로 옮긴다.
- '브레이크를 밟다'는 step on the brake, step on the brakes, with one's foot on the brake로 옮긴다.

(5) Keep going forward, and then you will definitely see the building.
Go straight ahead, and then you will be able to find the building.
If you continue to go straight forward, you will see the building for sure.
Keep on going straight forward. You won't be able to miss the building.

- '계속해서 앞으로 가다'는 keep going forward, go straight ahead, continue to go straight forward, keep on going straight로 옮긴다.

- '~가 틀림없이 보이다'는 will definitely see~, will be able to find~, will see~for sure, won't be able to miss~로 옮긴다.

(6) May you pass the company entrance exam!

I hope you pass the company employment exam!

I wish you success in the company entrance exam!

I wish you best of luck in passing the company employment exam!

- '그 입사시험'은 the company entrance exam, the company employment exam으로 옮긴다.
- '성공하다'는 동사 pass나 명사 success로 옮긴다.
- 한국어 문장은 기원을 나타내므로 기원을 나타내는 조동사 may를 주어 앞에 두어 옮기거나 동사 hope, wish를 사용하여 옮긴다.

(7) I don't know why you are against my bringing my friend there.

I don't understand why you dislike my bringing my friend there.

I don't understand why you object to my bringing my friend there.

I can't understand why you are against me bringing my friend there.

- '~에 반대하다'는 be against~, dislike~, object to~로 옮긴다.
- 첫째 예문의 against는 전치사이고 bringing은 전치사의 목적어인 동명사이며 bringing 앞의 my는 동명사의 주어이고 my friend는 동명사의 목적어인 명사구이다.
- 셋째 예문의 object to의 to는 전치사이므로 뒤의 동사 bring은 동명사 bringing으로 와야 한다.

(8) She is a little bit chubby but kind of cute.

She is a little chubby, but she is quite cute.

Although she is a little plump, she is still quite cute.

Even though she is a little chubby, she is quite cute.

- '약간 살이 찌긴 했지만 귀여운'은 a little bit chubby but kind of cute나 a little chubby, but~cute로 옮길 수도 있고 although~is a little plump, ~is still quite cute나 even though~is a little chubby, ~is quite cute로도 옮길 수 있다.
- 셋째 예문의 부사 still은 보통 be동사 is 뒤에 오며 앞에 오지 않는다.

(9) He went out for billiards, but he did not return yet.

He has not come back from going out to play billiards.

He still has not returned from going out to play billiards.

He went out to play billiards, and he has not come back yet.

- '당구를 치다'는 play billiards로 옮기며 '당구'는 billiard가 아니라 billiards이다.
- '치러가서 아직 돌아오지 않았다'는 과거의 사실로 보면 단순과거시제로 옮기며 과거에 치러가서 아직 돌아오지 않은 것으로 보면 현재와 과거가 연관되어 있으므로 현재완료시제를 써서 옮긴다.

(10) Neither he nor I have seen your keys.
He hasn't seen your keys, nor have I.
Both he and I haven't seen your keys.
He hasn't seen your keys, and I haven't either.

- '너의 열쇠'는 열쇠가 여러 개이면서 상대방의 소유인 것으로 보면 your keys로 옮긴다. 열쇠가 여러 개가 아니라 한 개인 때는 your key가 된다.
- '~도 ~도 ~아니다'는 의미는 neither~nor~나 not~, nor~로 옮기거나 both~and~not~이나 ~not~, and~either로 옮긴다.
- 둘째 예문의 부정의 접속사 nor 뒤는 '주어+조동사(I have)'가 '조동사+주어(have I)'로 어순이 도치된다.

2. (1) a. Why are you just standing there?
b. What are you just standing there for?
c. Are you just standing there for any reason?
d. Is there any reason why you are just standing there?

- '무엇 때문에'는 의문을 나타내는 부사 why나 what~for, for any reason, is there any reason why~로 옮긴다.
- 둘째 예문의 의문대명사 what은 전치사 for의 목적어이다.
- '서 있기만 하는'은 just standing으로 옮기며 standing은 현재분사이다.

(2) a. The tree lost a lot of its flowers when the wind blew.
b. The wind blew off many of the flowers from that tree.
c. Lots of flowers fell off from that tree when the wind blew.
d. Many of the flowers in that tree fell off because of the wind.

- '바람이 불어'는 when the wind blew, the wind~, because of the wind로 옮긴다.
- '그 나무의 꽃들'은 its flowers, the flowers from that tree, lots of flowers~from that tree, the flowers in that tree로 옮긴다.
- '떨어지다'는 the tree loses its~, blow off~from~, fall off from~, fall off로 옮긴다.

(3) a. On finishing dinner, they all start to go around the playground.
b. They all start to go around the playground as soon as they finish dinner.
c. The moment they finish their dinner, they all start to go around the playground.
d. Right after finishing dinner, they all start to go around the playground.

- '~하자마자'는 시간의 접촉을 나타내는 전치사 on을 이용하거나 as soon as, the moment that~, right after~로 옮긴다.
- '일제히'는 they all~로 옮긴다.

- '운동장을 돌다'는 go around the playground로 옮긴다.

(4) a. The unstable politics in that country is preventing economic growth.

b. That country's development in the economy is being hindered by its political unstability.

c. The country is politically unstable, which is an obstacle for economic development.

d. The country's economic development is being held back by its political unstability.

- '정치적 불안정'은 the unstable politics, its political unstability, be politically unstable로 옮긴다.
- '경제발전'은 economic growth, development in the economy, economic development로 옮긴다.
- '가로막다'는 prevent~, be hindered by~, be an obstacle for~, be held back by~로 옮긴다.

(5) a. With frequent haircuts, he always has short hair.

b. He gets haircuts often, so his hair is always short.

c. Because of his frequent haircuts, his hair is always short.

d. His hair is always short because he has a haircut very often.

- '머리를 너무 자주 깎아'는 전치사구 with frequent haircuts로 옮기거나 get haircuts often, so~로 옮길 수 있고 because of one's frequent haircuts나 have a haircut very often으로 옮길 수도 있다.
- '머리가 짧다'는 have short hair, one's hair is short로 옮긴다.
- 주어를 사람인 '그' he나 사물인 '그의 머리' his hair로 두어 옮긴다.

## 제5장 주 어

1. 정답 : c

- 이유 : 전치사 by가 수송수단이나 전달의 수단을 나타낼 때는 뒤에 오는 교통기관을 나타내는 명사에는 관사가 붙지 않는다. 따라서 plane과 car 앞의 부정관사 a를 빼야 한다.

2. 정답 : a

- 이유 : 명사 앞에 오는 한정사의 하나인 지시사(this, that, these, those)는 자신이 지시하는 명사가 단수이냐 복수이냐에 따라 다른 형태가 쓰인다. this나 that은 단수명사 앞에 오고 these나 those는 복수명사 앞에 온다. 따라서 명사 children이 복수이므로 this는 these가 된다.

3. 정답 : b

- 이유 : 버터 butter는 셀 수 없는 명사로 일반적으로 양의 개념으로 쓰인다. 따라서 수를 나타내

는 양화사 a few의 수식을 받을 수 없다. 그러나 양을 나타내는 양화사 some의 수식을 받을 수는 있다.

4. 정답 : d

• 이유 : 참외 melon은 개개의 참외를 가리킬 때는 셀 수 있는 명사이고 물질 자체를 가리킬 때는 셀 수 없는 명사이다. 예문에서처럼 수를 나타내는 양화사 a few의 수식을 받으면 복수형 melons가 되어야 한다.

5. 정답 : c

• 이유 : '몇 개의'는 수를 나타내는 양화사 a few를 쓰며 few는 '거의 없는'의 의미이다. 따라서 '몇 개의 삶은 고구마'는 a few steamed sweet potatoes이다.

6. 정답 : c

• 이유 : 재귀대명사는 일반적으로 문장의 주어와 동일한 지시대상을 가리킬 때 쓴다. 예문에서 동사 interests의 주어와 목적어가 동일한 지시대상을 가리킨다면 목적어가 재귀대명사로 바뀐다. 그러나 주어가 I가 아니라 Music이므로 재귀대명사 myself가 이 자리에 오지 못하므로 myself를 me로 바꾼다.

7. 정답 : c

• 이유 : 물 water는 셀 수 없는 명사이다. 따라서 일반적인 의미의 물은 한정사를 앞에 붙이지 않은 water로 표현한다. 예문에서 섭씨 100도에서 끓는 물은 일반적인 의미의 물이므로 정관사 the를 붙이지 않는다. the water는 특정한 물인 '그 물'을 의미하기 때문이다.

8. 정답 : b

• 이유 : 선생 teacher는 셀 수 있는 명사로 일반적으로 수의 개념으로 쓰인다. 따라서 '특정한 선생 한 사람'은 particular teacher가 아니라 a particular teacher이다.

9. 정답 : b

• 이유 : 동사 decide 뒤에 오는 동사는 to-부정사로 오며 동명사로 오지 않는다. 따라서 decided 뒤의 동명사 going을 to-부정사인 to go로 바꾼다.

10. 정답 : b

• 이유 : '~하는 게 좋겠다'는 'had better + 동사원형'으로 표현하므로 would를 had로 바꾼다.

## Ⅳ. 기본영작

1. How many fish did you catch?
   How many fish did you get?
   How many fish were you able to catch?
   You caught lots of fish, didn't you? How many?

• '얼마나 많은 물고기'는 how many fish로 옮기며 명사 fish의 복수형으로 fish와 fishes 둘 다 쓰인다.

- '물고기를 잡다'는 catch fish, get fish로 옮긴다.
- 넷째 예문은 부가의문문으로 옮긴 것이다.

2. My books here are more expensive than yours there.
   These books of mine cost more than those books of yours.
   These books of mine are more expensive than those books of yours.
   These books, which belong to me, are more expensive than those books belonging to you.

- '나의 이 책들'은 my books here, these books of mine이나 these books, which belong to me로 옮기고 '너의 저 책들'은 yours there, those books of yours, those books belonging to you로 옮긴다. 여기서 here와 there는 부사이다.
- '나의 이 책들'을 my these books, these my books로 옮기거나 '너의 저 책들'을 your those books, those your books로 옮길 수 없다. 소유격과 지시사가 나란히 나올 수 없기 때문이다.

3. I had a few sleepless nights.
   I had a few nights in which I could not sleep.
   There were some nights that I could not sleep.
   There were a few nights in which I could not sleep.

- '잠이 오지 않는 밤이 여러 번'은 a few sleepless nights, a few nights in which～cannot sleep, some nights that～cannot sleep으로 옮긴다.
- a few는 셀 수 있는 명사의 복수형을 수식하므로 뒤의 명사 night에 복수어미 -s가 붙어야 한다.

4. Learning a foreign language is not easy and requires patience.
   Learning a foreign language is not easy and needs a lot of patience.
   It is not easy to learn a foreign language, and it requires lots of patience.
   You need to be patient to learn a foreign language, because it is not easy to learn it.

- '외국어'는 '한 외국어'를 가리킬 때는 a foreign language로 표현하고 외국어의 수와 관계없이 일반적인 의미의 '외국어'를 가리킬 때는 한정사를 앞에 붙이지 않은 복수형 foreign languages로 옮긴다.
- '외국어를 배운다는 것'은 동명사를 사용하여 learning a foreign language로 표현하거나 가주어 it과 진주어인 to-부정사 to learn a foreign language로 옮긴다.

5. This item of clothing is dirtier than that one.
   This piece of clothing is dirtier than that piece of clothing.
   This article of clothing is less clean than that article of clothing.
   Compared to that piece of clothing, this piece of clothing is dirtier.

- '이 옷'은 this item of clothing, this piece of clothing, this article of clothing으로 옮긴다.
- clothing은 집합명사이므로 '이 옷'은 의류의 한 점을 의미하는 item, piece, article과 같은 단위를

나타내는 명사를 사용하여 옮긴다.

6. A lot of people got together on the street, but I did not know why.
   There were a lot of people on the street, but I did not know why they were there.
   Although there were many people on the street, I did not know why they were there.
   There were many people on the street, but I did not know why they went there.

- '사람들이 많다'는 a lot of people get together, be a lot of people, be many people로 옮긴다. get together는 '모이다'는 뜻이다.
- '왜 ~하는지 알지 못하다'는 do not know why, do not know why~로 옮긴다.

7. Many people work hard to earn lots of money.
   Many people work hard to make a lot of money.
   Lots of people make a constant effort to earn a lot of money.
   In order to make a lot of money, many people work diligently.

- '많은 사람들'은 many people, lots of people로 옮긴다.
- '돈을 벌다'는 earn money, make money로 옮긴다.
- '많은 돈'은 lots of money, a lot of money로 옮긴다.
- '열심히 일하다'는 work hard, make a constant effort, work diligently로 옮긴다.

8. Some of these ball-point pens are out of ink.
   Some of these ball-point pens are all out of ink.
   Out of these ball-point pens, some are out of ink.
   Of these ball-point pens, some are already out of ink.

- '이 볼펜 중 몇 개'는 some of these ball-point pens나 out of these ball-point pens, some~으로 옮기거나 Of these ball-point pens, some~으로 옮긴다.
- '잉크가 다 닳다'는 be out of ink로 옮긴다.

9. Some people have several houses, but I have none.
   While some people have many houses, I have none.
   Some people have not a few houses, but I have none.
   Some people have many houses, but I don't have any.

- '몇 채의 집을 가지고 있다'는 have several houses, have many houses, have not a few houses로 옮긴다.
- '~하지만'은 ~, but~이나 while~, ~로 옮긴다.
- '나는 한 채도 없다'는 I have none이나 I don't have any로 옮긴다.

10. Do you want to trade my fountain pen with yours?
    Would you like to exchange your fountain pen with mine?

How about exchanging that fountain pen of yours with this fountain pen of mine?

Do you want to change that fountain pen of yours with this fountain pen of mine?

- '너의 그 만년필'은 your fountain pen, that fountain pen of yours로 옮기며 your that fountain pen, that your fountain pen으로 옮길 수 없다. 또한 '나의 이 만년필'은 my this fountain pen, this my fountain pen으로 옮길 수 없다.
- '~을 ~와 바꾸다'는 trade~with~, exchange~with~, change~with~로 옮긴다.

## V. 심화영작

1. (1) We ordered squid and peanuts as side dishes for beer.

We ordered squid and some peanuts as side dishes for beer.

We ordered some squid and peanuts to accompany our beer.

We ordered some squid and peanuts as side dishes to go with our beer.

- '맥주 안주'는 side dishes for beer, ~to accompany one's beer, side dishes to go with one's beer로 옮긴다.
- '오징어와 땅콩'은 squid and peanuts, squid and some peanuts, some squid and peanuts로 옮긴다.
- 오징어 squid는 개체를 가리킬 때는 셀 수 있는 명사이지만 '오징어 살, 오징어 고기'를 가리킬 때는 셀 수 없는 명사이다.

(2) I went to a lake in the suburbs with some friends to fish.

I went to a lake in the suburbs to fish with some friends.

With some of my friends, I went fishing in a lake in the suburbs.

Accompanied by some friends, I went fishing in a lake in the suburbs.

- '친구 몇 명과'는 with some friends, with some of my friends, accompanied by some friends로 옮긴다.
- '교외의 호수에'는 to a lake in the suburbs, in a lake in the suburbs로 옮긴다.
- '낚시하러 가다'는 go to fish, go fishing으로 옮긴다.

(3) As the night went on, only the street lights shone brighter.

As the night went on, only the street lights were getting brighter.

As the night got deeper, only the street lights were getting brighter.

As the night became deeper, only the street lights were shining more brightly.

- '밤이 깊어지자'는 as the night went on, as the night got deeper, as the night became deeper 로 옮긴다.

- '가로등만이'는 가로등이 여러 개이면서 상대방도 알고 있는 대상으로 보아 정관사 the와 복수어미 -s를 붙여 only the street lights로 옮긴다.
- '더욱 빛을 발하다'는 shine brighter, get brighter, shine more brightly로 옮긴다.

(4) Most villagers left the village, leaving only a few people behind.
Most of the villagers left the village, and only a few remained there.
Most villagers went out of the village, and only a few remained there.
Most of the people living in the village left it, and only a few remained there.

- '그 마을 사람들 대부분'은 most villagers, most of the villagers, most of the villagers living in the village로 옮긴다.
- '그 마을을 떠나다'는 leave the village, go out of the village로 옮긴다.
- '몇 명만 남다'는 leave only a few people behind, only a few remain there로 옮긴다.

(5) He smokes almost two packs of cigarettes a day; however, he rarely drinks.
He smokes close to two packs of cigarettes a day, but he rarely drinks.
Even though he smokes about two packs of cigarettes a day, he seldom drinks liquor.
He rarely drinks, though he smokes about two packs of cigarettes a day.

- '담배 두 갑'은 two packs of cigarettes로 옮긴다. 담배 한 갑은 a pack of cigarettes로 옮기며 a pack of cigarette로 표현하지 않는다. '담배 한 개비'는 a cigarette이다.
- '술은 거의 마시지 않다'는 rarely drink, seldom drink liquor로 옮긴다.

(6) Can you lend me some money? I will pay you back in two days.
Can you lend me some money? I can give it back two days later.
Could I borrow a little money from you? I will give it back two days later.
Could I borrow some money from you? I will repay you two days later.

- '돈 약간'은 some money, a little money로 옮긴다.
- '빌려주다'는 lend로 옮기며 돈을 빌리는 쪽에서 보면 '빌리다'는 의미이므로 borrow로 옮길 수도 있다.
- '이틀 후에'는 in two days, two days later로 옮긴다.
- '갚다'는 pay back, give back, repay로 옮긴다.

(7) I cannot breathe because so much smoke is leaking out.
There is so much smoke leaking out that I cannot breathe.
Thick smoke is coming out, so it is impossible for me to breathe.
There is so much smoke leaking out, and this makes it impossible for me to breathe.

- '많은 연기'는 so much smoke, thick smoke로 옮긴다.

• '새어나오다'는 leak out, come out으로 옮긴다.
• '숨을 쉴 수가 없다'는 cannot breathe, it is impossible for~to breathe, make it impossible for ~to breathe로 옮긴다.
• 넷째 예문의 it은 가목적어이고 to breathe가 진목적어이다.

(8) Two fans, an electric fan, and an air conditioner were ready to fight off the heat.
Ready to fight off the heat were a couple of fans, an electric fan and an air conditioner.
A couple of fans, an electric fan, and air conditioning were ready to fight the heat.
To fight off the heat, two fans, an electric fan and an air conditioner were ready.

• '~두 개'는 two, a couple of~로 옮긴다.
• '에어컨'은 an air conditioner, air conditioning으로 옮긴다.
• '더위를 물리칠 준비를 하다'의 '더위'는 정관사를 붙여 the heat으로 표현하여 be ready to fight off the heat, be ready to fight the heat으로 옮긴다.

(9) He read about fifty pages of the book and went out to kick a ball.
He read about fifty pages of the book before going out to kick the ball.
He went out to kick the ball after reading about fifty pages of the book.
After reading about fifty pages of the book, he went out to kick the ball.

• '그 책을 약 50쪽 읽다'는 read about fifty pages of the book으로 옮긴다.
• '공을 차러 나가다'는 go out to kick a ball, go out to kick the ball로 옮긴다.
• 예문의 about은 '~에 관하여'라는 전치사가 아니라 '약'이라는 부사이다.

(10) He doesn't travel a lot, but he doesn't hate traveling.
He seldom travels; however, he doesn't hate traveling.
He doesn't hate traveling, even though he seldom travels.
Although he doesn't travel much, he doesn't hate traveling.

• '여행을 많이 하지는 않다'는 do not travel a lot, seldom travel, do not travel much로 옮긴다. much는 '많이'라는 부사이다.
• '~지만'은 ~, but으로 옮기거나 ~; however, ~로 옮길 수 있다.
• '~을 싫어하는 것은 아니다'는 do not hate~로 옮긴다.

2. (1) a. Many people know that knowledge of grammar is indispensable to writing in English.
b. It is a well-known fact that knowledge of grammar is the basis of English composition.
c. A knowledge of grammar is the basis of English composition; that is a well-known fact.
d. We know very well that we need knowledge of grammar to be good at English writing.

- ‘영작’은 writing in English, English composition, English writing으로 옮긴다.
- ‘문법지식’은 knowledge of grammar, a knowledge of grammar로 옮긴다.
- ‘~을 기초로 하다’는 be indispensable to~, be the basis of~, need~to do~로 옮긴다.

(2) a. With no experiences abroad, he speaks foreign languages very well.

b. His foreign languages are very good, even though he has never been to a foreign country.

c. Although he has never been abroad, he speaks foreign languages very well.

d. He has never been abroad, but he speaks foreign languages very well.

- ‘가 본적이 없는데’는 전치사구 with no experiences abroad나 현재완료시제 has never been to ~, has never been abroad로 나타낸다. abroad는 ‘해외에’라는 부사이다.
- ‘외국어’는 ‘한 외국어’를 가리킬 때는 a foreign language로 옮기고 일반적인 의미의 ‘외국어’를 가리킬 때는 foreign languages로 옮긴다.

(3) a. What you are saying is far from our common interest.

b. Our common interest is very distant from what you are saying.

c. You are saying something that is far from our common interest.

d. The subject you are talking about is far from our common interest.

- ‘네가 말하는 것’은 ‘네가 말하고 있는 것’의 의미인 현재진행시제로 what you are saying, you are saying something, the subject you are talking about으로 옮긴다.
- ‘~와 거리가 먼’은 far from~, very distant from~으로 옮긴다.
- 첫째, 둘째 예문의 what은 모두 명사절을 이끄는 관계대명사이다.

(4) a. While he was writing a book, a mosquito bit his leg.

b. A mosquito bit his leg when he was writing a book.

c. His leg was bitten by a mosquito while he was writing a book.

d. He was working on writing a book when a mosquito bit his leg.

- ‘~의 다리를 물다’는 bite one’s leg로 옮긴다.
- ‘모기’는 ‘한 마리의 모기’를 가리킬 때는 a mosquito로 옮기고 모기의 마릿수와는 관계없이 일반적인 의미의 ‘모기’를 가리킬 때는 한정사를 앞에 붙이지 않은 복수형 mosquitos로 옮긴다.
- 무는 행위의 행위자인 모기를 주어로 하면 능동문이 되고 물리는 대상인 his leg를 주어로 하면 수동문이 된다.

(5) a. Two or three days is too short to read all these books.

b. You cannot read all of these books just within two or three days.

c. It is impossible to read all of these books within two or three days.

d. Reading all these books just within two or three days is impossible.

- '이 책들'은 '이 책들 모두'의 의미로 all these books, all of these books로 옮긴다.
- '이삼일'은 two or three days로 옮기고 '이삼일 내에'는 전치사구 within two or three days로 옮긴다.
- '~은 불가능하다'는 be too short to do~, cannot~, be impossible로 옮긴다.

## 제6장 동 사

### Ⅲ. 심화연습

1. 정답 : d

- 이유 : 바람 wind는 보통 정관사 the를 앞에 붙여 the wind로 표현한다. 그러나 wind 앞에 이것을 수식하는 수식어가 있으면 바람의 한 종류나 유형을 나타내게 되어 부정관사가 붙는다. 따라서 wind 앞에 수식어 gentle이 있으므로 부정관사 a가 앞에 붙어 a gentle wind가 된다.

2. 정답 : c

- 이유 : 주어가 3인칭 단수이고 동사가 현재시제일 때 동사에 -s나 -es가 붙는다. 따라서 주어가 3인칭 단수 it이고 동사 thunder가 현재시제이므로 thunder 뒤에 -s를 붙여 thunders가 된다.

3. 정답 : d

- 이유 : 이중부정은 긍정의 의미가 된다. 부정의 부사 not 뒤에 또 다른 부정의 부사 nowhere가 나란히 나와 긍정의 의미가 되므로 nowhere를 anywhere로 바꾼다.

4. 정답 : b

- 이유 : 동사 make는 목적어와 목적보어를 취하여 '~을 ~하게 되게 하다'는 의미를 전한다. 따라서 목적어 him 뒤는 목적보어가 와야 하므로 부사 happily가 아닌 형용사 happy가 와야 한다.

5. 정답 : b

- 이유 : 관계대명사 who가 이끄는 관계절에서 등위접속사 and에 의해 두 개의 동사구가 연결된 구문이다. 따라서 동사 like의 주어가 3인칭 단수 a person이고 동사가 현재시제여서 -s가 붙어 likes가 되듯이 동사 enjoy의 주어 역시 같은 3인칭 단수 a person이고 동사가 현재시제이므로 동사 enjoy에 -s가 붙어 enjoys가 된다.

6. 정답 : d

- 이유 : 전치사 after 뒤는 전치사의 목적어인 명사구가 온다. 그러나 동사가 올 때는 동명사로 와야 전치사의 목적어가 될 수 있으므로 동사 finish는 동명사 finishing이 된다.

7. 정답 : b

• 이유 : 사역동사 뒤에 부정사가 올 때는 to-부정사가 아닌 원형부정사가 온다. 따라서 사역동사 make의 목적어인 her 뒤에 있는 to answer의 to를 뺀다.

8. 정답 : b

• 이유 : about이 '~에 관하여'라는 의미를 전하는 때는 전치사이다. 전치사 뒤는 보통 전치사의 목적어인 명사구가 오며 전치사의 목적어는 전치사 뒤에 있거나 그 문장 내에 반드시 존재해야 하며 그렇지 않으면 비문이 된다. 예문의 전치사 about 뒤는 목적어인 명사구가 와야 하므로 앞에서 언급한 내용(He walked so fast)을 가리키는 대명사 this를 넣는다.

9. 정답 : c

• 이유 : 명사절인 that-절의 내용이 전체 문장의 주어가 되어야 하므로 이 절을 진주어로 하는 가주어 it이 필요하다. 따라서 주어인 this 자리에 가주어 it이 온다.

10. 정답 : c

• 이유 : 고속도로 express highway는 셀 수 있는 명사로 일반적으로 수의 개념으로 쓰인다. 따라서 한정사(관사, 소유격, 지시사, 양화사)가 앞에 붙은 형태(*an* express highway, *the* express highway, *our* express highway, *this* express highway, *any* express highway)로 쓰이거나 아니면 한정사가 앞에 붙지 않은 복수형(express highway*s*)으로 쓰인다. 따라서 예문에서는 '한 고속도로'의 의미이므로 부정관사 an을 앞에 붙여 an express highway로 표현한다.

## Ⅳ. 기본영작

1. It was an hour and a half drive from my house to my school.
   It took an hour and a half from my house to the school by car.
   It took an hour and a half to get to the school from my home in a car.
   It took me an hour and a half to get to the school from my home by car.

• '집에서 학교까지'는 from one's house to one's school로 옮기며 어느 학교를 가리키는지 청자도 알고 있다고 볼 때는 school 앞에 정관사를 붙일 수 있다.

• '차로 한 시간 반이 걸리다'는 거리를 나타내는 it을 주어로 be an hour and a half drive로 옮기거나 시간을 나타내는 it을 주어로 take an hour and a half by car나 take an hour and a half to get to~in a car로 옮긴다.

2. The strong wind made us give up doing fishing.
   We had to give up fishing because of a strong wind.
   We had to forget about doing fishing because of the strong wind.
   It was impossible for us to do fishing because of strong winds, so we had to give it up.

- '강한 바람이 불어'는 the strong wind, because of a strong wind, because of the strong wind, because of strong winds로 옮긴다. a strong wind는 '하나의 강한 바람'을 뜻하고 the strong wind는 청자도 알고 있다고 화자가 보고 있는 '그 강한 바람'을 뜻하며 strong winds는 일반적인 의미의 '강한 바람'을 뜻한다.

3. He is clever, but not wise.
   He is more clever than wise.
   He is clever, but he is not wise.
   Clever though he is, he is not wise.

- '영리한'은 clever이고 '현명한'은 wise이다.
- '~하지만'은 ~, but으로 나타내거나 양보를 나타내는 though-절로 옮긴다.
- 동일인의 성격을 묘사할 때는 -er비교급 대신 more~비교급을 쓰므로 '현명하다기보다는 영리한'은 둘째 예문처럼 more clever than wise로 옮긴다.

4. We walked and walked never to arrive at the top of the mountain.
   We walked and walked, but could not get to the top of the mountain.
   Although we kept on walking, we could not arrive at the mountain top.
   Even after a continuous walk, we could not get to the top of the mountain.

- '걷고 또 걸어도 ~하지 못하다'는 walk and walk never to~나 walk and walk, but cannot~으로 옮길 수 있고 although~keep on walking, ~cannot~으로 옮기거나 even after a continuous walk, ~cannot~으로 옮긴다.
- '산 정상'은 the top of the mountain, the mountain top으로 옮긴다.
- '~에 다다르다'는 arrive at~, get to~로 옮긴다.

5. Her son is already attending elementary school because she married young.
   She married at a young age, and she even has a son who is an elementary school student.
   She got married at such a young age that her son is already in elementary school.
   She married her husband early, and her son is an elementary school student already.

- '어려서 결혼하다'는 marry young, marry at a young age, get married at a young age, marry one's husband early로 옮긴다.
- '초등학교에 다니다'는 attend elementary school, be an elementary school student, be in elementary school로 옮긴다.

6. After buying some fried chicken, fruit and drinks, they made towards the mountain.
   They bought fried chicken, fruit, and drinks, and headed for the mountain.
   They bought some roast chicken, fruit and drinks, and they started for the mountain.
   They left for the mountain after buying some fried chicken, fruit, and drinks.

- '통닭'은 some fried chicken, fried chicken, some roast chicken으로 옮기고 양화사 some이 들어간 표현은 '약간의'라는 의미를 전하고 some이 붙지 않은 fried chicken은 일반적인 의미의 통닭을 가리킨다.
- '~을 향해 출발하다'는 make towards~, head for~, start for~, leave for~로 옮긴다.

7. In summer, less people go to a public bath than ever.
   The number of people using a public bath largely reduces during the summer.
   In summer, the number of public bathhouse users significantly decreases.
   The number of people using the public bathhouse dramatically decreases in summer.

- '여름에는'은 in summer, in the summer, during the summer로 옮긴다.
- '대중목욕탕'은 a public bath, a public bathhouse로 옮긴다.
- '~의 수가 줄다'는 less people~, reduce, decrease로 옮긴다.
- 둘째, 넷째 예문의 using은 각각 a public bath와 the public bathhouse를 목적어로 취하면서 앞 명사구 people을 수식하는 현재분사이다.

8. Everything looks beautiful during your pleasure.
   When you are happy, everything looks beautiful.
   Everything looks beautiful with a delightful mind.
   When you have a joyful mind, everything looks beautiful.

- '마음이 즐거우면'은 전치사구 during your pleasure나 부사절 when you are happy로 옮길 수도 있고 전치사구 with a delightful mind나 부사절 when you have a joyful mind로 옮길 수도 있다.
- '만사'는 everything으로 표현한다.
- '아름다워 보이다'는 look beautiful로 옮기며 look이 '~해 보이다'는 의미를 전할 때는 보어인 형용사구가 뒤에 오기를 요구한다.

9. This weekend, I am going to Lake Soyang for a change.
   I will go to Lake Soyang to take a short rest this weekend.
   To get some fresh air, I will go to Lake Soyang on the weekend.
   I would like to go to Lake Soyang to enjoy some fresh air on the weekend.

- '바람 쐬러'는 for a change, to take a short rest, to get some fresh air, to enjoy some fresh air로 옮긴다.
- '가봐야겠다'는 '가려고 하다'는 의미로 be동사의 현재형과 동사원형 am going을 써서 예정되어 있는 미래로 옮기거나 '가겠다'는 의미로 보아 will go로 옮기거나 '가보고 싶다'는 의미로 보아 would like to go로 옮긴다.

10. I had breakfast late, so I don't want to eat lunch now.
    I don't feel like having lunch yet, for I had a late breakfast.

I'm not really up to lunch yet, because I had a late breakfast.

Because I had a late breakfast, I don't feel like having lunch yet.

- '아침식사를 늦게 하다'는 have breakfast late, have a late breakfast로 옮긴다.
- '~해서'는 ~, so나 ~, for~로 옮길 수도 있고 ~, because~나 because~, ~로 옮길 수도 있다.
- '아직 점심 생각이 없다'는 do not want to eat lunch now, do not feel like having lunch yet, be not really up to lunch yet으로 옮긴다.

## V. 심화영작

1. (1) She seems really busy preparing her doctoral dissertation.

She seems to be very busy preparing for a doctoral dissertation.

She may be very busy because she is in the process of preparing a dissertation for a doctor's degree.

It seems to me that she is really busy preparing her doctoral dissertation.

- '박사학위 논문'은 one's doctoral dissertation, a doctoral dissertation, a dissertation for a doctor's degree로 옮긴다.
- '~을 준비하다'는 prepare~, prepare for~로 옮긴다.
- '~하느라 바쁜'은 busy -ing, busy because~로 옮긴다.
- '~한 모양이다'는 seem~, seem to be~, may be~, seem that~으로 옮긴다.

(2) A car and a truck crashed, but luckily, nobody got hurt.

A car collided with a truck; fortunately, no one got hurt.

A car and a truck collided, but, luckily, no one was hurt.

Fortunately, no one was hurt when a car and a truck crashed.

- '자동차'는 한국어 문장에서 '한 대의 자동차'를 뜻하므로 a car로 옮기고 '트럭' 역시 '한 대의 트럭'을 뜻하므로 a truck으로 옮긴다.
- '충돌하다'는 crash, collide with, collide로 옮긴다.
- '다행히'는 luckily, fortunately로 옮긴다.
- '다치다'는 get hurt, be hurt로 옮긴다.

(3) It is fun to in-line skate through the air along the Han River.

It feels good to in-line skate through the air along the Han River.

It is enjoyable to race through the air in in-line skates along the Han River.

You may find it pleasant to roller-blade through the air along the Han River.

- '한강'은 강 이름 앞에는 정관사가 붙으므로 the Han River로 옮긴다.
- '한강을 따라'는 전치사구 along the Han River로 옮긴다.

- '바람을 가르며'는 전치사구 through the air로 옮긴다.
- '인라인스케이트를 타다'는 동사 in-line skate, roller-blade로 옮기거나 전치사구 in in-line skates로 옮긴다.

(4) He used to play table tennis, but now he hardly plays it.
He often used to play ping-pong but hardly plays it now.
He often used to play ping-pong. However, he hardly plays it nowadays.
He used to play table tennis from time to time, but now he rarely goes to play it.

- '탁구를 치다'는 play table tennis, play ping-pong으로 옮긴다.
- '~하곤 했지만 더 이상 ~아니다'는 used to do~로 옮긴다.
- '거의 치지 않다'는 hardly play~, rarely go to play~로 옮긴다.

(5) A human being just receives benefits from nature but rarely repays it.
Mankind only receives the benefits given from the nature, and is stingy about repaying.
Human beings only take the benefits nature gives them, but rarely repay it.
Man only takes the benefits of nature, and is ignorant about giving back to nature.

- '인간'은 '한 인간'을 가리킬 때는 부정관사를 붙인 a human being으로 나타내고 일반적인 의미의 인간을 가리킬 때는 한정사를 붙이지 않은 복수형 human beings나 한정사를 붙이지 않은 mankind, man으로 나타낸다.
- '받기만 하고'는 just receive~, only receive~, only take~로 옮긴다.
- '보답하는 데 인색하다'는 rarely repay~, be stingy about~, be ignorant about giving back to ~로 옮긴다.

(6) He wants to be a diplomat in the future, so he is studying foreign languages hard.
In order to become a diplomat in the future, he is studying foreign languages very hard.
He is diligently studying foreign languages to become a diplomat in the future.
He is studying foreign languages hard to become a diplomat in the future.

- '장차'는 전치사구 in the future로 나타낸다.
- '외교관'은 한국어 원문에서 '한 사람의 외교관'을 가리키므로 a diplomat으로 옮긴다.
- '외국어'는 셀 수 있는 명사로 어떤 외국어이건 '한 외국어'를 의미할 때는 a foreign language로 나타내고 '일반적인 의미의 외국어'를 가리킬 때는 한정사를 붙이지 않은 복수형 foreign languages로 나타낸다.

(7) I cannot see the far away mountain top because the newly built apartments are in the way.
The newly built apartments prevent me from seeing the top of the mountain far away.
The newly built apartments have blocked the view of the far away mountain top.

The view of far away mountains can no longer be seen because of the newly built apartments.

- '멀리 보이던 산봉우리'는 the far away mountain top, see the top of the mountain far away, the view of the far away mountain top, the view of far away mountains로 옮긴다.
- '~에 가려 보이지 않다'는 cannot see~because~be in the way, prevent~from seeing~, have blocked the view of~, can no longer be seen because of~로 옮긴다.

(8) She said she wanted to be good at everything: English composition, English reading comprehension, and English conversation.
She said that she wanted to be good at English composition, English reading and comprehension, and English conversation altogether.
She said she wants to be a good English speaker, writer, and reader.
She said, "I want to excel in English composition, English reading and comprehension, and English conversation altogether."

- '영어작문'은 English composition이나 to be a good English writer로 옮기고 '영문독해'는 English reading comprehension, English reading and comprehension, to be a good English reader로 옮기고 '영어회화'는 English conversation, to be a good English speaker로 옮긴다.
- '~을 잘하다'는 be good at~, be a good~, excel in~으로 옮긴다.

(9) Why do people usually use blue in men's wear and red in women's?
Why do they usually use blue tones for men's wear and red ones for women?
Why is it that blue is often used for men's wear and red is often used for women's wear?
How come in men's clothing blue is used often and in women's clothing red is used often?

- '왜'는 의문부사 why로 옮기거나 how come으로 옮긴다.
- '남자 옷'은 men's wear, men's clothing으로 옮기고 '여자 옷'은 women's wear, women's clothing으로 옮긴다.
- '푸른색'은 blue, blue tones로 옮기면 무난하다.
- 둘째 예문의 they는 막연하게 세상 사람들을 가리키는 말이다.

(10) They all scattered away, but they got together soon.
They all separated, but soon gathered together again.
They were scattered everywhere, but they were soon back together.
Although they were dispersed all over the place, they were soon back together.

- '뿔뿔이 흩어지다'는 scatter away, separate, be scattered everywhere, be dispersed all over the place로 옮긴다.

- '곧 다시 모이다'는 get together soon, soon gather together again, be soon back together로 옮긴다.

2. (1) a. They got to the west sea and watched the sunset.
   b. After arrival at the west sea, they watched the sunset.
   c. When they reached the west sea, they watched the sun setting.
   d. On their arrival at the west sea, they watched the sun going down.

- '서해안'은 the west sea로 옮긴다.
- '도착하여'는 get to~, after arrival~, when~reach~, on one's arrival로 옮긴다.
- '일몰을 지켜보다'는 watch the sunset, watch the sun setting, watch the sun going down으로 옮긴다.

(2) a. It was very difficult for me to drive because the sudden shower blurred the field of vision.
   b. The sudden shower blurred the field of vision, and this made it very difficult for me to drive.
   c. The field of vision was blurred by the sudden shower, and this made it very difficult for me to drive.
   d. I found it very difficult to drive because my field of vision was blurred by the sudden shower.

- '소나기'는 the sudden shower로 옮긴다.
- '시야를 가리다'는 blur the field of vision, the field of vision is blurred, one's field of vision is blurred로 옮긴다.
- '운전하기가 어렵다'는 be difficult for a person to drive, make it difficult for a person to drive, find it difficult for a person to drive로 옮긴다.

(3) a. The printer was out of ink, so he could not print anything.
   b. He could not print anything, for the printer was out of ink.
   c. The ink in the printer was all out; therefore, he could not do any printing jobs.
   d. It was impossible for him to do any printing jobs because the printer was out of ink.

- '잉크가 다 떨어지다'는 be out of ink, the ink is all out으로 옮긴다.
- '인쇄를 할 수 없다'는 cannot print anything, cannot do any printing jobs, be impossible for a person to do any printing jobs로 옮긴다.
- 주어는 '그 프린터' the printer, '그' he, '그 프린터의 잉크' the ink in the printer, 가주어 it으로 할 수 있다.

(4) a. Whenever his students play with their cell phones in class, the professor feels bothered by this.

b. The professor is bothered by his students playing with their cell phones in class.

c. Students playing with their cell phones in class get on the professor's nerves.

d. It bothers the professor that his students play with their cell phones in class.

- '그 교수'는 화자가 자신의 청자도 그 지시대상이 누구인지 알고 있다고 보고 있는 한 사람의 교수를 가리키므로 the professor로 옮긴다.
- '수업시간에'는 전치사구 in class로 옮긴다.
- '휴대폰을 만지작거리다'는 play with one's cell phone으로 옮긴다.
- '신경이 쓰이다'는 feel bothered, is bothered, get on one's nerves, bother~로 옮긴다.

(5) a. With the late lunch, I am starting to feel drowsy.

b. The late lunch I have had is making me start to feel sleepy.

c. Because I have had a late lunch, I am starting to feel sleepy.

d. I am starting to feel drowsy because I have had a late lunch.

- '점심을 늦게 먹고 나니'는 with the late lunch, the late lunch I have had, because I have had a late lunch로 옮긴다. lunch 앞의 정관사 the는 화자가 가리키는 점심이 어떤 것인지 그의 청자도 알고 있다고 보는 경우이고 부정관사 a는 화자가 어떤 점심을 가리키는지 그의 청자는 모른다고 보는 경우이다.
- '졸리기 시작하다'는 start to feel drowsy, start to feel sleepy로 옮긴다.

## 제7장 보 어

### Ⅲ. 심화연습

1. 정답 : c

- 이유 : '~을 ~한 채'는 '전치사 with + 전치사의 목적어 + 목적보어'로 나타낼 수 있으므로 '팔짱을 낀 채'는 전치사 with 뒤에 전치사의 목적어와 목적보어로 표현할 수 있다. 문장의 주어인 he가 자신의 팔이 겹쳐지게 한다는 의미이므로 전치사의 목적어 his arms 뒤에 올 타동사 fold는 현재분사 folding이 아닌 과거분사 folded가 된다. 타동사의 현재분사는 능동의 의미를 가지는 데 반해 과거분사는 수동의 의미를 가지기 때문이다.

2. 정답 : c

• 이유 : 타동사 find의 진목적어가 to-부정사인 to keep이고 형용사 difficult가 목적보어이므로 동사 find 바로 뒤에 가목적어 it이 필요하다.

3. 정답 : b

• 이유 : 타동사 welcome의 목적어로 대명사 him이 나와 있다. 그러나 이 동사는 목적어 뒤에 목적보어가 나오기를 요구하지는 않는 동사이므로 목적어 뒤는 목적보어가 아니라 동사의 행위가 어떤 모양으로 이루어지는가를 나타내는 양태부사가 올 수 있다. 따라서 형용사구 most glad가 아닌 부사구 most gladly가 와야 한다.

4. 정답 : d

• 이유 : 한정사(관사, 소유격, 지시사, 양화사) 중 관사, 소유격, 지시사는 둘이 나란히 나와 직접 명사를 한정할 수 없다. 예문은 소유격(His)과 부정관사(a)가 나란히 나와 모두 명사(daughter)를 한정하고 있어 비문이다. 따라서 His a young daughter를 His young daughter 또는 A young daughter of his로 바꾼다.

5. 정답 : b

• 이유 : 동사 find는 뒤에 목적어와 목적보어를 취하여 '~가 ~하다는 것을 알다'는 의미를 전한다. 예문에서 가목적어 it과 진목적어인 to-부정사(to hear)가 나와 있으므로 가목적어 뒤에 목적보어가 되는 형용사구가 필요하므로 부사 hardly는 형용사 hard가 되어야 한다.

6. 정답 : d

• 이유 : both~and는 명사구와 명사구를 연결하는 데 쓰인다. 예문처럼 both 뒤는 명사구(the room)가 오고 and 뒤는 동사구(helps her mother to do the dishes)가 오면 비문이 된다. 이와 달리 not only~but also는 동사구와 동사구를 연결할 수 있다. 따라서 동사구인 sweeps the room 앞에 not only를 두고 또 다른 동사구 helps her mother to do the dishes 앞에 but also를 둔다.

7. 정답 : c

• 이유 : '정열적으로 연구하다'는 study passionately이다. 동사 study는 연구하는 모양이 어떻게 이루어지는가를 나타내는 양태부사는 취할 수 있지만 보어가 나타나기를 요구하지는 않는다. 따라서 예문에서 형용사 passionate가 보어로 오지 않으므로 이것을 양태부사 passionately로 바꾼다.

8. 정답 : a

• 이유 : 둘 이상의 절이 연결될 때는 일반적으로 접속사가 필요하다. 예문은 두 개의 절이 접속사 없이 단지 쉼표로만 연결되어 비문이다. 따라서 뒷 절의 주어 this가 앞 절의 내용 전체를 가리키는 대명사이므로 이것을 주격 관계대명사 which로 바꾼다.

9. 정답 : b

• 이유 : 날씨 weather는 셀 수 없는 명사로 일반적으로 앞에 정관사 the를 붙여 the weather로 표현한다. 그리고 이 명사 앞에 수식어가 붙어도 부정관사는 붙일 수 없어서 '더운 날씨'는 a hot weather가 아닌 hot weather로 나타낸다.

10. 정답 : d

• 이유 : 대명사는 자신이 가리키는 명사구와 성(gender)과 수(number)가 일치해야 한다. 예문의 대명사 his는 앞에 나온 명사구 human beings를 가리켜야 하므로 복수인 their가 된다.

## Ⅳ. 기본영작

1. There goes your girlfriend.
   Your girlfriend is going by.
   Your girlfriend is walking by.
   There's your girlfriend walking by.

• '걸어가고 있다'는 현재 걸어가는 행위가 일시적으로 진행 중에 있다고 보면 현재진행시제 is going by, is walking by로 표현한다. 그러나 '저기 ~가 가다'는 의미는 첫째 예문처럼 부사 there 뒤에 go의 단순현재시제 goes가 오고 뒤에 주어 your girlfriend가 온다.

2. Place the book on the desk and shut it.
   Put the book on your desk and close it.
   Put the book on top of the desk and then close it.
   After putting the book on top of the desk, close it.

• '~을 ~위에 올려놓다'는 place~on~, put~on~으로 표현한다.

• '올려놓고'는 place~on~ and~, put~on~ and~, put~on~ and then~, after putting~on~으로 표현한다.

• 넷째 예문의 after putting the book은 전치사구로 after는 전치사이고 putting은 동명사이고 명사구 the book은 동명사의 목적어이다.

3. The girl student is not good at her studies, but tries her best.
   Although the girl student is not very good at her studies, she is very sincere.
   The girl student is not very successful at her studies, but she is very diligent.
   The girl student is not very good at her studies. Nevertheless, she is very sincere.

• '그 여학생'은 the girl student로 옮긴다.

• '공부를 잘하지 못하다'는 be not good at one's studies, be not very good at one's studies, be not very successful at one's studies로 옮긴다.

• '매우 성실하다'는 try one's best, be very sincere, be very diligent로 옮긴다.

4. These words touched her deeply.
These words impressed her greatly.
She was deeply moved by these words.
She was greatly impressed by these words.

- '이 말'은 these words로 옮긴다.
- '깊은 감동을 받다'는 touch~deeply, impress~greatly, be deeply moved, be greatly impressed로 옮긴다.
- 한국어 문장은 과거의 사실을 말하는 것으로 보아 단순과거시제 touched, was impressed, impressed, was moved로 옮긴다.

5. Many modern people are troubled with beer bellies.
A worry of many modern people is that they have a potbelly.
Getting a potbelly is one of the factors that trouble many people in the modern age.
One of the concerns that many people in the modern age have is getting a potbelly.

- '현대인들'은 modern people, people in the modern age로 옮긴다.
- '고민거리'는 be troubled with, a worry, the factors that trouble~, the concerns로 옮긴다.
- '똥배'는 a beer belly, a potbelly로 옮기고 '똥배가 나오다'는 with beer bellies, have a potbelly, get a potbelly로 옮긴다. beer bellies는 일반적인 의미의 똥배를 가리킨다.

6. Actually, he went on a blind date and had drinks with her until late at night.
In truth, he went on a blind date with her and drank with her till very late at night.
The truth is that he went on a blind date with her, and they had drinks until late at night.
It is true that he went on a blind date with her and drank liquor with her until late at night.

- '사실은'은 actually, in truth, the truth is~, it is true that~으로 옮긴다.
- '선보러 가다'는 go on a blind date로 옮긴다.
- '밤늦게까지 술을 마시다'는 have drinks until late at night, drink till very late at night, drink liquor until late at night으로 옮긴다.

7. I keep yawning because I slept late last night.
I went to bed late last night, so I cannot stop yawning.
I cannot stop yawning because I went to sleep late last night.
I am continuing to yawn because I went to bed late last night.

- '어제'는 한국어 문장에서 '어제 밤에'의 의미로 last night으로 옮긴다.
- '늦게 잠들다'는 sleep late, go to bed late로 옮긴다.
- '~했더니'는 ~because~로 옮기거나 ~, so~로 옮긴다.
- '계속 하품이 나오다'는 keep yawning, cannot stop yawning, be continuing to yawn으로 옮긴다.

8. Whenever he is tired, he looks far out the window.
He usually looks far out the window when he is tired.
He often looks far out of the window when he feels tired.
When he is tired, he usually looks far out through the window.

- '피로할 때면'은 '피로할 때마다'의 의미로 whenever~is tired, when~is tired, when~feels tired로 옮긴다.
- '멀리 창밖을 내다보다'는 look far out the window, look far out of the window, look far out through the window로 옮긴다.
- 한국어 문장은 현재의 사실을 말하므로 시제는 단순현재시제를 쓴다.

9. She is still single, though she is tall and pretty.
Although she is tall and pretty, she still remains single.
She is still unmarried even though she is tall and pretty.
Despite her pretty appearance and tall height, she still remains unmarried.

- '키도 크고 얼굴도 예쁜'은 tall and pretty, one's pretty appearance and tall height로 옮긴다.
- '아직 미혼이다'는 be still single, still remain single, be still unmarried, still remain unmarried로 옮긴다.
- '~한데'는 '~하지만'의 의미로 양보의 접속사 though~, although~로 옮기거나 even though~로 옮길 수도 있고 양보의 전치사 despite~로 옮긴다.

10. Very clever though he is, he seems to lack sincerity.
Although he is very clever, he seems to lack sincerity.
He is very clever, but he seems insincere.
It seems as though he lacks sincerity, but he is very clever.

- '매우 영리하지만'은 형용사구 very clever가 앞으로 이동된 very clever though he is나 although he is very clever로 옮겨도 좋고 he is very clever, but~이나 ~, but he is very clever로 옮겨도 좋다.
- '성실성이 부족하다'는 lack sincerity, seem insincere로 옮긴다.

## V. 심화영작

1. (1) When he got his doctor's degree, his mother was very happy.
He got his doctor's degree, and this made his mother very happy.
His mother was very happy the moment he got his doctor's degree.
The mother was very pleased when her son got his doctor's degree.

- '박사학위'는 a doctor's degree, a doctorate으로 표현한다.

- '박사학위를 취득하다'는 get one's doctor's degree로 표현한다.
- '매우 기쁘다'는 be very happy, make~very happy, be very pleased로 표현한다.

(2) You must use writing utensils in ink for important exams.

You must use writing instruments in ink during an important test.

It is required that you use writing tools in ink for important exams.

Important tests require that you use writing utensils in ink instead of pencils.

- '하나의 중요한 시험'은 an important exam, an important test로 옮기고 일반적인 의미의 중요한 시험은 한정사를 붙이지 않은 복수형 important exams, important tests로 옮긴다.
- '반드시 ~하다'는 must~, be required, require~로 옮긴다.
- '잉크 필기구'는 writing utensils in ink, writing instruments in ink, writing tools in ink로 옮긴다.

(3) He enjoys a great view from his room, which is on the eighth floor of a ten-story building.

He lives on the eighth floor of a ten-story building, and his room has a great view.

His room is on the eighth floor of a ten-story building, and it has a fine view.

His room is on the eighth floor of a ten-story building, and it commands a fine view.

- '10층 건물 8층에'는 on the eighth floor of a ten-story building으로 옮긴다. 한 건물의 개개의 층을 가리킬 때는 floor를 쓰고 한 건물이 몇 개의 층으로 되어 있는가를 가리킬 때는 story를 쓴다.
- '전망이 매우 좋다'는 enjoy a great view, have a great view, have a fine view, command a fine view로 옮긴다.

(4) These days, he is exercising and sweating a lot to lose weight.

To lose weight, he is doing a lot of exercise and sweating a lot these days.

These days, he is taking exercise and sweating a lot to lose his weight.

He is exercising with much sweat so that he may reduce his weight these days.

- '체중을 줄이다'는 lose weight, lose one's weight, reduce one's weight로 옮긴다.
- '땀을 흘리며 운동하다'는 exercise and sweat a lot, do a lot of exercise and sweat a lot, take exercise and sweat a lot, exercise with much sweat로 옮긴다.

(5) She decided to break up with her boyfriend and cut her hair short.

She cut her hair short and decided that she would break up with her boyfriend.

She made up her mind to break up with her boyfriend and cut her hair short.

Deciding that she would break up with her boyfriend, she also cut her hair short.

- '~와 헤어지다'는 break up with~로 옮긴다.

- '~하기로 결심하다'는 decide to~, decide that~, make up one's mind to로 옮긴다.
- '머리를 짧게 깎다'는 cut one's hair short로 옮긴다.

(6) It can be very dangerous to fall asleep in an enclosed area while an electric fan is on.
It is very dangerous to sleep in a closed area with an electric fan on.
Falling asleep in a closed area with an electric fan on is very dangerous.
It is very dangerous to fall asleep in a closed area with an electric fan on.

- '밀폐된 공간에서'는 in an enclosed area, in a closed area로 옮긴다.
- '선풍기를 켜 놓고'는 while an electric fan is on, with an electric fan on으로 옮긴다. with an electric fan on은 전치사구로 명사구 an electric fan이 전치사 with의 목적어이고 on은 '켜져'라는 부사로 전치사의 목적보어이다.

(7) The clear sky makes me feel much better.
The sky has cleared up, so I feel a lot better.
Now that the sky has cleared up, I feel much better.
I am feeling far better because the sky has cleared up.

- '하늘이 맑게 개어'는 the clear sky나 the sky has cleared up, so~로 옮길 수도 있고 now that the sky has cleared up으로 옮기거나 because the sky has cleared up으로 옮긴다.
- '기분이 한결 좋다'는 feel much better, feel a lot better, be feeling far better로 옮긴다.

(8) He was way over sixty, but he was learning to in-line skate.
Although he was way over sixty, he was learning in-line skating.
He was learning how to in-line skate, even though he was way over sixty.
He was learning in-line skating, despite the fact that he was way over sixty.

- '예순 살이 훨씬 넘다'는 be way over sixty로 옮긴다.
- '인라인스케이트를 배우다'는 learn to in-line skate, learn in-line skating, learn how to in-line skate로 옮긴다.
- '배우고 있었다'는 과거의 일시적으로 진행 중인 행위를 나타내므로 과거진행시제 was learning으로 옮긴다.

(9) It is not so bad to jog with music.
It is not that bad to jog listening to music.
Listening to music while jogging is not that bad.
It is not that bad to jog while listening to music.

- '음악' music은 셀 수 없는 명사로 앞에 부정관사 a를 붙이거나 뒤에 복수 어미 -s를 붙일 수 없다.
- '음악을 들으면서'는 전치사구 with music이나 현재분사를 써서 listening to music으로 옮길 수

도 있고 동명사를 써서 listening to music으로 옮기거나 접속사를 사용하여 while listening to music으로 옮길 수도 있다.

- 예문의 that은 '그렇게, 그 정도로'를 의미하는 부사이다.

(10) Her voice is so attractive that it is pleasant to listen to her.

Her attractive voice entertains people when they listen to her.

Her voice is so attractive that it is a pleasure to listen to her talk.

She has a voice that is so attractive that it is a pleasure to listen to her talk.

- '너무나 ~해서 ~하다'는 so~that~으로 옮긴다.
- '그녀의 이야기를 들으면 즐겁다'는 '그녀의 이야기를 듣는 것은 즐겁다'의 의미로 가주어 it과 진주어인 to-부정사 to listen으로 옮기거나 Her attractive voice entertains people로 옮긴다.

2. (1) a. His confident story made the people around him more interested.

b. People around him got more interested by his story full of confidence.

c. He told a story with confidence, and this made the people around him more interested.

d. The story, on which he had a firm belief, made the people around him be more interested.

- '그의 확신에 찬 이야기'는 his confident story, his story full of confidence, he tells a story with confidence나 the story, on which he has a firm belief로 옮긴다.
- '주위 사람들'은 the people around him, people around him으로 옮기며 people around him은 일반적인 의미의 주위 사람을 말하며 the people around him은 '주위의 그 사람들'이란 뜻이다.

(2) a. The rain was gradually getting absorbed into our clothes. Nevertheless, we continued to walk.

b. We continued to walk even though the rain was gradually getting absorbed into our clothes.

c. Although the rain was gradually getting absorbed into our clothes, we kept on walking.

d. Despite the fact that the rain was gradually getting absorbed into our clothes, we went on walking.

- '빗물이 스며들다'는 the rain gets absorbed로 옮긴다.
- '스며들고 있었지만'은 과거의 진행 중인 행위를 나타내므로 과거진행시제 was getting으로 나타낸다.
- '계속 걷다'는 continue to walk, keep on walking, go on walking으로 옮긴다.

(3) a. These colors in clothing make you look older.

b. Clothes with these colors make you look older.

c. You will look older with clothes of these colors.

d. When you wear clothes with these colors, you will look older.

- '이런 색의 옷'은 these colors in clothing, clothes with these colors, clothes of these colors로 옮긴다.
- '나이가 더 들어 보이게 하다'는 make~look older, ~look older로 옮긴다.
- 첫째, 둘째 예문의 사역동사 make 뒤에서 to-부정사 to look이 원형부정사 look으로 바뀌었다.

(4) a. After painting his roof blue, the young man from the small rural community waited to take a wife.

b. Having painted his roof blue, the young man from the agricultural village waited to take a wife.

c. To take a wife, the young man living in the rural farming village painted his roof blue and waited for his bride.

d. The young man from the farming village painted his roof blue and waited to take a wife.

- '그 농촌 총각'은 the young man from the small rural community, the young man from the agricultural village, the young man living in the rural farming village, the young man from the farming village로 옮긴다.
- '지붕을 푸르게 칠하다'는 paint one's roof blue로 옮긴다.
- '배우자가 생기길 기다리다'는 wait to take a wife, wait for his bride로 옮긴다.

(5) a. With time can we grow younger?

b. Can a person grow younger as time goes by?

c. Is it possible to restore youth as time goes by?

d. As time passes by, can a person grow young again?

- '시간이 지남에 따라'는 with time, as time goes by, as time passes by로 옮긴다.
- '사람'은 we, a person으로 표현하거나 셋째 예문처럼 일반인을 가리키는 주어 one을 to-부정사 to restore 앞에 생략할 수도 있다.
- 동사 grow는 '~하게 되다'는 의미를 전할 때 형용사보어를 요구한다.

# 제8장 목적어

## Ⅲ. 심화연습

1. 정답 : d

• 이유 : 양태부사는 일반적으로 타동사의 목적어가 있으면 목적어 뒤에 오며 -ly로 끝나는 양태부사는 이 자리는 물론 문장 가운데 위치에도 온다. 양태부사 easily는 조동사 can 뒤에 오거나 transmitting towers for mobile phones 뒤에 와야 한다.

2. 정답 : d

• 이유 : '우산을 쓴 채'는 전치사 with 뒤에 전치사의 목적어를 두고 그 뒤에 목적보어를 두어 표현할 수 있다. 예문에서 전치사 with의 목적어인 an umbrella가 hold up의 행위자가 아니라 행위를 받는 대상이므로 hold up의 동사 hold는 현재분사 holding이 아닌 과거분사 held가 된다.

3. 정답 : c

• 이유 : 여행 trip은 셀 수 있는 명사로 일반적으로 수의 개념으로 쓰인다. '영어연수여행'은 trip을 셀 수 없는 명사처럼 사용한 English study trip이 아니라 셀 수 있는 명사로 사용한 an English study trip이나 일반적인 의미의 영어연수여행을 가리키는 English study trips로 표현한다.

4. 정답 : b

• 이유 : 형용사 difficult 뒤에 진주어인 to-부정사가 오고 앞의 주어 자리에 가주어 it이 온다. 예문에서 to-부정사 to see가 진주어이므로 주어 자리에 가주어 it이 필요하다. 따라서 주어 I를 가주어 It으로 바꾼다.

5. 정답 : c

• 이유 : 이발 haircut은 셀 수 있는 명사로 수의 개념으로 쓰인다. 따라서 '이발을 하다'는 get haircut이 아니라 get a haircut이다.

6. 정답 : b

• 이유 : '그 집 지붕'은 of-소유격을 써서 the roof of the house로 표현하며 어포스트로피 에스 소유격('s)을 쓰지 않는다. 따라서 the house's roof를 the roof of the house로 바꾼다.

7. 정답 : d

• 이유 : '고개를 돌렸다'는 과거의 사실을 말하는 것으로 보아 단순과거시제로 표현한다. 예문에서 동사 turn은 단순현재시제로 되어 있어 현재의 사실을 전한다. 따라서 앞 절과 같은 단순

과거시제(felt)로 바꾸어 두 절 모두 과거의 사실을 전하는 문장으로 만든다.

8. 정답 : c

• 이유 : 동사 lend는 '~에게 ~을 빌려주다'는 의미를 뒤에 간접목적어와 직접목적어를 두어 전한다. 이 때 간접목적어 자리에 오는 간접목적어는 전치사 없이 온다. 간접목적어가 전치사와 오는 때는 직접목적어 뒤에 온다. 따라서 예문의 동사 lend 뒤의 간접목적어 to you는 전치사를 빼고 you로 하거나 전치사와 함께 쓸 때는 직접목적어 this book 뒤에 두어야 한다.

9. 정답 : b

• 이유 : the cook은 '그 요리사'의 의미로 그녀가 요리하는 것을 좋아한다는 의미와는 거리가 멀다. 따라서 the cook을 동명사 cooking이나 to-부정사 to cook으로 바꾼다.

10. 정답 : b

• 이유 : '어딘가'는 some place로 표현하며 some place 앞에 부정관사 a를 두지 않는다. 부정관사 a가 전하는 의미가 양화사 some과 셀 수 있는 명사의 단수형 place에 의해 전달되기 때문이다.

## Ⅳ. 기본영작

1. We went downstream and then returned upstream.
   We went down the stream and then came back up.
   We went downstream and then came upstream again.
   We went down to the lower part of the stream and then came back to the upper part of the stream.

• '하류로'는 부사 downstream으로 '상류로'는 부사 upstream으로 옮긴다.
• '하류로 내려가다'는 go downstream, go down the stream, go down to the lower part of the stream으로 옮긴다.
• '다시 상류로 올라오다'는 return upstream, and then come back up, come upstream again, and then come back to the upper part of the stream으로 옮긴다.

2. I could tell exactly what that object was from here.
   From here, I was clearly able to discern what the object was.
   I was able to identify exactly what that object was from here.
   From here, it was possible for me to tell exactly what that object was.

• '그 물체가 무엇인지 분명히 식별하다'는 tell exactly what the object is, clearly discern what the object is, identify exactly what that object is, tell exactly what that object is로 옮긴다.
• '~할 수 있었다'는 could do~, was able to do~, it was possible to do~로 옮긴다.

3. I know your name, but not your age.
   Your name I know, but your age I don't.
   Although I know your name, I don't know your age.
   I know what your name is, but I don't know how old you are.

- '네가 누구인지 알다'는 know your name이나 타동사 know의 목적어인 your name을 문장의 앞으로 이동시킨 구조로 옮길 수도 있고 know what your name is로 옮길 수도 있다.
- '몇 살인지는 알지 못하다'는 know~, but not your age나 ~know, but your age I don't로 옮기거나 don't know your age나 don't know how old you are로 옮긴다.

4. The country strongly insisted that North Korea give up its nuclear development.
   The country emphasized that North Korea should give up its nuclear development.
   That country made it clear that North Korea must give up its nuclear development.
   That country clearly conveyed that North Korea must give up its nuclear development.

- '~해야 한다는 것을 분명히 하다'는 strongly insist that~, emphasize that~, make it clear that ~, convey that~으로 옮긴다.
- 주장을 나타내는 동사 insist 뒤의 that-절에서는 동사가 가정법으로 와야 하므로 동사 give의 가정법 give가 온 것이다. give 앞에 조동사 should는 올 수 있다.

5. The girl knew very well that the boy liked her.
   The boy liked the girl, which she knew very well.
   The boy liked the girl, and she knew this very well.
   The boy liked the girl, and this was well-known to her.

- '~을 잘 알고 있다'는 know very well that~이나 ~, which~know very well로 옮길 수 있고 ~, and ~know this very well이나 ~, and this is well-known to~로 옮길 수도 있다.
- 둘째 예문의 which는 목적격 관계대명사로 앞 절 전체를 선행사로 취한다.
- this는 앞의 절(The boy liked the girl)을 가리키는 지시대명사이다.

6. He likes to listen to music, and he does this while driving, too.
   He enjoys listening to music, and listens even while he is driving.
   He likes music so much that he listens to it even while he is driving.
   Being a lover of listening to music, he listens to music even while he is driving.

- '음악을 즐겨 듣다'는 like to listen to music, enjoy listening to music, like music so much, being a lover of listening to music으로 옮긴다. 동사 enjoy 뒤에 오는 동사는 to-부정사가 아닌 동명사로 와야 한다.
- '운전 중에도'는 while driving, while~is driving, even while~is driving으로 옮긴다. while driving의 접속사 while과 현재분사 driving 사이에 주어와 be동사 he is가 생략되어 있다.

7. Maybe it is hard to continue our trip.
   It might be difficult to keep going on our trip.
   It might be difficult to continue with our journey.
   There might be some difficulties in continuing with our journey.

- '여행을 계속하다'는 continue one's trip, keep going on one's trip, continue with one's journey로 옮긴다.
- '~하는 것이 어려울지 모르다'는 maybe it is hard to do~, it might be difficult to do~, there might be some difficulties in~으로 옮긴다.
- trip은 가장 흔히 쓰이는 구어로 보통 짧은 여행을 말하며 journey는 voyage가 긴 해상여행을 말하는 데 반해 보통 육지에서의 긴 여행을 말한다.

8. Because it is vacation time, less students come to the library.
   There aren't many students in the library since it is vacation time.
   Less students make visits to the library because it is vacation time.
   There are less students who are visiting the library, for it is vacation time.

- '방학이라'는 '방학이기 때문에'의 의미로 이유를 나타내는 because-절인 because it is vacation time이나 이유를 나타내는 since-절인 since it is vacation time으로 옮길 수 있다. 이유를 나타내는 since-절은 because-절과 달리 상대방에게 이미 알려져 있는 이유일 때 사용한다. 이유를 나타내는 for-절은 이유를 가볍게 덧붙일 때 사용한다.

9. He missed his wife and children overseas, but could not go to see them.
   He missed his wife and children living abroad, but could not go to meet them.
   He missed his wife and children who were in a foreign country, but could not go to see them.
   Although he missed his wife and children who were overseas, he could not go and see them.

- '외국에 있는'은 부사 overseas나 현재분사를 사용한 living abroad, 관계대명사를 사용한 who are in a foreign country, who are overseas로 옮긴다.
- '~가 보고 싶다'는 '~을 그리워하다'는 의미로 miss~로 옮긴다.
- '~을 보러 갈 수 없다'는 cannot go to see~, cannot go to meet~, cannot go and see~로 옮긴다.

10. It is not easy to try writing in English every day.
    Writing in English every day is not an easy thing to do.
    It is not easy to practice writing something in English every day.
    Writing something in English every day is not an easy thing to do.

- '영어로 글을 써보다'는 try writing in English, write in English, practice writing something in

English, write something in English로 옮긴다.

- '쉬운 일은 아니다'는 is not easy, is not an easy thing으로 옮긴다.
- 첫째, 셋째 예문은 가주어와 to-부정사를 진주어로 하여 옮긴 것이고, 둘째, 넷째 예문은 동명사를 주어로 옮긴 것이다.

## V. 심화영작

1. (1) I will look after you and your family as long as you follow me.

   As long as you follow me, I will take care of you and your family.

   You and your family shall be looked after as long as you follow me.

   You and your family will be taken care of as long as you follow me.

- '~을 돌보다'는 look after~, take care of~, be taken care of~로 옮긴다.
- '~하겠다'는 말을 하면서 앞으로 무엇을 하겠다고 할 때 쓰는 조동사 will을 써서 옮길 수 있다. 셋째 예문처럼 2인칭이나 3인칭 주어와 shall을 쓰면 화자의 의지가 들어가게 되어 '네가 나를 따르는 한 내가 너와 너의 가족을 돌보겠다'는 뜻이 되며 격식을 차린 딱딱한 표현이다.

(2) One can rarely see a woman breast-feeding her baby nowadays.

Nowadays it is not easy to see a woman breast-feeding her baby.

These days it is not easy to see a woman who gives the breast to her baby.

These days you may find it difficult to see a woman breast-feeding her baby.

- '갓난아이에게 젖을 물리는 여성'은 a woman breast-feeding her baby, a woman who gives the breast to her baby로 옮긴다. breast-feeding은 명사구 her baby를 목적어로 가지면서 앞 명사 woman을 수식하는 현재분사이다.
- '~을 보기가 쉽지 않다'는 can rarely see~, it is not easy to see~, may find it difficult to see~로 옮긴다.

(3) I peeled a big Korean melon and ate it, so I am full now.

I am full now because I peeled and ate a big Korean melon.

Because I peeled and ate a big Korean melon, I am full now.

Now, I am full because I peeled and ate a large Korean melon.

- '커다란 참외 하나'는 a big Korean melon, a large Korean melon으로 옮긴다.
- '깎아 먹다'는 peel~and eat~으로 옮기거나 eat~으로 옮긴다.
- '배가 부르다'는 be full로 나타낸다.

(4) A woman bought him a car and he sometimes drives it.

He sometimes drives the car that he got from a woman.

A woman bought him a car, and he drives the car sometimes.

A car was bought for him by a woman and he sometimes drives it.

- '그에게 차를 사주다'는 buy him a car, the car that he gets from a woman, a car is bought for him by~로 옮긴다.
- 한 여성이 차를 사준 것은 과거의 사실로 단순과거시제 bought, got, was bought으로 옮기고 타고 다니는 것은 현재의 사실로 보아 단순현재시제 drives로 옮긴다.

(5) I think you are very smart, but I want you to study hard.

I admit that you are clever; nevertheless, I want you to study hard.

I believe that you are smart, but I wish that you would study hard.

Even though I have no doubt that you are smart, I hope that you will study hard.

- '머리가 좋다'는 be smart, be clever로 옮긴다.
- '~하다고 생각하지만'은 think~, but~이나 admit that~; nevertheless, ~로 옮길 수도 있고 believe that~, but~이나 even though~have no doubt that~으로 옮길 수도 있다.

(6) His belief was that he was able to get to his destination for himself without relying on a road map.

He thought that he could arrive at the destination by himself without a road map.

He thought he could get to his destination by himself without a road map.

He thought it possible for him to get to his destination by himself without relying on a road map.

- '도로지도 없이'는 전치사구 without relying on a road map, without a road map으로 옮긴다.
- '~하다고 생각하다'는 one's belief is that~, think that~으로 옮긴다.
- 넷째 예문의 it은 동사 think의 가목적어로 to get이 진목적어이고 형용사 possible은 목적보어이다. him은 부정사의 주어이고 for는 부정사의 주어 앞에 오는 전치사이다.

(7) He knew that she was innocent, but he could not prove this.

Although he knew that she was innocent, he could not prove her innocence.

Even though he knew her innocence, he was unable to establish it.

He knew she was innocent; however, he failed to prove her innocence.

- '결백하다'는 be innocent로 옮긴다.
- '결백하다는 것을 증명하다'는 prove one's innocence, establish one's innocence로 옮긴다.
- 넷째 예문의 동사 fail 뒤에 오는 동사는 동명사가 아닌 to-부정사로 와야 한다. 따라서 failed to prove는 되지만 failed proving은 안 된다.

(8) Nobody knows what will happen in the future.

We cannot tell what may happen in the future.

No one knows what is going to happen in the future.

Everyone is unaware of what is going to happen in the future.

- '무슨 일이 일어날 지'는 what will happen, what may happen, what is going to happen으로 옮긴다.
- '~을 아무도 모르다'는 nobody knows~, we cannot tell~, no one knows~, everyone is unaware of~로 옮긴다.
- 넷째 예문의 what-절은 간접의문문으로 전치사 of의 목적어이다.

(9) Listen to fast music or chew gum when you feel drowsy when driving.
When you feel sleepy while driving, listen to lively music or chew gum.
Listen to upbeat music or chew gum when feeling drowsy while driving.
When you feel sleepy while driving, listen to upbeat music or chew gum.

- '운전 중'은 when driving, while driving으로 옮기며 접속사 when이나 while과 현재분사 driving 사이에 주어와 be동사 you are가 생략되어 있다.
- '졸리면'은 when you feel drowsy, when you feel sleepy, when feeling drowsy로 옮긴다.
- '신나는 음악을 듣다'는 listen to fast music, listen to lively music, listen to upbeat music으로 옮긴다.

(10) She always wears the necklace that he gave her as a birthday present.
She got a necklace from him as a birthday present, and she has it on all the time.
Wherever she goes, she always wears the necklace that he gave her as a birthday present.
The necklace she received from him as a birthday present is always hung around her neck wherever she goes.

- '목걸이를 하고 다니다'는 wear a necklace, have a necklace on, a necklace is hung around one's neck으로 옮긴다.
'생일 선물' birthday present는 셀 수 있는 명사로 일반적으로 수의 개념으로 쓰인다. '하나의 생일선물'을 가리키므로 부정관사 a를 붙여 a birthday present로 옮긴다.

2. (1) a. Instead <u>of me, you should get the praises</u>.
b. You <u>should be the one to be praised, not me</u>.
c. It <u>is you, not me, that should get the praises</u>.
d. The person <u>who should get the praises is you, not me</u>.

- '칭찬을 듣다'는 get the praises, be praised로 옮긴다.
- 셋째 예문은 it~that~ 강조구문으로 it와 that 사이의 요소 you를 강조한다. that은 주격 관계대명사로 쓰인 것이다.
- 예문의 should는 당연함을 나타내는 조동사이다.

(2) a. Sounds of grass insects came out from everywhere as the summer night got deeper.

b. As the summer night got deeper, sounds of grass insects came out from all over the place.

c. With the deepening summer's night, the sounds of grass insects came out from all over the place.

d. I could hear the sounds of grass insects coming out from everywhere as the summer's night got deeper.

- '여름밤이 깊어지다'는 the summer night gets deeper, the deepening summer's night, the summer's night gets deeper로 옮길 수 있다.
- '풀벌레 우는 소리'는 sounds of grass insects, the sounds of grass insects로 옮기며 sounds 앞에 the가 없으면 일반적인 의미의 '풀벌레 소리'를 뜻하고 있으면 청자도 알고 있다고 보는 '그 풀벌레 소리들'을 뜻한다.

(3) a. It seems to me that the demand for air conditioners will decrease because it is not very hot this summer.

b. Because of this summer's mild weather, I think the demand for air conditioners will decrease.

c. I think the demand for air conditioners will decrease, because it is not very hot this summer.

d. The demand for air conditioners may decrease this summer because of the mild weather.

- '별로 덥지 않다'는 동사구 is not very hot이나 명사구 mild weather로 옮길 수도 있고 절인 it is not very hot이나 명사구 the mild weather로 옮길 수도 있다. 정관사 the가 붙은 형태는 화자가 가리키는 지시대상에 대해 그의 청자도 알고 있다고 보고 말할 때 쓴다.

(4) a. The rain had just stopped, and then a swarm of dragonflies appeared in the air and were flying about.

b. A swarm of dragonflies appeared just after the rain stopped, and they were flying around in the air.

c. No sooner had the rain stopped than a swarm of dragonflies appeared and they were flying around in the air.

d. As soon as the rain stopped, a swarm of dragonflies appeared and they were flying around in the air.

- '~하자마자'는 ~, and then~이나 just after~로 옮길 수도 있고 no sooner had~than~이나 as soon as~로 옮길 수도 있다.

- '잠자리 떼'는 a swarm of dragonflies로 옮긴다.
- '상공에서'는 in the air로 옮긴다.
- '이리저리 날다'는 fly about, fly around로 옮기며 about과 around는 '이리저리'를 뜻하는 부사이다.

(5) a. As soon as he heard his cell phone ring, he hurried out of the classroom to get it.

b. He quickly went out of the classroom as soon as he heard his cell phone ring, because he wanted to answer it.

c. In order to answer his cell phone, he quickly went out of the classroom as soon as he heard it ring.

d. When he heard his cell phone ring, he hurried out of the classroom to get the phone.

- '휴대폰'은 셀 수 있는 명사로 하나의 휴대폰은 a cell phone이고 일반적인 의미의 휴대폰은 cell phones이며 그의 휴대폰은 his cell phone이다.
- '전화를 받다'는 get the phone, answer the phone으로 옮긴다.
- '서둘러 교실 밖으로 나가다'는 hurry out of the classroom, quickly go out of the classroom으로 옮긴다.

## 제9장 부 사

### Ⅲ. 심화연습

1. 정답 : a

- 이유 : that-절이 나타내는 의미가 나를 기쁘게 한다는 의미로 that-절이 진주어이고 It은 이것을 가리키는 가주어이다. 동사 make는 목적어와 목적보어를 취하여 '~을 ~하게 만들다'는 의미를 전할 수 있는 동사로 뒤에 목적어(me)가 나와 있으므로 이 목적어 뒤에 목적보어가 필요하므로 부사 gladly는 형용사 glad가 되어야 한다.

2. 정답 : b

- 이유 : 그가 그 일을 겪은 것과 그가 제 정신이 아닌 것은 모두 과거의 사실을 나타내므로 동사의 현재시제 undergoes는 과거시제 underwent가 된다. 과거시제 underwent 대신 과거완료시제 had undergone을 쓸 수도 있다.

3. 정답 : d

- 이유 : 동사 lay는 무엇을 어디에 '두다'는 타동사이고 동사 lie는 '놓여 있다'는 자동사이다. 따라서 전자의 현재분사 laying이 아니라 후자의 현재분사 lying이 필요하다.

4. 정답 : b

• 이유 : 동사의 행위가 어떤 모양으로 이루어지는가를 나타내는 양태부사는 일반적으로 자동사가 있는 문장에서는 자동사 뒤에 오고 타동사가 있는 문장에서는 타동사의 목적어 뒤에 온다. 그리고 -ly로 끝나는 양태부사는 일반동사 앞에도 올 수 있다. 따라서 예문의 양태부사 beautifully는 자동사 danced 뒤에 오거나 일반동사 danced 앞에 온다.

5. 정답 : c

• 이유 : 가주어 it과 진주어인 to-부정사가 나오는 문장에서 be동사의 보어로 인간행위를 판단하는 형용사가 나올 때 이 to-부정사의 의미상의 주어 앞에는 전치사 of가 온다. 따라서 전치사 for를 of로 바꾼다.

6. 정답 : b

• 이유 : enough가 부사로 쓰일 때는 자신이 수식하는 형용사나 부사의 뒤에서 수식한다. 따라서 예문에서 형용사 fortunate을 수식해야 하므로 이 형용사 뒤에 온다.

7. 정답 : a

• 이유 : 일반적으로 타동사와 그 짧은 목적어 사이에 부사가 들어가 방해해서는 안 되므로 부사 completely를 동사 finish의 목적어인 this manuscript 뒤로 이동시킨다.

8. 정답 : d

• 이유 : 부정의 부사 never가 문장의 첫 머리로 이동하면 뒤의 절 전체의 어순이 도치된 어순으로 의무적으로 바뀐다. 따라서 정상적인 어순인 '주어(I) + 동사(bothered)'가 도치된 어순인 '조동사(did) + 주어(I) + 본동사(bother)'로 바뀐다. 만약 부정의 부사 never가 문장의 첫머리가 아니라 문장 가운데 위치인 일반동사 bothered 앞에 오면 어순이 도치되지 않는다.

9. 정답 : a

• 이유 : 형용사 vain은 동사 pedal을 수식할 수 없다. 따라서 이것을 '헛되이'라는 부사 vainly나 in vain으로 바꾼다.

10. 정답 : b

• 이유 : 보행자 pedestrian은 셀 수 있는 명사로 일반적으로 수의 개념으로 쓰인다. 예문에서는 마치 셀 수 없는 명사인 것처럼 앞에 한정사도 붙지 않고 뒤에 복수어미 -s도 붙지 않아서 비문이다. 따라서 셀 수 있는 명사의 일반적인 의미를 전하는 형태는 그 명사 앞에 한정사를 붙이지 않은 복수형을 쓰므로 pedestrian을 pedestrians로 바꾼다.

## Ⅳ. 기본영작

1. She hardly goes out late at night.

   She scarcely goes out late at night.

   She usually stays at home late at night.

   At the middle of night, she rarely goes out.

- '심야에'는 late at night, at the middle of night로 옮긴다.
- '거의 외출하지 않다'는 hardly go out, scarcely go out, usually stay at home, rarely go out으로 옮긴다.
- 한국어 문장은 현재의 사실을 말하므로 goes, stays처럼 단순현재시제를 쓴다.

2. I had never heard of hamburgers at your age.
   When I was your age, I had never heard of hamburgers.
   Never did I hear of a "hamburger" when I was your age.
   I had never heard of hamburgers when I was as young as you are.

- '너의 나이였을 때는'은 at your age, when~was your age, when~was as young as you are로 옮긴다.
- '~을 들어보지 못하다'는 never hear of~로 옮긴다.
- '햄버거란 이름'은 일반적인 의미의 햄버거는 한정사를 붙이지 않은 복수형 hamburgers로 옮기고 '어떤 햄버거이건 햄버거'를 가리키는 a "hamburger"로 옮길 수도 있다.

3. She put on sportswear, looked in the mirror, and went out to meet her boyfriend.
   She went out to meet her boyfriend in sportswear after looking into the mirror.
   She put on her training outfit, looked in the mirror, and went out to meet her boyfriend.
   After getting dressed in sportswear and looking in the mirror, she went out to meet her boyfriend.

- '운동복을 입다'는 put on sportswear, in sportswear, on one's training outfit, get dressed in sportswear로 옮긴다.
- '거울을 보다'는 look in the mirror, look into the mirror로 옮긴다.
- '남자친구를 만나러 나가다'는 go out to meet one's boyfriend로 옮긴다.
- 넷째 예문의 동명사 getting과 looking은 전치사 after의 목적어이다.

4. She goes up a mountain every week, and this is primarily to keep her healthy.
   She goes up a mountain every week mainly because she wants to remain healthy.
   The main reason she climbs the mountain every week is to maintain good health.
   Maintaining good health is the main reason she goes up the mountain every week.

- '산에 오르다'는 go up a mountain, climb up a mountain으로 옮기며 전자는 보통 높지 않은 산에 쓰고 후자는 험하고 높은 산에 힘들여 오를 때 쓴다.
- '~하는 주된 이유는'은 primarily, mainly because~, the main reason~으로 옮긴다.
- '건강을 유지하다'는 keep a person healthy, remain healthy, maintain good health로 옮긴다.

5. He became a rich person, then a poor person, and finally a rich person again in a different sense this time.

He became rich and then poor, and he became rich again in a different sense this time.

After becoming rich and poor, he once again became rich in a different way.

He became rich, then he became poor, and then, he became rich once again in a different manner.

- '부자가 되다'는 become a rich person, become rich로 옮긴다.
- '가난해지다'는 become a poor person, become poor로 옮긴다.
- '다른 의미의'는 in a different sense, in a different way, in a different manner로 옮긴다.

6. Regrettably, they had already left there.

   It was unfortunate that they had already left there.

   It was a regrettable thing that they had already left there.

   Unfortunately, they were not there. They had already left.

- '유감스럽게도'는 regrettably, it is unfortunate that~, it is a regrettable thing that~, unfortunately로 옮긴다.
- '이미 그곳을 떠나고 없었다'는 과거의 시점에서 보았을 때 이미 완료된 것이므로 과거완료시제로 had already left there나 had already left로 옮긴다.
- 둘째, 셋째 예문의 it은 모두 가주어이고 that-절이 진주어이다.

7. In any case, you must admit to your mistake.

   At any rate, you must recognize your mistake.

   Anyway, you must not deny that it's your fault.

   You must admit that you made a mistake any way you look at it.

- '어쨌든'은 in any case, at any rate, anyway, any way you look at it으로 옮긴다.
- '너의 실수를 인정하다'는 admit to your mistake, recognize your mistake, not deny that it's your fault, admit that you made a mistake로 옮긴다.

8. He must be living abroad, far from Korea.

   He must be living in a foreign country, not Korea.

   He must be out of Korea, and living in a foreign country.

   It is almost certain that he is no longer in Korea, but is living overseas.

- '한국을 떠나'는 far from Korea, not Korea, out of Korea, no longer in Korea로 옮긴다.
- '외국에'는 전치사구 in a foreign country나 부사 abroad, overseas로 옮긴다.
- '~하고 있는 게 분명하다'는 must be -ing, must be~, be almost certain으로 옮긴다.

9. I got up a little late, so I nearly missed the train.

   I almost did not catch the train, for I got up a bit late.

   I almost missed the train because I woke up a little late.

Because I woke up a little late, I got on the train just on time.

- '좀 늦게 일어나다'는 get up a little late, get up a bit late, wake up a little late로 옮긴다.
- '그 기차를 거의 놓칠 뻔하다'는 nearly miss the train, almost do not catch the train, almost miss the train, get on the train just on time으로 옮긴다.
- '기차' train 앞에 정관사 the를 붙인 것은 '한 대의 기차'가 아니라 타기로 되어 있던 '그 기차'를 가리키기 위한 것이다.

10. She visits her old parents in the countryside every week.
    Every week, she visits her aged parents who live in the countryside.
    She makes visits to her aged parents who live in the countryside every week.
    She makes it a rule to visit her old parents living in the countryside every week.

- '시골에 있는 노부모'는 one's old parents in the countryside, one's aged parents who live in the countryside, one's old parents living in the countryside로 옮긴다.
- 매주 방문하는 것은 규칙적으로 방문하는 것이므로 '규칙적으로 ~하다'는 의미의 make it a rule to do~로 옮긴다. 대명사 it은 동사 make의 가목적어이고 명사구 a rule은 목적보어이며 to-부정사 to do는 진목적어이다.

## V. 심화영작

1. (1) She kept walking forward without looking back.
    Keeping her eyes straight forward, she kept walking forward.
    She kept her eyes straight forward and kept on walking without looking back.
    Without looking back, she kept on walking forward with her eyes looking in the same direction.

- '뒤도 돌아보지 않고'는 전치사구 without looking back이나 현재분사를 사용하여 keeping one's eyes straight forward로 옮기거나 전치사구 without even looking back, with one's eyes looking in the same direction으로 옮길 수도 있다.
- '계속해서 ~하다'는 keep -ing나 keep on -ing로 옮긴다.

   (2) I will go my own way whether you like it or not.
    Whether you like it or not, I will go my own way.
    I will do as I like regardless of you liking it or not.
    Regardless of your liking it or not, I will keep going my own way.

- '네가 좋아하든 그렇지 않든'은 whether you like it or not, regardless of you liking it or not으로 옮긴다. 전치사 of 뒤의 전치사의 목적어 자리에 오는 동명사 liking의 주어는 보통 소유격 your를 쓰며 구어체에서는 목적격 you를 쓰기도 한다.

- '나의 갈 길을 가다'는 go my own way로 옮긴다.

(3) Because of rain, I had to finish jogging hurriedly somewhat earlier than usual yesterday.

I was jogging yesterday when it started to rain, so I had to finish quickly a little earlier than usual.

Yesterday I hurriedly ended jogging earlier than usual because it began to rain.

Yesterday I had to finish jogging quickly a little earlier than usual because it rained.

- '조깅하다'는 동사 jog로 옮기고 '조깅을 끝내다'는 finish jogging, end jogging으로 옮긴다.
- '비가 와서'는 because of rain, when it started to rain, because it began to rain, because it rained로 옮긴다.
- '일찍'은 earlier than usual로 옮기거나 '좀 일찍'의 의미이므로 somewhat earlier than usual, a little earlier than usual로 옮긴다.

(4) The kid was running so quickly that it looked as if he would fall at any time.

The child was running very fast, so I felt that he would fall down at any time.

The child was running so fast that he was likely to fall down at any time.

It looked as if the kid would fall at any time because he was running with so much speed.

- '그 아이'는 the kid, the child로 옮기며 kid는 child의 의미로 구어에서 주로 쓴다.
- '너무나 ~해서'는 so~that~이나 ~, so~로 옮길 수도 있고 전치사구 with so much~로 옮길 수도 있다.
- '~할 것처럼 보이다'는 look as if~, feel that~, be likely to~로 옮긴다.

(5) A cool wind began to blow as soon as we came out onto the street.

We went out onto the street and suddenly, a cool wind began to blow.

A cool wind started to blow suddenly when we came out to the street.

As soon as we came out to the street, a cool wind suddenly started to blow.

- '거리에 나오다'는 come out onto the street, go out onto the street, come out to the street으로 옮긴다.
- '~하자'는 as soon as~나 ~and suddenly, ~로 옮길 수도 있고 ~suddenly when~이나 ~suddenly~로 옮길 수도 있다.
- '서늘한 바람'은 a cool wind로 옮기지만 '바람'은 정관사를 붙여 the wind로 쓴다.

(6) As the night became darker, the streetlights lighted one by one.

The streetlights began to shine one by one, as the night went on.

It was getting dark, so the streetlights began to shine one by one.

As the darkness fell, the streetlights started to shine brightly one by one.

- '어둠이 짙어지다'는 the night becomes darker, the night goes on, it gets dark, the darkness falls로 옮긴다.
- '가로등'은 셀 수 있는 명사로 복수형 앞에 the를 붙이면 가로등이 여러 개이면서 화자가 자신의 청자도 알고 있다고 보는 것이다.
- '하나 둘 빛을 발하다'는 light one by one, shine one by one, shine brightly one by one으로 옮긴다.

(7) He went out after he woke up and had several slices of watermelon.
He woke up from his sleep, ate some pieces of sliced watermelon and went out.
After waking up from his sleep, he ate some pieces of sliced watermelon and went out.
He woke up from his sleep, ate a few slices of watermelon and went out.

- '잠에서 깨다'는 wake up, wake up from one's sleep으로 옮긴다.
- '수박' watermelon은 개개의 수박을 가리킬 때는 셀 수 있는 명사이지만 수박이라는 물질 그 자체를 가리킬 때는 셀 수 없는 명사로 본다. 예문의 watermelon은 셀 수 없는 명사로 쓰인 것이다.
- a slice는 '썬 것 한 조각'을 가리킨다.

(8) Let's go shopping on Saturday at three in the afternoon, shall we?
Would you like to go shopping with me on Saturday at three in the afternoon?
What do you say to our going shopping together on Saturday at three o'clock in the afternoon?
How about going shopping with me on Saturday at three o'clock in the afternoon?

- '토요일 오후 3시에'는 on Saturday at three in the afternoon, on Saturday at three o'clock in the afternoon으로 옮긴다.
- '쇼핑가다'는 go shopping으로 옮긴다.
- '~하는 게 어때?'는 Let's~, shall we?나 What do you say to~?, How about~?, Would you like to~?로 옮긴다.

(9) He delighted the kids and also himself.
He made both the kids and himself happy.
He entertained the children, and he was also joyful.
He made the kids happy, and he was also happy himself.

- '~을 즐겁게 하다'는 delight~, make~happy, entertain~으로 옮긴다. 동사 make의 목적어 뒤의 형용사 happy는 목적보어이다.
- '그 역시 즐거웠다'는 also delighted himself, make both~and himself happy, he was also joyful, he was also happy himself로 옮긴다.

(10) Dropping classroom temperature resulted in an increasing number of students coughing.
As the classroom got cold, more and more students started to cough.
The temperature inside the classroom started to drop, and this brought about the increase of coughing students.
As the temperature inside the classroom started to drop, the number of students coughing started to increase.

- '교실 안이 추워지다'는 dropping classroom temperature, as the classroom gets cold, the temperature inside the classroom drops로 옮긴다.
- '기침하는 학생의 수가 늘다'는 result in an increasing number of students coughing, more and more students start to cough, bring about the increase of coughing students, the number of students coughing starts to increase로 옮긴다.

2. (1) a. Walking her dog, she skated slowly in her in-line skates.
b. While walking her dog, she skated slowly in her in-line skates.
c. As she walked her dog, she skated slowly in her in-line skates.
d. She skated slowly in her in-line skates while she walked her dog.

- '개를 걸리다'는 walk one's dog으로 옮기며 동사 walk는 '~을 걸리다'는 의미를 가지고 있다.
- '~하면서'는 현재분사로 옮길 수도 있고 while-절로 옮길 수도 있으며 동시동작을 나타내는 as-절로 옮길 수도 있다.
- '인라인스케이트를 타다'는 skate in one's in-line skates로 옮긴다.

(2) a. His wet hair that he just shampooed started to dry slowly with the gentle breeze.
b. The gentle breeze started to dry his just shampooed wet hair slowly.
c. It was gently windy and his freshly shampooed wet hair began to dry slowly.
d. He just came out with his freshly shampooed wet hair, and it began to dry slowly with the gentle breeze.

- '산들바람이 불어'는 with the gentle breeze, the gentle breeze, it was gently windy로 옮긴다.
- '막 감고 나온 그의 머리'는 his wet hair that he just shampooed, his just shampooed wet hair, his freshly shampooed wet hair로 옮긴다.
- '마르기 시작하다'는 start to dry, begin to dry로 옮긴다.

(3) a. He studied English composition hard, and this was greatly helpful in getting a good job.
b. The fact that he studied English composition hard helped him greatly in getting a nice job.
c. His experiences in studying English composition diligently helped him greatly in getting a nice job.

d. If he had not studied English composition hard, he couldn't have got a good place to work.

- '좋은 일자리를 얻다'는 get a good job, get a nice job, get a good place to work으로 옮긴다.
- '~하는 데 도움이 되다'는 be greatly helpful in~, help~greatly in~이나 가정법 과거완료로 옮길 수 있다.

(4) a. They discussed that problem for a long time, only to get no results.

b. Although they discussed that problem for a long time, they could not reach a conclusion.

c. Despite their long discussion about the problem, they did not get any results.

d. Their long discussion about the problem came to an end without any results.

- '~에 관해 오랫동안 토의하다'는 discuss~for a long time, one's long discussion about~으로 옮긴다.
- '아무런 결론도 얻지 못하다'는 only to get no results, cannot reach a conclusion, do not get any results, come to an end without any results로 옮긴다.

(5) a. The plane that they were on was slowly soaring into the sky.

b. The plane on which they were was gradually rising into the sky.

c. They were on a plane, and their plane was slowly soaring into the sky.

d. Having taken them in, the plane was gradually going up into the sky.

- '천천히'는 slowly, gradually로 옮긴다.
- '하늘로 높이 치솟다'는 soar into the sky, rise into the sky, go up into the sky로 옮긴다.
- Having taken은 완료분사로 주절동사가 나타내는 때보다 분사가 나타내는 때가 먼저 일어난 때라는 것을 나타낸다.

## 제10장 부정사

### III. 심화연습

1. 정답 : b

- 이유 : 타동사의 주어와 목적어가 동일한 지시대상일 때 목적어는 재귀대명사로 바뀐다. 예문에서 타동사 feigned의 주어인 The man과 목적어인 him이 동일한 대상을 가리키는 데도 불구하고 이 목적어가 재귀대명사로 바뀌지 않아 비문이다. 따라서 이것을 재귀대명사 himself로 바꾼다.

2. 정답 : d

• 이유 : 명령, 요구, 주장, 제안, 소망을 나타내는 동사나 그 동사의 명사형 뒤에 오는 that-절에서는 동사의 가정법이 온다. 따라서 요구를 나타내는 동사 require 뒤에 that-절이 왔으므로 동사는 조동사 must 없이 be가 된다. must 대신 조동사 should를 동사원형 be 앞에 두어도 된다.

3. 정답 : d

• 이유 : 사역동사 let 뒤는 목적어가 오고 그 뒤에 원형부정사가 온다. 그리고 목적어로 인칭대명사가 올 때는 목적격으로 와야 한다. 예문은 이 동사 뒤에 인칭대명사의 주격 she가 와서 비문이다. 따라서 주격 she를 목적격 her로 바꾼다.

4. 정답 : b

• 이유 : 동사 seem 뒤에 오는 동사는 to-부정사의 형태로 온다. 따라서 to 뒤의 동명사 having은 have가 되어야 한다. to have met은 to meet의 완료부정사이다.

5. 정답 : b

• 이유 : 확신부사 certainly는 일반적으로 문장 가운데 위치(be동사 뒤, 일반동사 앞, 조동사 뒤)에 온다. 그러나 예문 (a)에서처럼 조동사 뒤에 나올 요소가 생략(go to your house)되어 있는 때는 조동사(will) 앞에 온다. 따라서 확신부사 certainly를 조동사 will 뒤에 둔다.

6. 정답 : d

• 이유 : '그는 거의 두 시간 전에 신문을 읽기 시작해서 여전히 그것을 읽고 있는 중인 것 같다'는 의미이므로 타동사의 현재분사 reading 뒤에 이미 나온 명사구 a newspaper를 가리키는 대명사 it이 필요하다.

7. 정답 : c

• 이유 : to-부정사가 진주어이므로 이것을 가리키는 가주어 it이 필요하다. 따라서 That을 가주어 It으로 바꾼다.

8. 정답 : b

• 이유 : 그 여대생이 가장한 시점이 과거(feigned)이므로 만난 적이 없는 것은 과거 이전부터 과거까지를 의미하므로 과거완료시제가 된다. 따라서 현재완료 has met은 과거완료 had met이 된다.

9. 정답 : d

• 이유 : 주어가 등위접속사 or로 결합되어 있을 때는 주어가 모두 단수이면 동사는 단수 취급하고 주어가 모두 복수이면 복수 취급한다. 따라서 예문에서는 Jogging과 in-line skating 모두 단수로 되어 있으므로 동사는 단수취급하여 are가 아니라 is가 된다.

10. 정답 : d

• 이유 : 부정사를 부정할 때는 부정사 바로 앞에 부정의 부사를 둔다. 따라서 to-부정사인 to have를 부정하는 부사 not은 to have 뒤가 아니라 앞에 온다.

## Ⅳ. 기본영작

1. Your car needs washing.
   You need to wash your car.
   Your car needs to be washed.
   You had better wash your car.

• '세차를 하다'는 wash one's car로 옮긴다.

• 동사 need의 목적어가 동명사일 때는 이 동사의 주어가 동명사의 목적어이므로 동명사는 수동의 의미를 가진 동명사이다. 따라서 첫째 예문의 동명사 washing은 부정사로 바꾸면 셋째 예문처럼 수동부정사가 된다.

2. Frankly speaking, our friendship is not very close.
   To tell the truth, I cannot say we are best friends.
   To be honest, I cannot really say that we are very close friends.
   To be frank with you, I cannot say we are very thick with each other.

• '솔직하게 말하면'은 frankly speaking, to tell the truth, to be honest, to be frank with you로 옮긴다.

• '아주 친한 친구이다'는 our friendship is very close, we are best friends, we are very close friends, we are very thick with each other로 옮긴다.

• '~라고 할 수는 없다'는 cannot say~, cannot really say~로 옮긴다.

3. He saw her get into the car and drive far off right away.
   He saw her get into the car and go far away immediately.
   He saw her driving far away just as soon as she got into the car.
   He saw her going into the car and going off right away to somewhere far.

• '(차로)멀리 떠나다'는 drive far off, go far away, drive far away, go off로 옮긴다.

• '~하는 것을 보다'는 see~do~, see~doing~으로 옮기며 지각동사 see 뒤에서 to do 대신 do가 쓰인다. 또한 see 뒤의 목적어 뒤에 현재분사가 올 수 있으므로 do가 doing으로 온 것이다.

4. I wanted her to go there, but she wanted me to go there.
   I wanted her to go there, and she wanted me to go there too.
   I hoped that she would go there, but she hoped that I would go there.
   I was hoping that she would go there, while she was hoping that I would go there.

- '~가 ~하길 바라다'는 동사 want 뒤에 목적어와 to-부정사를 쓰거나 hope 뒤에 that-절을 써서 옮길 수 있다.
- while-절은 양보를 나타내는 종속절로 '~하지만'의 의미이다.

5. You won't speak a foreign language more fluently than your native tongue.
   It is nearly impossible to speak a foreign language more fluently than one's mother tongue.
   It is almost impossible to speak a foreign language better than one's mother tongue.
   You will find it difficult to speak a foreign language better than your native tongue.

- '모국어보다 더 잘하다'는 speak~more fluently than one's mother tongue, speak~better than one's native tongue으로 옮긴다.
- '~하는 것은 거의 불가능하다'는 won't do~, it is nearly impossible to do~, it is almost impossible to do~, will find it difficult to do~로 옮긴다.

6. I persuaded my friend to go some place away from the rain because it started to rain.
   As it began to rain, I persuaded my friend to go somewhere to avoid the rain.
   Because it began to rain, I persuaded my friend to hide from the rain for a while.
   It started to rain, so I persuaded my friend to hide from the rain for a while.

- '비가 내리기 시작하다'는 it starts to rain, it begins to rain으로 옮긴다.
- '몸을 피하다'는 go some place away from~, go somewhere to avoid~, hide from~으로 옮긴다.
- '~을 ~하도록 설득하다'는 persuade~to do~로 옮긴다.
- 예문의 it은 모두 날씨를 나타내는 대명사이다.

7. He will meet his girlfriend's parents tomorrow.
   He is to meet his girlfriend's parents tomorrow.
   He is meeting his girlfriend's parents tomorrow.
   He is going to meet his girlfriend's parents tomorrow.

- '여자 친구의 부모님'은 one's girlfriend's parents로 옮긴다.
- '~하기로 되어 있다'는 미래에 대한 예언이나 예측을 나타내는 'will + 동사원형'으로 나타내거나 예정을 나타내는 'be동사 + to-부정사'나 예정되어 있는 미래를 나타내는 'be동사의 현재형 + 동사의 -ing형'으로 옮길 수도 있고 be going to do로 옮긴다.

8. Shall we send her friend there instead of her?
   How about sending her friend there instead of her?
   Let's send her friend there instead of her, shall we?
   What do you think about sending her friend there instead of her?

- '그녀 대신'은 instead of her로 옮긴다.

- '~하는 게 어떨까?'는 Shall we~?나 How about~?으로 옮길 수 있고 부가의문문 Let's~, shall we?나 What do you think about~?으로 옮길 수도 있다.
- 예문의 about은 부사가 아니라 전치사이므로 뒤의 동사가 동명사 sending이 된 것이다.

9. He was due to get here at ten o'clock, but he hasn't come yet.
   He was supposed to get here at ten o'clock, but he has not come yet.
   He was supposed to arrive here at ten o'clock but has not arrived yet.
   He still has not arrived here, even though he was supposed to get here at ten o'clock.

- '열 시 정각에'는 at ten o'clock으로 옮긴다.
- '여기 도착하다'는 get here, arrive here로 옮긴다.
- '~하기로 되어 있다'는 be due to do~, be supposed to do~로 옮긴다.
- '~지만'은 ~, but~으로 옮기거나 even though~로 옮긴다.

10. I will send her over to you if you are looking for her.
    If you are looking for her, I will send her to you soon.
    If it is her that you are for, I will send her over to you.
    If you want to see her, I will send her over to you soon.

- '~을 찾다'는 look for~, be for~, want to see~로 옮긴다.
- '~을 ~에게 보내다'는 send~over to~, send~to~로 옮긴다.
- '~하겠다'는 말을 하면서 앞으로 무엇을 하겠다고 결정을 내리는 것으로 'will + 동사원형'으로 옮긴다.

## V. 심화영작

1. (1) That friend is diligently saving up money to study abroad.
   That friend is diligently saving up money to go abroad for study.
   To go abroad for study, the friend is working hard at saving money.
   The friend is diligently saving money for the purpose of studying abroad.

- '그 친구'는 that friend, the friend로 옮긴다.
- '유학을 가다'는 study abroad, go abroad for study로 옮기며 abroad는 '해외에'라는 부사이다.
- '열심히 ~하다'는 diligently~, work hard at~으로 옮긴다.
- '돈을 저축하다'는 save up money, save money로 옮긴다.

   (2) He started lecturing at an academy again to pay for his living costs.
   He started to lecture at an academy again in order to earn his living expenses.
   His lecture at an academy began again, because he needed to earn his cost of living.
   His lecture at an academy began again, because he needed to earn his bread and butter.

• '생활비를 벌다'는 pay for one's living costs, earn one's living expenses, earn one's cost of living, earn one's bread and butter로 옮긴다.
• '학원에서 강의하다'는 lecture at an academy, one's lecture at an academy begins로 옮긴다.
• 동사 start 뒤는 동명사(lecturing)와 to-부정사(to lecture) 모두 올 수 있다.

(3) I think the boy is reading a fairy tale with his friends in the room.
I think the boy is in the room reading a fairy tale with his friends.
The boy seems to be reading a fairy tale with his friends in the room.
It seems that the boy is reading a children's story with his friends in the room.

• '동화책을 읽다'는 read a fairy tale, read a children's story로 옮긴다.
• '~을 읽고 있는 중인'은 현재진행시제 is reading~으로 옮긴다.
• '~인 것 같다'는 think~, seem to be~, seem that~으로 옮긴다. 동사 seem 뒤는 to-부정사와 that-절 모두 올 수 있다.

(4) I think the foreigner is sending someone an e-mail.
The foreigner seems to be sending an e-mail to somebody.
It seems that the foreigner is sending an e-mail to someone.
It seems as though the foreigner is sending someone an e-mail.

• '누군가'는 someone이나 somebody로 옮기며 이 둘의 의미는 차이가 없지만 somebody가 someone보다 구어적이다.
• '전자메일' e-mail은 일반적인 의미의 전자메일을 가리킬 때는 앞에 한정사가 붙지 않은 셀 수 없는 명사 e-mail로 나타내고 전자메일 하나를 가리킬 때는 셀 수 있는 명사로 an e-mail로 나타낸다.

(5) Although he needed money himself, he lent some money to his junior.
Even though he did not have enough money for himself, he lent some money to his junior.
He lent money to his junior when he himself did not have enough money.
He did not have enough money for himself; however, he lent money to his junior.

• '자신이 쓸 돈도 모자라다'는 needs money himself, does not have enough money for himself, he himself does not have enough money로 옮긴다.
• '~에게 돈을 빌려주다'는 lend some money to~, lend money to~로 옮긴다.
• '후배'는 one's junior로 옮긴다.

(6) What must politicians do for their citizens?
What must politicians do for their citizens?
What is a politician's obligation to the people?
What is it that politicians must do for their citizens?

- '정치가' politician은 셀 수 있는 명사로 '한 사람의 정치가'는 a politician이고 일반적인 의미의 정치가는 politicians이다.
- '국민'은 one's citizens, the people로 옮긴다.
- '~해야 하다'는 must do~, one's obligation으로 옮긴다.

(7) You need to check your car regularly every year.
Your car needs to be regularly checked every year.
You need to give your car an annual checkup regularly.
You need to have your car checked regularly every year.

- '매년'은 every year, an annual~로 옮긴다.
- '차를 정기적으로 점검하다'는 check one's car regularly, one's car is regularly checked, give one's car an annual checkup regularly, have one's car checked regularly로 옮긴다.

(8) He was pleased that his friend had come, and his friend was pleased to have been warmly welcomed.
He was happy because his friend came, and his friend was happy because he was warmly welcomed.
He was happy because his friend came, and his friend was happy to get a warm welcome.
He was happy that his friend came. His friend was happy too, because he received a warm welcome.

- '~해서 기쁘다'는 be pleased that~, be happy because~, be happy that~으로 옮긴다.
- '~의 환영을 받아 기쁘다'는 be pleased to have been warmly welcomed, be happy because~ was warmly welcomed, be happy to get a warm welcome이나 be happy, because~received a warm welcome으로 옮긴다.

(9) It is natural that we should be helpful to others if we want to be respected by them.
Doing helpful things for others naturally results in being respected by them.
To be respected by others, one naturally needs to do helpful things for them.
You should do helpful things for others if you want to be respected by them.

- '남의 존경을 받다'는 be respected by others로 옮긴다.
- '남에게 도움이 되는 일을 하다'는 be helpful to others, do helpful things for others로 옮긴다.
- result in은 '결국 ~가 되다'는 뜻으로 동명사 being이 전치사 in의 목적어이다.

(10) He thought he couldn't drive safely before calming himself down.
He thought that he could not drive safely without calming down.
He thought it was impossible for him to drive safely before making himself calm.
He thought it impossible for him to drive safely before calming himself down.

- '마음을 가라앉히다'는 calm oneself down, calm down, make oneself calm으로 옮긴다.
- '~않고는'은 before~, without~으로 옮긴다. 예문의 before와 without은 전치사이므로 뒤의 동사 calm, make가 동명사 calming, making이 된 것이다.
- 셋째 예문의 it은 가주어이고 넷째 예문의 it은 가목적어이다.

2. (1) a. His objective these days is how to make lots of money.
   b. These days, he is looking for ways to earn a lot of money.
   c. He is searching for ways to earn a lot of money these days.
   d. The topic of his research these days is how to make a lot of money.

- '돈을 많이 버는 방법'은 how to make lots of money, ways to earn a lot of money로 옮긴다.
- '~을 연구 중이다'는 one's objective is~, be looking for~, be searching for~, the topic of one's research is~로 옮긴다.
- 주어를 '그의 목표' his objective, '그' he, '그의 연구의 주제' the topic of his research로 두어 옮길 수 있다.

(2) a. The waves from the blowing wind prevented them from fishing, so they came back.
   b. They had to give up fishing because the wind made big waves, so they came back.
   c. The wind made big waves, so they gave up fishing and came back.
   d. Because the wind made big waves, they had to give up fishing and came back.

- '바람이 파도를 일으키다'는 the waves from the blowing wind, the wind makes big waves로 옮긴다.
- '낚시를 포기하다'는 come back, give up fishing으로 옮긴다.
- prevent~from -ing는 '~가 ~하지 못하게 하다'는 의미이다.

(3) a. He hurried out of his house and got in the taxi, for he had to catch the plane.
   b. As he had to catch the plane, he hurried out of his house and got in the taxi.
   c. It was necessary for him to be on time for the plane, so he came out of his house hurriedly and got in the taxi.
   d. Because he had to catch the plane, he hurriedly came out of his house and got in the taxi.

- '비행기를 놓치지 않으려고'는 for he has to catch the plane, as he has to catch the plane, it is necessary for him to be on time for the plane, because he has to catch the plane으로 옮긴다.
- '서둘러 집을 나오다'는 hurry out of one's house, come out of one's house hurriedly, hurriedly come out of one's house로 옮긴다.
- '택시를 타다'는 get in the taxi로 옮긴다.

(4) a. Young though she is, she understands like an adult.

b. She is young but she understands as well as an adult.

c. Although she is young, she has the understanding of an adult.

d. Despite her young age, her power to understand is as good as an adult.

- '나이는 어리지만'은 young though~is, ~is young but~, although~is young, despite one's young age로 옮긴다.
- '어른에 못지않을 정도로 이해력이 있다'는 understand like an adult, understand as well as an adult, have the understanding of an adult, one's power to understand is as good as an adult로 옮긴다.

(5) a. That adult was so short that I mistook him for a child.

b. The adult's short height made me mistake him for a child.

c. Because of his short stature, I mistakenly thought that adult was a child.

d. I mistakenly thought that adult was a child, because he was so short.

- '그 어른'은 that adult나 the adult로 옮긴다.
- '키가 너무 작아서'는 so short that~, one's short height~, because of one's short stature, because~is so short로 옮긴다.
- '~을 ~로 착각하다'는 mistake~for~, mistakenly think that~으로 옮긴다.

## 제11장 동명사

### Ⅲ. 심화연습

1. 정답 : c

- 이유 : instead는 '그 대신에'라는 부사이므로 동명사 talking을 목적어로 취할 수 없다. 예문은 동명사 talking이 앞의 부사와 문장구조상 연결이 되지 않아 비문이다. 따라서 '~의 대신에'라는 의미의 instead of를 사용하면 전치사 of의 목적어가 동명사 talking이 되어 문법적으로 문제가 없다.

2. 정답 : d

- 이유 : 종속절의 주어가 she이고 make a fool of의 목적어가 주어 she와 동일한 지시대상일 때 이 목적어가 재귀대명사 herself가 된다. 그러나 주어가 she가 아니라 others이므로 목적어가 재귀대명사가 될 수 없어 비문이다. 따라서 목적어인 재귀대명사 herself를 대명사 her로 바꾼다.

3. 정답 : b

• 이유 : 대명사의 지시대상이 동일할 때는 대명사가 통일성을 유지해야 한다. 예문에서 주어 자리에 동명사 exerting의 목적어로 일반인을 가리키는 3인칭 one의 재귀대명사 oneself가 나와 있는데 이와는 달리 전치사 to의 목적어 자리에 있는 명사구 your success에서는 인칭대명사가 2인칭 you의 소유격 your이다. 이와 같이 대명사가 서로 일관성을 유지하지 않아 비문이므로 your를 one's로 바꾸거나 oneself를 yourself로 바꾼다.

4. 정답 : d

• 이유 : 명사 thing은 셀 수 있는 명사이므로 일반적으로 수의 개념으로 쓰인다. 예문은 이 셀 수 있는 명사가 앞에 한정사(관사, 소유격, 지시사, 양화사)도 붙지 않고 복수형으로 쓰인 것도 아니어서 명사구가 아니므로 비문이다. 따라서 일반적으로 서수 앞에는 정관사가 붙으므로 서수 first 앞에 the를 붙여 first thing을 명사구 the first thing으로 바꾼다.

5. 정답 : a

• 이유 : 완료동명사(having + 과거분사)를 부정할 때는 부정의 부사 not을 완료동명사 바로 앞에 둔다. 따라서 having not met을 not having met으로 바꾼다.

6. 정답 : c

• 이유 : 진주어가 that-절이고 이것을 가리키는 가주어 It이 나와 있는 문장이다. '매일 열심히 일하는 것'은 미래의 일이 아니라 현재의 사실이므로 단순현제시제로 나타낸다. 따라서 단순미래시제 will do를 단순현재시제 do로 바꾼다.

7. 정답 : b

• 이유 : 타동사 read의 동명사 reading이 good books를 목적어로 취하고 있다. 따라서 문장의 주어는 복수형 good books가 아니라 동명사 reading이므로 동사는 복수형 are가 아니라 단수형 is이다.

8. 정답 : a

• 이유 : 동사 like 뒤에 이미 존재하고 있거나 존재했던 일이 올 때는 to-부정사가 아니라 동명사로 온다. 그 노인이 현재 도시에 살고 있는데 이것을 싫어한다는 의미는 like 뒤에 to-부정사가 아니라 동명사로 나타낸다. 따라서 to live를 living으로 바꾼다.

9. 정답 : b

• 이유 : 동사 inform은 간접목적어와 직접목적어인 that-절을 취하여 '~에게 ~가 ~하다는 것을 알리다'는 의미를 전한다. 따라서 예문에서 informed 뒤에는 전치사 of 없이 간접목적어인 명사구 others가 오고 그 뒤에 직접목적어인 that-절이 온다.

10. 정답 : a

• 이유 : 명사 time이 횟수의 의미를 전할 때는 셀 수 있는 명사이다. 따라서 일반적으로 수의 개념으로 쓰인다. 따라서 '몇 번'은 a few time이 아니라 a few times이다.

## Ⅳ. 기본영작

1. Downsizing your meals is helpful for losing weight.
   Reducing your food intake will be of help for losing weight.
   Reducing the amount of your meals is one way to lose weight.
   Reducing the size of meals is helpful for taking off your weight.

- '식사량을 줄이다'는 downsize one's meals, reduce one's food, reduce the amount of one's meals, reduce the size of meals로 옮긴다.
- '체중을 줄이다'는 lose weight, take off one's weight로 옮긴다.
- '도움이 되다'는 be helpful, be of help, be one way to do~로 옮긴다.

2. The child's favorite thing to do is writing about books.
   What that child likes most is to write his impressions of books.
   Writing down impressions of books is what that child likes most.
   Of all things, the child enjoys writing down his own impressions of books.

- '~가 가장 좋아하는 것'은 one's favorite thing to do나 what~like most로 옮기거나 of all things, ~enjoy~로 옮긴다.
- '독후감을 쓰다'는 write about books, write one's impressions of books, write down impressions of books, write down one's own impressions of books로 옮긴다.

3. Both abuse and being abused are unpleasant to see.
   Both abuse and being abused are not good to look at.
   It is not nice to see both being abusive and getting abused.
   It is not pleasant to watch abuse, and to see yourself being abused.

- '구타하는 것과 구타당하는 것'은 both abuse and being abused, both being abusive and getting abused로 옮긴다.
- '보기에 아름답지 않다'는 be unpleasant to see, be not good to look at, be not nice to see~, be not pleasant to watch~로 옮긴다.

4. A hasty decision leads to zero results.
   Making hasty decisions results in nothing.
   To come to a conclusion too fast cannot bring any results.
   You cannot lead to any results if you come to a hasty conclusion.

- '성급하게 결론을 내리는 것'은 a hasty decision, making hasty decisions, to come to a conclusion too fast, come to a hasty conclusion으로 옮긴다.
- '아무런 결과도 가져오지 못하다'는 lead to zero results, result in nothing, cannot bring any

results, cannot lead to any results로 옮긴다.

- lead to~는 '~에 이르다'는 의미로 to가 전치사이므로 뒤는 명사구가 온다.

5. Is it a bad thing to kill mosquitoes or flies because it may mean taking life?
Do you think it wrong to kill mosquitoes or flies merely because it may mean taking life?
Is it bad to kill a mosquito or a fly because this is destroying a form of life?
Is it wrong to kill a mosquito or a fly because it is equal to destruction of life?

- '모기나 파리를 죽이다'는 kill mosquitoes or flies, kill a mosquito or a fly로 옮긴다. mosquitoes와 flies는 일반적인 의미의 모기와 파리를 가리키며 a mosquito와 a fly는 한 마리의 모기와 한 마리의 파리를 뜻한다.
- '살생을 하다'는 take life, destroy a form of life, destruction of life로 옮긴다.

6. It is not good for all of us that you end the work incompletely.
Your finishing the work incompletely is not desirable for all of us.
It is not desirable for all of us that you do not finish the work thoroughly.
It is not preferable for all of us that you do not complete the job thoroughly.

- '그 일을 대충 끝내다'는 end the work incompletely, finish the work incompletely, do not finish the work thoroughly, do not complete the job thoroughly로 옮긴다.
- '~에게 바람직하지 않다'는 is not good for~, is not desirable for~, is not preferable for~로 옮긴다.

7. The coed does not like being a student.
The coed dislikes the fact that she is a student.
The girl student does not like herself as a student.
The female student dislikes the fact that she is a student.

- '그 여학생'은 the coed, the girl student, the female student로 옮긴다. coed는 남녀공학대학의 여학생을 가리킨다.
- '학생인 것을 좋아하지 않다'는 do not like being a student, dislike the fact that~is a student, do not like oneself as a student로 옮긴다. 동사 like 뒤는 보통 to-부정사와 동명사 모두 오지만 이미 존재하거나 존재했던 일을 나타낼 때는 후자만 가능하다. 현재 학생인 경우 being 대신 to be는 쓰지 않는다.

8. Giving your children too much money tends to spoil them.
If you give your children too much money, you are apt to spoil them.
Giving too much money to children does not teach them the value of it.
Giving too much money to one's child leads to their ignorance of the value of it.

- '너무 많은 돈을 주다'는 give too much money로 옮기며 money는 셀 수 없는 명사로 양의 양

화사 much 대신 수의 양화사 many를 쓰지 못한다.

- '인생을 그르치다'는 spoil one's children, do not teach the value of money, lead to one's ignorance of the value of money로 옮긴다.

9. He is afraid of getting punished, while his mother is afraid of punishing him.
   He is afraid of being punished, but his mother is also afraid of punishing him.
   He is afraid of being punished, whereas his mother is afraid of punishing him.
   He is afraid of being punished, and his mother is afraid of punishing him.

- '벌 받다'는 get punished, be punished로 옮기고 '벌주다'는 punish~로 옮긴다.
- '~을 두려워하다'는 be afraid of~로 옮긴다.
- '~하고'는 ~, while~이나 ~, but~으로 옮길 수도 있고 ~, whereas~나~, and~로 옮길 수도 있다.

10. It is bad for your eyes to read a book in the dark.
    Reading a book in the dark is not good for your eyes.
    You'd better not read in the dark for the sake of your eyes.
    You should not read in the dark, for it is bad for your eyes.

- '어두운 데서 독서를 하다'는 read a book in the dark, read in the dark로 옮긴다.
- '너의 눈에'는 '너의 눈을 위하여'의 의미로 전치사구 for your eyes, for the sake of your eyes로 옮긴다.
- '좋지 않다'는 '~해서는 안 된다'는 의미로 be bad, be not good, had better not~, should not ~으로 옮긴다.

## V. 심화영작

1. (1) If you sleep on the street in midwinter, you could freeze to death.
   One might die from cold if one sleeps on the street in midwinter.
   You could freeze to death if you sleep on the street in midwinter.
   Sleeping on the street in midwinter may lead to one's death from cold.

- '한겨울에'는 in midwinter로 옮긴다.
- '길거리에서'는 on the street으로 옮긴다.
- '동사하다'는 freeze to death, die from cold, lead to one's death from cold로 옮긴다.
- 일반인을 가리키는 one은 구어체에서는 one 대신 he로 받기도 한다.

   (2) You are apt to get tired after you type on the computer too long.
   You naturally become tired if you type on the computer too much.
   It is only natural to be tired after typing on the computer keyboard for a long time.
   One naturally gets tired if one types on the computer keyboard for a long time.

- '컴퓨터 자판을 두드리다'는 type on the computer, type on the computer keyboard로 옮긴다.
- '피곤해지다'는 get tired, become tired, be tired로 옮긴다.
- '~하기 마련이다'는 be apt to do~, naturally become~, it is only natural to do~, naturally get~으로 옮긴다.

(3) Yawning is a sign of your tiredness.
Yawning is an indication that you are tired.
Yawning is one of the proofs of your being tired.
Yawning is one of the signs that show you are tired.

- '하나의 증거'는 a sign, an indication, one of the proofs, one of the signs로 옮긴다.
- 둘째 예문의 that은 접속사이고 넷째 예문의 that은 관계대명사이다.
- 셋째 예문의 being tired는 수동동명사이고 your는 동명사의 주어이다.

(4) If you pick that flower, others cannot have a chance to appreciate it.
If you pick that flower, other people won't have the chance to admire it.
If you break off that flower, other people won't get a chance to enjoy it.
With your breaking off that flower, you are taking away others' chance to appreciate it.

- '그 꽃을 꺾다'는 pick that flower, break off that flower로 옮긴다.
- '다른 사람'은 남이나 타인을 뜻하는 others나 other people로 옮긴다.
- '~을 감상할 기회가 없어지다'는 cannot have a chance to appreciate~, won't have the chance to admire~, won't get a chance to enjoy~, take away one's chance to appreciate~로 옮긴다.

(5) Spitting on busy streets makes other people disgusted.
Spitting on a busy street makes others feel unpleasant.
It makes others feel unpleasant to see people spitting on a busy street.
People feel unpleasant when they see someone spitting on a busy street.

- '많은 사람이 다니는 길에'는 on busy streets, on a busy street로 옮긴다.
- '침을 뱉다'는 동사 spit으로 옮긴다.
- '~을 불쾌하게 하다'는 make~disgusted, make~feel unpleasant, ~feel unpleasant로 옮긴다.

(6) He works very hard till late at night to care for his family.
In order to support his family, he works very hard until late at night.
The reason he works very diligently until late at night is to support his family.
He works very hard till late at night, and this is to look after his family.

- '밤늦게까지'는 till late at night, until late at night으로 옮긴다.
- '열심히 일하다'는 work hard, work diligently로 옮긴다.
- '가족을 부양하다'는 care for one's family, support one's family, look after one's family로 옮긴다.

(7) Watching TV too much results in exhaustion and decreased work efficiency.

Watching too much TV will make you tired, thus making you unable to work at your best ability.

If you watch TV too much, you tend to get tired, consequently bringing about decreased work efficiency.

If you watch TV too much, you get tired, and this might lead to decreased work efficiency.

- 'TV를 너무 많이 보다'는 watch TV too much, watch too much TV로 옮긴다.
- '피로하여'는 result in exhaustion, make~tired, get tired로 옮긴다.
- '일할 때 능률이 떨어지다'는 result in decreased work efficiency, make~unable to work at one's best ability, bring about decreased work efficiency, lead to decreased work efficiency로 옮긴다.

(8) The girl's hobby is to pick pretty leaves and put them in a book.

The girl's hobby is to get pretty leaves from trees and place them inside a book.

The girl collects pretty leaves from trees, and places them in between the pages of a book. This is her hobby.

As a hobby, the girl likes to pick pretty leaves from trees, and insert them inside a book.

- '그 소녀의 취미'는 the girl's hobby나 as a hobby, the girl~로 옮긴다.
- '예쁜 나뭇잎을 따다'는 pick pretty leaves, get pretty leaves from trees, collect pretty leaves from trees, pick pretty leaves from trees로 옮긴다.
- '책갈피에 끼워두다'는 put~in a book, place~inside a book, place~in between the pages of a book, insert~inside a book으로 옮긴다.

(9) You can get swollen eyes if you cry too much.

If you cry too much, your eyes can get swollen.

Your eyes will become swollen if you cry too much.

Too much crying may cause your eyes to be swollen.

- '너무 많이 울다'는 동사구 cry too much나 명사구 too much crying으로 옮긴다.
- '눈이 붓다'는 get swollen eyes, one's eyes get swollen, one's eyes become swollen, cause one's eyes to be swollen으로 옮긴다.
- '~할 수도 있다'는 can get~, will become~, cause~to do~로 옮긴다.

(10) Reading at the same time every day may help you to find mental stability.

You may feel peace of mind if you read at the same time every day.

Regular reading at the same time every day may bring about mental calmness.

Reading at the same time every day may be helpful in stabilizing your mental health.

- '매일 같은 시간에'는 at the same time every day로 옮긴다.
- '정신적인 안정에 도움이 되다'는 help~to find mental stability, feel peace of mind, bring about mental calmness, be helpful in stabilizing one's mental health로 옮긴다.

2. (1) a. Cell phones should be put on vibrate in classes.

b. During classes, you should put your cell phone in silent or vibration mode.

c. In class, one should put one's cell phone in silent or vibration mode.

d. You should put your cell phone in silent or vibration mode when you are in class.

- '교실에서는'은 '수업 중에는'의 의미이므로 전치사구 in classes, during classes, in class로 옮긴다.
- '휴대폰'은 cell phones, one's cell phone, one's mobile phone으로 옮긴다.
- '무음이나 진동으로 설정하다'는 put~on vibrate, put~in silent or vibration mode로 옮긴다.

(2) a. Whether or not one always eats fruit after having a meal tells you how rich he is.

b. One of the factors determining your wealth is whether or not you always eat fruit after each meal.

c. Wealth can be seen from whether a person always has fruit after having a meal or not.

d. Always having fruit as a dessert is a factor determining whether a person is rich or not.

- '식후에'는 after having a meal, after each meal로 옮긴다. each 뒤는 셀 수 있는 명사가 단수형으로 와야 한다.
- '빈부의 차이를 드러내다'는 tell~how rich~is, determine one's wealth, wealth can be seen from~, determine whether a person is rich or not으로 옮긴다.

(3) a. I hear that eating vegetables is much better than eating meat for health.

b. People say that it is healthier to have a vegetable diet than a meat diet.

c. They say that a vegetable diet is better for health than a meat diet.

d. It is said that for health, a diet composed of vegetables is better than that of meat.

- '채식'은 eating vegetables나 a vegetable diet, a diet composed of vegetables로 옮긴다.
- '육식'은 eating meat이나 a vegetable diet, a diet composed of vegetables로 옮긴다.
- '~라고들 하다'는 I hear~, People say that~, They say~, It is said that~으로 옮긴다.

(4) a. A person becomes healthier by walking ten thousand steps a day.

b. Walking more than ten thousand steps a day is very good for health.

c. I advise you to walk more than ten thousand steps a day if you want to remain healthy.

d. It is very good for health to walk more than ten thousand steps a day.

- '만보 이상 걷다'는 walk more than ten thousand steps로 옮긴다.
- '건강에 매우 좋다'는 become healthier, be very good for health, remain healthy로 옮긴다.
- 주어를 A person, walking, I, 가주어 it으로 두어 작문할 수 있다.

(5) a. Time creates new things and makes old things disappear.

b. With time, new things are created and old things are made to disappear.

c. It is time that creates new things and makes old things disappear.

d. As time goes by, new things are created and old things are made to disappear.

- '세월'은 시간을 가리키므로 time으로 옮긴다.
- '새것을 만들어내다'는 create new things, new things are created로 옮긴다.
- '오래된 것을 사라지게 하다'는 make old things disappear, old things are made to disappear로 옮긴다.

## 제12장 분 사

### Ⅲ. 심화연습

1. 정답 : c

- 이유 : 동사 have는 목적어를 취하지만 목적보어를 요구하지는 않는다. 따라서 목적어인 명사구 your meal 뒤에 부사는 올 수 있지만 형용사는 올 수 없다. 따라서 형용사 hasty를 부사 hastily로 바꾼다.

2. 정답 : d

- 이유 : 접속사 until은 시간의 계속을 나타내는 데 반해 한국어 문장은 정해진 시간까지의 동작의 완료를 나타낸다. 따라서 이 문장에 쓰일 수 없다.

3. 정답 : d

- 이유 : 등위접속사로 연결된 두 절의 주어가 동일한 때는 일반적으로 뒷 절의 주어는 생략할 수 있다. 그러나 종속접속사로 연결된 절에서는 그렇지 않다. 따라서 종속접속사 though 뒤에 주어 I가 필요하다.

4. 정답 : b

- 이유 : 직접의문문이 주절의 일부가 되는 때는 간접의문문으로 바뀐다. 따라서 where was I

going은 where I was going이 된다.

5. 정답 : b

• 이유 : 앞 절 전체의 내용을 목적어로 취할 수 있는 관계대명사는 계속적 용법(관계대명사 앞에 쉼표가 있음)의 관계대명사 which이다. 따라서 that을 which로 바꾼다.

6. 정답 : a

• 이유 : 독자 reader는 셀 수 있는 명사이므로 일반적으로 수의 개념으로 쓰인다. 그러나 예문의 reader는 앞에 한정사도 붙지 않고 복수어미 -s도 붙어있지 않다. 따라서 명사이지만 명사구가 아니어서 비문이다. 따라서 reader's를 일반적인 의미의 독자를 가리키는 readers의 소유격인 readers'로 바꾼다.

7. 정답 : c

• 이유 : 등 back과 머리 head는 셀 수 있는 명사로 일반적으로 수의 개념으로 쓰인다. 그러나 예문에서는 마치 셀 수 없는 명사인 것처럼 앞에 한정사도 붙어 있지 않고 또한 복수어미 -s도 붙어 있지 않아서 비문이다. 따라서 back과 head 앞에 각각 정관사를 넣어 the back과 the head로 고치거나 소유격을 앞에 붙여 her back과 her head로 고친다.

8. 정답 : a

• 이유 : 전체 문장의 주어가 명사구 wind이고 전체 문장의 동사는 excites가 되어야 하므로 동사 goes는 주어 wind를 수식하는 현재분사 going이 되어야 한다.

9. 정답 : a

• 이유 : 축구 soccer는 셀 수 없는 명사이므로 일반적으로 수의 개념으로 쓰이지 않는다. 따라서 a soccer의 부정관사 a를 뺀다. 그러나 a soccer ball의 부정관사 a는 soccer에 붙은 것이 아니라 셀 수 있는 명사 ball에 붙은 것이므로 빼서는 안 된다.

10. 정답 : c

• 이유 : 동사 walk는 '걷다'는 자동사로 뒤의 대명사 him을 목적어로 취할 수 없다. 그리고 up 역시 전치사가 아니라 '~쪽으로'를 뜻하는 부사로 대명사 him을 목적어로 취할 수 없다. 결과적으로 대명사 him이 앞의 어떤 요소와 문장구조상 연결이 되지 않아 비문이다. 따라서 전치사 to를 up 다음에 넣어 him이 전치사의 목적어가 되게 하면 좋은 문장이 된다.

## Ⅳ. 기본영작

1. Although he has never been to a foreign country, he speaks many languages fluently.
   He speaks several languages fluently, despite the fact that he has never been abroad.
   Even though he has never been abroad, he is fluent in many languages.
   He has never been to foreign countries, but he can speak several languages fluently.

• '외국'은 '한 외국'을 가리킬 때는 a foreign country로 옮기고 일반적인 의미의 외국은 foreign countries로 옮긴다.

- '~에 가본 적이 없다'는 현재완료시제를 사용하여 have never been to~나 have never been~으로 옮긴다.

2. Who is the man that is entertaining you?
   Who is the man that gives you pleasure?
   Who is the man that brings you pleasure?
   Who is the man that is making you be happy?

- '~을 즐겁게 하다'는 entertain~, give~pleasure, bring~pleasure, make~be happy로 옮긴다. give와 bring은 간접목적어와 직접목적어를 취할 수 있는 동사이다.
- who는 의문대명사이고 that은 주격 관계대명사이다.

3. If a child is seen crying alone on the street, you should take him to his parents.
   If you see a child crying by himself on the street, you should find him his parents.
   If you find a child crying alone on the street, you should help him find his parents.
   If you meet with a child crying alone on the street, you should help him to find his parents.

- '혼자 울다'는 cry alone, cry by oneself로 옮긴다.
- '~를 만나면'은 if~is seen, if~see~, if~find~, if~meet with~로 옮긴다.
- '부모를 찾아주다'는 take~to one's parents, find~one's parents, help~find one's parents, help ~to find one's parents로 옮긴다.
- 둘째 예문의 find는 '~에게 ~을 찾아주다'는 의미이다.

4. The teacher came in by the time the student had been studying for two hours.
   The student had been studying for two hours when the teacher came in.
   The teacher came in when the student had been studying for two hours.
   When the teacher came in, the student had been studying for two hours.

- '들어오다'는 come in으로, come은 자동사이고 in은 '안으로'라는 부사이다.
- '두 시간 동안 공부를 하고 있었다'는 두 시간 이전인 과거이전부터 기준시점인 과거까지 행위가 진행 중이었으므로 과거완료진행시제 had been studying for two hours로 옮긴다.

5. Disappointed at his girlfriend, he decided to find another.
   He made up his mind to look for a new girlfriend because his girlfriend disappointed him.
   His girlfriend disappointed him, so he decided to look for a new girlfriend.
   Because he was disappointed by his girlfriend, he decided to look for a new girlfriend.

- '~에 실망해서'는 disappointed at~이나 because~disappointed~로 옮기거나 ~, so~나 because ~was disappointed by~로 옮긴다.
- '다른 여자친구'는 '또 다른 여자친구'이므로 another girlfriend이지만 앞에 이미 his girlfriend에

서 girlfriend가 나왔으므로 반복을 피하기 위해 another로 나타낸다.

- '~을 찾다'는 find~, look for~로 옮긴다.

6. The professor was feeling exhausted because he had been writing a manuscript for three hours.

   The professor felt very tired, for he had been writing a manuscript for three hours.

   The professor was very tired from writing a manuscript for three hours.

   The professor was very tired because he had been writing a manuscript for three hours.

- '원고' manuscript는 셀 수 있는 명사로 '하나의 원고'를 가리킬 때는 a manuscript로 옮긴다.
- 피곤한 것은 과거이므로 과거시제 was feeling exhausted, felt tired로 옮기고 세 시간 동안 원고를 써 오고 있었던 것은 과거이전부터 과거까지이므로 과거완료진행시제 had been writing으로 옮긴다.

7. It is my son that is reading out a book loud.

   The boy who is reading a book out loud is my son.

   The child who is reading the book out loud is my son.

   A kid is reading a book out loud. That kid is my son.

- '큰소리로 책을 읽다'는 read out a book loud, read a book out loud로 옮긴다.
- '읽고 있는'은 현재의 일시적으로 진행 중에 있는 행위로 현재진행시제 is reading이 되며 reading은 진행형을 만드는 현재분사이다.
- '그 아이'는 the boy, the child, that kid로 옮긴다.

8. The woman looking very happy is the one that I met yesterday.

   That woman looks very happy. She is the one I met yesterday.

   The woman who is looking very happy is the person I met yesterday.

   The woman who looks very happy is the woman whom I met yesterday.

- '내가 어제 만났던 여자'는 the one that I met yesterday, the person I met yesterday, the woman whom I met yesterday로 옮긴다.
- looking은 첫째 예문에서는 형용사구 very happy를 보어로 취하면서 앞 명사 woman을 수식하는 현재분사이고 셋째 예문에서는 be동사와 함께 진행형을 만드는 현재분사이다.

9. Do you know that woman who is having coffee by herself?

   Do you know that woman who is drinking a cup of coffee alone?

   You see that woman who is having a cup of coffee alone. Do you know who she is?

   Can you see that woman who is drinking a cup of coffee alone? Do you know her?

- '혼자'는 전치사구 by oneself나 부사 alone으로 옮긴다.
- '커피를 마시다'는 have coffee, drink a cup of coffee, have a cup of coffee로 옮긴다.

• '마시고 있는'은 현재의 일시적으로 진행 중에 있는 행위이므로 현재진행시제 is having, is drinking으로 옮긴다.

10. She was standing there, giving the children something.
She was standing there, giving something to the children.
She was standing there as she handed something out to the children.
She was standing there, and she was giving something to the children.

• '아이들에게 뭔가를 건네주다'는 give the children something, give something to the children, hand something out to the children으로 옮긴다. children 앞의 정관사는 아이들이 여러 명일 뿐 아니라 화자가 그의 청자도 알고 있는 대상으로 보아 붙인 것이다.

## V. 심화영작

1. (1) The incredibly happy looking couple are newly married.
That couple who seem very happy have just got married.
The man and woman who seem very happy are newlyweds.
The couple, who look incredibly happy, is a newly married couple.

• '매우 행복해 보이는'은 incredibly happy looking, who seem very happy, who look incredibly happy로 옮긴다.

• '막 결혼한 사람들'은 ~are newly married, ~have just got married, newly weds, a newly married couple로 옮긴다. couple은 한 쌍의 부부를 뜻할 때는 단수로 부부인 남자와 여자 개개인을 뜻할 때는 복수로 본다.

(2) Two men are digging potatoes. They are brothers.
The two people who are digging potatoes are brothers.
Those two men that are digging potatoes are brothers.
Those two people, who are digging potatoes, are brothers.

• '감자를 캐다'는 dig potatoes로 옮긴다. 일반적인 의미의 감자는 한정사를 붙이지 않은 복수형 potatoes, 감자 하나는 a potato, 감자라는 물질 그 자체를 가리킬 때는 셀 수 없는 명사로 한정사를 붙이지 않은 형태 potato로 나타낸다는 데 유의해야 한다.

• '캐고 있는'은 현재 캐는 행위가 일시적으로 진행 중에 있다는 의미로 현재진행시제 are digging ~으로 옮긴다.

(3) Generally, we feel pleasant when we see a sunrise.
Few people will feel unhappy upon seeing the sunrise.
Few people will feel unpleasant when they look at a sunrise.
Most people will feel happy when they see the sun rising.

• '떠오르는 해를 보다'는 see a sunrise, see the sunrise, see the sun rising으로 옮긴다.
• '~를 보고'는 when~see~, upon seeing~으로 옮긴다. upon은 전치사이고 seeing은 전치사의 목적어인 동명사이다.
• '기분이 좋지 않은 사람은 별로 없다'는 feel pleasant, few people feel unhappy, few people feel unpleasant, feel happy로 옮긴다.

(4) I met with the woman who is entertaining everyone not long ago.
Only a short time ago, I met with the woman who is entertaining everyone.
The woman is making everyone happy. I met with her not long ago.
Not long ago, I met with the woman, the one who is making everyone happy.

• '모두를 즐겁게 하다'는 entertain everyone, make everyone happy로 옮긴다.
• '얼마 전'은 not long ago, only a short time ago로 옮긴다.
• meet with는 '~을 우연히 만나다'는 뜻이다.
• 그 여자를 만난 것은 과거의 사실로 단순과거시제가 되고 모두를 즐겁게 하고 있는 것은 현재의 일시적으로 진행 중인 행위로 현재진행시제가 된다.

(5) How do you feel when you see that bird flying up in the sky?
When you see that bird flying high up in the sky, what kind of thought enters your mind?
What do you think of when you see that bird flying high up in the sky?
What comes into your mind when you see that bird flying up in the sky?

• '하늘 높이 날다'는 fly up in the sky, fly high up in the sky로 옮긴다.
• '저 새를 보면'은 when~see that bird로 표현한다.
• '무슨 생각이 드니?'는 How do you feel~? What kind of thought enters your mind? What do you think of~? What comes into your mind~?로 옮긴다.

(6) The man, who is walking fast, is the husband, and the woman, who is following him, is his wife.
The man who is walking fast is the husband, and the woman behind him is his wife.
The man who is walking quickly is the husband, and his wife is following him.
The man walking fast is the husband, and the woman following him is his wife.

• '빨리 걷고 있는 남자'는 the man, who is walking fast나 the man who is walking fast로 옮기거나 the man who is walking quickly, the man walking fast로 옮긴다.
• '그 뒤에 가는'은 following~, behind~로 옮긴다.
• '남편'은 '한 사람의 남편' a husband가 아니라 화자가 그의 청자도 알고 있다고 보는 '그 여자의 남편'을 가리키므로 the husband로 옮긴다.

(7) Is that man singing loudly your husband?

A man is singing loudly. Is he your husband?

Is the man, who is singing loudly, your husband?

Is that man who is singing loudly your husband?

- '큰 소리로 노래를 부르다'는 sing loudly로 옮긴다.
- 셋째 예문은 관계대명사 who를 계속적 용법으로, 넷째 예문은 제한적 용법으로 사용한 것이다. 셋째 예문은 who가 이끄는 관계절이 관계대명사의 선행사 the man에 대해 부연설명을 하는 데 반해 넷째 예문은 who가 이끄는 관계절이 선행사 that man을 한정한다.

(8) Soon he will live in that blue house.

He will soon live in that blue house.

That blue house will soon be his new home.

He will be living in that blue house before long.

- '머지않아'는 soon, before long으로 옮긴다.
- '저 파란색 집'은 that blue house로 옮기며 that은 명사 앞에 오는 한정사의 하나인 지시사이다.
- '~하게 될 것이다'는 미래에 대한 예언이나 예측을 나타내므로 미래조동사 will을 사용한다.

(9) I don't know that woman smiling at me.

That woman smiling at me is a stranger to me.

I don't know that woman, the one who is smiling at me.

That woman who is smiling at me is someone I don't know.

- '~에게 미소 짓다'는 smile at~으로 옮긴다.
- '잘 알지 못하는 여자'는 don't know that woman, a stranger, someone I don't know로 옮긴다.
- smiling은 첫째, 둘째 예문에서 앞 명사 woman을 수식하는 현재분사이고, 셋째, 넷째 예문에서는 be동사와 함께 진행형을 만드는 현재분사이다.

(10) My daughter is the kid with a doll on her back, and my son is the one kicking a ball.

The kid who has a doll on her back is my daughter, and the kid who is kicking a ball is my son.

The girl who has a doll on her back is my daughter, and the boy who is kicking a ball is my son.

The child with a doll on her back is my daughter, and the child kicking a ball is my son.

- '인형을 업고 있는'은 목적어와 목적보어를 취할 수 있는 전치사 with를 사용한 전치사구 with a doll on one's back이나 have a doll on one's back으로 옮긴다.
- '공을 차고 있는'은 현재분사를 사용하여 ~kicking a ball로 옮기거나 관계절 who is kicking a

ball로 옮긴다.

2. (1) a. Under the hot summer sun, they were working diligently.

b. Over them was the hot summer sun, and they were working hard.

c. They were working diligently with the hot summer sun shining upon them.

d. With the hot summer sun shining upon them, they were working hard.

• '뜨거운 여름 햇살을 받으면서'는 전치사구 under the hot summer sun이나 over them was the hot summer sun으로 옮기거나 전치사구 with the hot summer sun shining upon them으로 옮긴다. 위치를 나타내는 부사적 기능의 전치사구 over them이 문장의 첫머리로 이동하여 주어 the hot summer sun과 동사 was의 어순이 도치되었다.

(2) a. I will be finished with my homework by the time you are finished with yours.

b. At around the same time as you finish your homework, I will finish mine.

c. By the time you finish your homework, I will finish my homework as well.

d. My homework will be completed when your homework gets completed.

• '숙제를 끝마치다'는 be finished with one's homework, finish one's homework, one's homework is finished로 옮긴다.

• 첫째, 셋째 예문의 by는 기한을 나타내는 전치사로 어떤 것이 특정한 때나 그 이전에 일어난다는 것을 나타낸다.

(3) a. That foreigner sent a letter written in difficult English.

b. The letter sent from that foreigner was written in difficult-to-understand English.

c. It was hard to understand the letter sent from that foreigner, for it was written in difficult English.

d. The English letter written by that foreigner was hard to understand.

• '편지' letter는 첫째 예문에서 '한 통의 편지'를 가리키기 위해 부정관사를 붙여 a letter로 옮기고 나머지 예문에서는 화자가 그의 청자도 알고 있다고 보는 특정한 편지인 '그 편지'를 가리키기 위해 정관사를 붙여 the letter로 옮긴 것이다.

• 셋째 예문의 앞의 it은 뒤의 진주어 to understand를 가리키는 가주어이고 뒤의 it은 앞에 나온 명사구 the letter를 가리키는 대명사이다.

(4) a. Continuous study is a prerequisite for mastering a foreign language.
This is a widely known fact.

b. A foreign language requires patience, and this is a well-known fact.

c. Everyone knows that mastering a foreign language requires continuous study.

d. It is a well-known fact that you can master a foreign language only if you continuously study it.

- '꾸준히 공부하다'는 명사구 continuous study나 동사구 require patience, continuously study~로 옮긴다. 명사 study가 공부를 의미할 때는 셀 수 없는 명사이므로 continuous study 대신 a continuous study를 쓰지 않도록 주의해야 한다.
- 둘째 예문의 this는 앞 절 전체를 가리키는 대명사이다.

(5) a. After having dyed their hair with different colors, the women were walking along the street.

b. With their hair dyed with different colors, the women were walking along the street.

c. The women were walking down the street with their hair dyed with different colors.

d. Having their hair dyed with different colors, the women were walking along the street.

- '제각기 다른 색으로 머리를 염색한 채'는 전치사구 after having dyed one's hair with different colors, with one's hair dyed with different colors나 분사 구문 having one's hair dyed with different colors로 옮긴다.
- '거리를 거닐다'는 walk along the street, walk down the street으로 옮긴다.

## 제13장 시 제

### Ⅲ. 심화연습

1. 정답 : a

- 이유 : '너무 ~해서 ~할 수 없다'는 too~to do~로 표현한다. 따라서 부사 so를 부사 too로 바꾼다.

2. 정답 : b

- 이유 : 동사를 단순현재시제로 쓰면 현재의 일반적인 사실을 나타낸다. 예문은 동사 do를 단순현재시제로 표현하여 일반적인 사실을 나타내고 있는 데 반해 같은 문장 내의 부사 right now는 '바로 지금'이라는 특정한 시점만을 고려대상으로 하고 있다. 이 점에서 관점의 일관성이 결여되어 있다. 따라서 단순현재시제의 do를 현재진행시제 am doing으로 바꾼다.

3. 정답 : c

- 이유 : 때나 조건을 나타내는 부사절 내에서는 현재시제가 미래를 대신한다. 종속접속사 until이 이끄는 절(until~an apartment)이 때나 조건의 부사절이므로 단순미래시제 will buy는 단순현재시제 buys가 된다.

4. 정답 : a

• 이유 : 한국어 문장은 정부가 과거에 조치를 취하지 않은 데 대해 현재 유감을 표현하고 있다. 따라서 과거의 사실에 반하는 상황을 한 번 가정해 보는 것이므로 가정법 과거완료에 해당한다. 따라서 should take는 should have taken이 된다.

5. 정답 : c

• 이유 : 어머니 mother는 셀 수 있는 명사로 일반적으로 수의 개념으로 쓰인다. 예문의 mother는 앞에 한정사도 붙지 않고 뒤에 복수어미 -s도 붙지 않아서 마치 셀 수 없는 명사처럼 쓰여 비문이다. 따라서 또 다른 아이의 어머니는 일반적인 의미의 어머니가 아니라 특정한 어머니를 가리키므로 mother 앞에 정관사 the를 붙인다.

6. 정답 : d

• 이유 : 물이 섭씨 100도에서 끓는 것은 일반적인 사실이며 일시적인 상황을 나타내는 것이 아니라 영속적인 상황을 나타낸다. 따라서 앞 절의 현재진행시제 is boiling은 단순현재시제 boils가 된다. 그러나 but 이하의 절은 특정한 물이 섭씨 90도에서 끓고 있는 중이라는 의미이므로 현재진행시제 is boiling을 쓸 수 있다.

7. 정답 : a

• 이유 : 동사 look은 '~처럼 보이다'는 의미를 전할 때 뒤에 형용사구인 보어가 오거나 부사구가 온다. 예문에서 look은 명사구 rain을 보어로 취할 수 없어 비문이다. 따라서 앞에 전치사를 두어 like rain처럼 부사적인 기능을 하는 전치사구로 표현한다.

8. 정답 : c

• 이유 : 종속절은 현재완료시제 has revisited로 되어 있는 데 반해 주절은 과거완료시제 had passed로 되어 있어 논리적으로 서로 맞지 않다. 따라서 과거에 방문하니 이미 세상을 떠나고 없었다는 의미로 보아 종속절의 현재완료시제 has revisited를 단순과거시제 revisited로 고친다.

9. 정답 : b

• 이유 : '~에 가 본적이 있다'는 have / has been to~로 표현하며 have / has gone to~로 표현하지 않는다. 따라서 gone을 been으로 고친다.

10. 정답 : b

• 이유 : 현재완료수동진행형은 일반적으로 쓰이지 않는다. 따라서 현재완료수동진행형 have been being provided를 현재완료수동형 have been provided로 고친다.

## Ⅳ. 기본영작

1. I called you yesterday, but you did not answer.

   Yesterday I called you, but you did not answer the phone.

You did not pick up the phone when I called you yesterday.

I called you yesterday. However, you did not answer the phone.

- '어제' yesterday는 시간부사로 주로 문장의 끝에 오지만 문장의 첫머리에 올 수도 있다.
- '~에게 전화하다'는 call~로 옮긴다.
- '전화를 받지 않다'는 do not answer, do not answer the phone, do not pick up the phone으로 옮긴다.

2. They will finish talking soon.

Their conversation will soon be over.

Their conversation will soon be finished.

Their conversation will be finished before long.

- '곧'은 soon, before long으로 옮긴다.
- '끝나다'는 finish~, be over, be finished로 옮긴다.
- '~할 것이다'는 미래에 대한 예언이나 예측을 나타내므로 미래조동사 will 뒤에 동사원형을 써서 옮긴다.

3. Tomorrow he is going to catch cicadas with his young son.

He plans to go cicada catching with his little son tomorrow.

He plans to go out to catch cicadas with his little son tomorrow.

He is planning on going out to catch cicadas with his young son tomorrow.

- '매미' cicada는 셀 수 있는 명사로 '한 마리의 매미'는 a cicada이고 매미의 수와 관계없는 일반적인 의미의 매미는 관사, 소유격, 지시사, 양화사와 같은 한정사가 붙지 않은 복수형 cicadas로 옮긴다.
- '매미를 잡으러 가다'는 go to catch cicadas, go cicada catching, go out to catch cicadas로 옮긴다.

4. I will have written three books if I write one more next year.

If I write another book next year, I will have written three books.

I will be the author of three books if I write another book next year.

If another of my books is published next year, I will have written three of them.

- '한 권 더 쓰다'는 write one more, write another book, another of my books is published로 옮긴다.
- '세 권의 책을 쓰는 셈이 될 것이다'는 미래완료시제를 써서 will have written three books로 옮기거나 단순미래시제인 will be the author of three books로 옮긴다.

5. I was out when you called yesterday.

I was not in when you called me yesterday.

Yesterday you called me during my absence.

When you called me yesterday, I had gone out.

- '외출하고 집에 없다'는 be out, be not in, during one's absence, have gone out으로 옮긴다.
- be out의 out과 be not in의 in은 부사로 각각 '외출하여' '집에'라는 뜻이다.
- 첫째 예문의 call은 '전화하다'는 자동사이고 나머지 세 예문에서는 '~에게 전화하다'는 타동사이다.

6. I will lend you this book as soon as I finish reading it.

   As soon as I finish reading this book, I will lend it to you.

   When I have read this book, I will lend it to you immediately.

   When I finish reading this book, I will lend it to you right away.

- '이 책'은 this book으로 옮기며 this는 한정사의 하나인 지시사로 명사가 복수형 books인 때는 복수형 these로 반드시 바뀌어야 한다.
- '~하자마자'는 as soon as~나 when~으로 옮기며 이 두 접속표현이 이끄는 절은 때나 조건의 부사절이므로 이 절 내에서 미래의 의미로 현재시제를 쓴다.

7. He wakes up at six o'clock in the morning, goes running around the athletic field, and has breakfast at seven o'clock.

   He gets up at six and then runs around the athletic field before having breakfast at seven.

   He wakes up at 6 o'clock, jogs on the athletic field, and has breakfast at 7 o'clock.

   After getting up at 6:00 a.m., he goes running around the athletic field, and has breakfast at 7:00 a.m.

- '일어나다'는 get up과 '잠이 깨다'는 wake up을 구별해 사용해야 한다.
- '운동장을 돌다'는 run around the athletic field로 옮기며 around는 '~을 돌아'라는 전치사로 명사구 the athletic field가 전치사의 목적어이다. 이 표현 대신 jog on the athletic field를 써도 좋다.

8. Our meeting will not be held if it rains tomorrow.

   If it rains tomorrow, our meeting will be canceled.

   Our meeting is to be canceled if it rains tomorrow.

   Our meeting will be canceled tomorrow if it is rainy.

- '비가 오면'은 if it rains, if it is rainy로 옮긴다.
- '취소되다'는 not be held, be canceled로 옮긴다.
- '~될 것이다'는 미래에 대한 예언이나 예측을 나타내므로 미래조동사 will 뒤에 동사원형을 두어 옮기거나 be동사 뒤에 to-부정사를 두어 예정을 나타내는 용법으로 옮긴다.

9. She has been writing the letter for half an hour.

   She has been writing the letter since thirty minutes ago.

It has been thirty minutes since she started to write the letter.

Thirty minutes have passed since she started to write the letter.

- '30분 동안'은 for half an hour, ~since thirty minutes ago, have been thirty minutes since~, thirty minutes have passed since~로 옮긴다.
- '~ 동안 하고 있는 중이다'는 과거부터 현재까지 하고 있는 중이라는 의미로 과거와 현재가 연관이 되어 있어 현재완료시제나 현재완료진행시제로 옮긴다.

10. I will buy you some cool beer if you help me.

If you help me, I will buy you some cool beer.

If you help me, I will buy some cool beer for you.

If you help me, I will treat you to some cool beer.

- '~하면 ~하겠다'는 조건문 현재로 현재 ~하면 앞으로 ~하겠다는 의미로 조건절에 현재시제를 쓰고 주절에 미래시제를 쓴다.
- '시원한 맥주'는 some cool beer로 옮긴다.
- '~살게'는 동사 buy 뒤에 간접목적어와 직접목적어를 두어 옮기거나 직접목적어와 전치사구 for you로 옮길 수도 있고 동사 treat 뒤에 목적어와 전치사구 to some cool beer를 두어 옮긴다.

## V. 심화영작

1. (1) I am going to see the sea tomorrow.

I plan to go to see the sea tomorrow.

I am planning on going to the sea tomorrow.

Tomorrow I am going somewhere to see the sea.

- '바다'는 정관사를 붙여 the sea로 옮긴다. 우리에게 너무나 잘 알려져 있는 물리적 자연환경인 태양은 the sun, 달은 the moon, 지구는 the earth, 날씨는 the weather, 바람은 the wind, 안개는 the fog, 산은 the mountains, 바다는 the sea로 쓴다.
- somewhere는 '어딘가에'를 의미하는 부사이다.

(2) The student has broken his leg, so he cannot come to take the test.

The student cannot come to take the test because his leg is broken.

The student cannot come to take the test, for his leg has been broken.

Because he has broken his leg, the student cannot come to take the test.

- '다리가 부러지다'는 break one's leg로 옮긴다. 과거에 다리가 부러진 것이 현재 시험을 보러 올 수 없는 직접적인 원인인 때는 현재완료시제 has broken으로 옮긴다. 그러나 둘째 예문처럼 be동사의 현재형을 사용하여 is broken으로 옮길 수도 있다.

(3) The driver was drowsy, so the car swayed right and left.

The car joggled right and left because the driver was drowsy.

Because the driver was dozing off, the car was not going straight.

The car was going in a zig-zag pattern because the driver was dozing off.

- '운전자' driver는 셀 수 있는 명사로 원문은 화자가 그의 청자도 알고 있다고 보는 그 차의 '그 운전자'를 말하므로 정관사를 붙여 the driver로 옮긴다.
- '졸고 있다'는 be drowsy, be dozing off로 옮긴다.
- '좌우로 흔들리다'는 sway right and left, joggle right and left, is not going straight, go in a zig-zag pattern으로 옮긴다.

(4) I love her, and I have never loved another woman.

I love her, and she is the only woman I've ever loved.

I love her, and I have never loved another woman before.

She is the one I love, and I've never loved another woman before.

- '전에 어떤 여자도 사랑한 적이 없다'는 과거부터 현재까지 사랑한 적이 없다는 의미로 현재와 과거가 연관이 있으므로 현재완료시제를 써서 have never loved another woman, is the only woman I've loved, have never loved another woman before로 옮긴다.

(5) When he arrived at the subway station, the train had already left.

The train was already gone when he arrived at the subway station.

By the time he got to the subway station, the train had already left.

The moment he reached the subway station, he found that the train had left.

- 역에 도착한 것은 과거로 이 때 기차는 이미 떠나고 없었으므로 기차가 떠난 것은 과거보다 이전이므로 과거완료 had left로 옮긴다. 둘째 예문처럼 be동사의 과거형 was 뒤에 자동사의 과거분사 gone을 써서 옮길 수도 있다.
- '기차' train 앞에 정관사 the를 붙인 것은 화자가 그의 청자도 알고 있다고 보는 특정한 기차인 '그 기차'를 가리키기 위한 것이다.

(6) I cannot take your call just now because I am shaving.

I cannot answer your call because I am shaving right now.

I am shaving right now, so I cannot talk with you on the phone.

I cannot talk to you on the phone, because I am shaving right now.

- '지금 면도를 하는 중이어서'는 because I am shaving right now나 I am shaving right now, so ~로 옮긴다. 한국어 문장에서 면도를 하는 것은 현재의 일시적으로 진행 중인 행위이므로 현재진행시제로 옮긴다.
- '전화를 받다'는 take one's call, answer one's call, talk with you on the phone, talk to you

on the phone으로 옮긴다.

(7) It will be his fifth year of lecturing at this school this time next year.

This time next year, he will have been lecturing at this school for five years.

If he goes on lecturing at this school, he will have been lecturing for five years this time next year.

By this time next year, he will have been lecturing at this school for five years.

- '내년 이맘때'는 this time next year, by this time next year로 옮긴다.
- '5년 동안 강의를 하는 셈이 되다'는 내년 이맘때가 5년이 되는 때로 그 때에도 여전히 강의를 하고 있는 중이므로 미래완료시제진행시제 will have been lecturing으로 옮긴다. 또한 단순미래 시제를 써서 will be one's fifth year of lecturing으로 옮길 수도 있다.

(8) I also know that the earth goes around the sun.

I also know that the earth moves round the sun.

I, too, know that the earth revolves around the sun.

I am also aware of the fact that the earth goes around the sun.

- '~의 주위를 돌다'는 go around the sun, move around the sun, revolve around the sun으로 옮긴다. around는 모두 전치사이다.
- '~도 알고 있다'는 also know~나 ~too, know~로 옮기거나 am also aware of~로 옮긴다.

(9) He has been smoking and will smoke even in the future.

He smoked in the past, is smoking now, and will smoke even in the future.

He smoked cigarettes before, he still does, and he will continue to do this in the future.

He was a smoker before, is currently a smoker, and will continue to be a smoker in the future.

- 과거에 담배를 피운 것은 과거의 사실로 단순과거시제 smoked로 나타낸다. 그러나 과거에 피웠고 현재도 피우고 있는 중이라는 의미는 현재완료진행시제 has been smoking으로 옮길 수 있다.
- 셋째 예문의 does는 동사 smoke를 대신하는 대동사이다.

(10) It was while she was studying at her desk for her tests that a thief broke into her house.

While she was at her desk doing studies for her exams, a thief broke into her house.

When she was studying for her exams at her desk, a thief broke into her house.

When she was studying at her desk for her exams, a thief broke into her house.

- '책상에서'는 at one's desk로 옮긴다.
- '시험공부를 하다'는 study for one's tests, do studies for one's exams, study for one's exams로 옮긴다.

- '집에 도둑이 침입하다'는 a thief breaks into one's house로 옮긴다.
- 첫째 예문은 it와 that 사이의 부사절인 while-절을 강조하는 구문이다.

2. (1) a. Practicing English writing every day will enable you to do English composition very well.

b. Your ability in English composition will be improved if you practice writing in English every day.

c. You will be able to do English composition very well if you practice writing in English every day.

d. With daily writing practice in English, you will be able to do English composition very well.

- '영어로 문장을 써 보다'는 practice English writing, practice writing in English, writing practice in English로 옮긴다.
- '영작을 잘하다'는 do English composition well, one's ability in English composition is improved로 옮긴다.

(2) a. Your first book may not turn out as well as you might have wanted.

b. Writing a good book does not always turn out as nicely as you might have thought.

c. It does not always turn out as nicely as you might have thought when you are trying to write a good book.

d. To write a good book does not always turn out as nicely as you might have planned.

- '좋은 책을 쓰다'는 '~의 첫 책'을 의미하는 것으로 보아 one's first book으로 옮기거나 write a good book으로 옮긴다.
- '생각대로 잘 되다'는 turn out as well as~might have wanted, turn out as nicely as~might have thought, turn out as nicely as~might have planned로 옮긴다.

(3) a. Despite the fact that he avoids talking about himself, he likes questioning about others closely.

b. Although he dislikes talking about himself, he likes asking many questions about others.

c. While he is not fond of talking about himself, he is fond of making inquiries about others.

d. He does not like to talk about himself, but he likes to question about others closely.

- '~에 관해서 말하기 싫어하다'는 avoid talking about~, dislike talking about~, be not fond of talking about~, do not like to talk about~으로 옮긴다.
- '캐묻기 좋아하다'는 like questioning~closely, like asking many questions, be fond of making

inquiries, like to question으로 옮긴다.

(4) a. People say that we should take care of our health while we are healthy, and this is truly right.

b. The saying is true that people should take care of their health while they are healthy.

c. It is true that one should take care of his health while he is healthy.

d. You should take care of your health while you are healthy, and this is undeniable.

- 건강 health는 셀 수 없는 명사로 일반적인 의미의 건강은 앞에 한정사를 붙이지 않은 health로 표현한다. 예문에서는 앞에 한정사의 하나인 소유격 our, their, his, your를 붙여 특정한 대상의 건강을 가리킨다.
- '맞는 말이다'는 is truly right, is true, is undeniable로 옮긴다.

(5) a. You must be careful not to get food poisoning because food gets spoiled easily in summer.

b. Food gets spoiled easily in summer; therefore, you must be cautious not to get food poisoning.

c. To prevent getting food poisoning in summer, when food gets easily spoiled, one must be careful.

d. Since food gets spoiled easily in summer, you must be cautious not to get food poisoning.

- '여름에는'은 in summer나 in the summer로 표현하지만 특정한 여름을 가리킬 때는 in the summer를 써야 한다는 데 유의해야 한다.
- '부패하다'는 get spoiled로 옮긴다.
- '식중독'은 food poisoning으로, '식중독에 걸리다'는 get food poisoning으로 옮긴다.

## 제14장 태

### Ⅲ. 심화연습

1. 정답 : a

- 이유 : 예문의 등위접속사 and 뒷 부분은 It is not easy to get this book과 같은 문장에서 진주어인 to-부정사 to get의 목적어인 this book이 가주어 It의 자리로 이동하여 This book is not easy to get이 파생되는 것으로 본다. 따라서 예문에 it이 있으면 비문이 되므로 뺀다.

2. 정답 : d

• 이유 : 타동사의 목적어가 주어가 되면 수동형이 된다. run over의 목적어 자리에 있던 her가 주어자리로 이동하여 주어 she가 되었다. 따라서 run over는 수동형이 되어야 하므로 능동형 running over는 수동형 being run over가 된다.

3. 정답 : c

• 이유 : 종속절에서 타동사 beat의 목적어가 주어 he가 되었으므로 과거완료시제인 능동형 had beaten은 과거완료수동형 had been beaten이 된다.

4. 정답 : d

• 이유 : 동사 bury는 '~을 묻다'는 타동사로 목적어였던 His son이 주어가 되었으므로 능동형 buried는 수동형 was buried가 된다.

5. 정답 : c

• 이유 : '~와 우연히 만나다'는 meet with로 전치사 with의 목적어가 주어가 된 것이 아니므로 동사가 수동태가 되지 않는다. 따라서 were를 뺀다.

6. 정답 : a

• 이유 : '~의 대신에'는 instead of를 쓴다. 동명사 trying이 전치사 of의 목적어가 된다.

7. 정답 : a

• 이유 : 타동사 learn의 목적어 it이 주어가 되었으므로 to-부정사는 수동부정사가 된다. 따라서 능동형 부정사 to learn이 수동형 부정사 to be learned가 된다.

8. 정답 : c

• 이유 : '~하면서'는 분사구문을 사용하여 표현할 수 있다. 따라서 '~라고 주장하면서'는 insisting that~으로 표현할 수 있다. 예문처럼 동사 insist를 등위접속사 and 없이 앞 절과 쉼표로만 연결하면 비문이 된다.

9. 정답 : d

• 이유 : 얼마 전에 some time ago는 명백한 과거를 나타내는 시간 표현이므로 단순과거시제와 쓰인다. 따라서 현재완료수동태를 사용한 has been deeply moved는 수동태의 단순과거형 was deeply moved가 된다.

10. 정답 : c

• 이유 : 동사 escort는 타동사로 뒤에 목적어가 나오기를 요구한다. 따라서 현재분사 escorting 뒤에 앞서 나온 명사구 His car를 가리키는 대명사 it이 필요하다.

## Ⅳ. 기본영작

1. Some people are constantly criticized by others because of their jobs.
   There are people who get constant criticism from others because of their jobs.

Some people are always getting constant criticism from others on account of their jobs.

There are people who are constantly criticized by others due to occupational reasons.

- '직업상'은 '직업 때문에'의 의미로 because of one's job, on account of one's job, due to occupational reasons로 옮긴다.
- '항상'은 constantly, constant~, always로 옮긴다.
- '남에게 비난을 받다'는 be criticized by others, get criticism from others로 옮긴다.

2. In the subway train, a man trod upon her foot.

A man stepped on her foot in the subway train.

Her foot was stepped on by a man in the subway train.

She had her foot stepped on by a man in the subway train.

- '전철 객차 안에서'는 in the subway train으로 옮긴다.
- '한 남자에게 발이 밟히다'는 a man treads upon one's foot, a man steps on one's foot, one's foot is stepped on by a man, have one's foot stepped on by a man으로 옮긴다.
- 주어를 '한 남자' a man, '그녀의 발' her foot, '그녀' she로 두어 작문한다.

3. This car drives well, but it is so expensive that I cannot buy it.

This car runs very well, but it is too expensive for me to afford.

This high performance automobile is too expensive for me to buy.

Although this car drives nicely, I cannot buy it because of its high price.

- '(차가)잘 나가다'는 drive well, run well, high performance~, drive nicely로 옮긴다.
- '너무 비싸서 살 수 없다'는 so expensive that~cannot buy~, be too expensive to buy, cannot buy~because of its high price로 옮긴다.
- 예문의 it은 모두 앞에 나온 명사구 this car를 가리키는 대명사이다.

4. If you walk across the stream, you could get swept away by the strong force of water.

If you cross the stream on foot, you are apt to get washed down by the strong force of flowing water.

If you walk across the stream, you could get washed down by the strong force of flowing water.

The strong force of flowing water may sweep you away, in case you try to walk across the stream.

- '~을 걸어서 건너다'는 walk across~, cross~on foot으로 옮긴다.
- '물살에 휩쓸리다'는 get swept away by the strong force of water, get washed down by the strong force of flowing water, the strong force of flowing water may sweep~away로 옮긴다.

5. Who is that man singing surrounded by a big audience?

A person is singing surrounded by a big audience. Who is he?

Do you know that man who is singing, surrounded by a big audience?

A singer is singing with lots of people around him. Do you know who he is?

- '관중' audience는 관중을 덩어리로 볼 때는 단수취급하고 덩어리 내의 개개인으로 볼 때는 복수 취급한다.
- '~으로 둘러싸여'는 surrounded by~, with lots of people around~로 옮긴다.
- '노래하고 있는'은 현재의 일시적으로 진행 중인 행위이므로 현재진행시제나 현재분사로 옮긴다.

6. A child suddenly ran in front of the car and almost got run over.

A child who suddenly ran in front of the car narrowly escaped being run over.

A young child suddenly came running out in front of the car, and he was almost hit.

A young child was almost hit by the car because he suddenly came running out into the front of it.

- '한 어린아이'는 a child, a young child로 옮긴다.
- '~앞으로 뛰어 나오다'는 run in front of~, come running out in front of~로 옮긴다.
- '치일 뻔하다'는 almost get run over, narrowly escape being run over, be almost hit로 옮긴다.

7. Every monsoon season, the stream overflows in this area and it gets damaged by the flood.

Every year, this region is damaged by the flooded stream in the rainy season.

This area annually gets damaged by the flood because of the overflow of the stream in the rainy season.

In the rainy season, this region is annually damaged by the inundation from the stream.

- '매년 장마철'은 every monsoon season, in the rainy season으로 옮긴다.
- '개울이 범람하다'는 the stream overflows, the flooded stream, the overflow of the stream, the inundation from the stream으로 옮긴다.
- '홍수피해를 입다'는 get damaged by the flood, be damaged by the flooded stream, be damaged by the inundation으로 옮긴다.

8. One should avoid beating a wife and being beaten by her.

Beating a wife and being beaten by her should both be avoided.

Beating your wife and being beaten by her should both be avoided.

You should avoid not only beating your wife, but also being beaten by her.

- '아내를 구타하다'는 beat a wife, beat one's wife로 옮긴다.
- '~에게 구타당하다'는 be beaten by~로 옮긴다.
- '피해야 할 일이다'는 당연함을 나타내는 조동사 should를 써서 should avoid~, should be avoided로 옮긴다.

9. He was respected by many people, but not by his wife.

He was held in respect by many people, but not by his own wife.

Despite the fact that he was respected by many people, he was not respected by his wife.

Although many people respected him, his wife was not one of them.

- '~의 존경을 받다'는 be respected by~, be held in respect by~, ~respect~로 옮긴다.
- '~지만'은 ~, but~으로 옮기거나 despite~로 옮길 수도 있고 양보를 나타내는 접속사를 써서 although~로 옮긴다.
- 넷째 예문의 them은 앞 명사구 many people을 가리키는 대명사이다.

10. Long ago, people were often bitten by mad dogs.

People getting bitten by mad dogs were common long ago.

In old times, it often happened that people were bitten by mad dogs.

In the old days, there were many incidents of people being bitten by mad dogs.

- '옛날에는'은 long ago, in old times, in the old days로 옮긴다.
- '미친개' mad dog은 한국어 문장에서 일반적인 의미의 미친개를 뜻하므로 한정사를 붙이지 않은 복수형 mad dogs로 옮긴다.
- '물리다'는 be bitten, get bitten으로 옮긴다.
- '종종 있다'는 be often~, be common, often happen~, be many~로 옮긴다.

## V. 심화영작

1. (1) The children followed and teased the stranger.

The children followed the stranger and teased him.

The children followed the stranger and made fun of him.

The stranger was followed by the children who were making fun of him.

- '그 이방인'은 화자가 그의 청자도 알고 있다고 보는 대상이며 한 사람이므로 the stranger로 옮긴다.
- '~을 쫓아다니다'는 follow~, be followed by~로 옮긴다.
- '~을 놀리다'는 tease~, make fun of~로 옮긴다.

(2) I saw the two walking out of the movie theater.

I saw both of them coming out of the movie theater.

I saw the two of them coming out of the movie theater.

I saw those two people coming out of the movie theater.

- '그 두 사람'은 the two, both of them, the two of them, those two people로 옮긴다.
- '그 영화관'은 the movie theater로 옮긴다.
- '~에서 나오다'는 walk out of~, come out of~로 옮긴다.

(3) The beggar went into the house to beg, but he was kicked out by the owner.

The beggar went into the house to beg. However, he was turned away by the owner.

The beggar was turned away by the house owner when he went into the house to beg for food.

The beggar went into the house to beg for food, but he was turned away by its owner.

- '그 거지'와 '그 집'은 화자가 그의 청자도 알고 있다고 보는 특정한 한 사람의 거지와 한 집을 가리키므로 정관사를 붙여 the beggar와 the house로 옮긴다.
- '~에 들어가다'는 go into~로 옮긴다.
- '~에게 쫓겨나다'는 be kicked out by~, be turned away by~로 옮긴다.

(4) Despite the fact that he previously failed at his attempt to join the company, he tried again and succeeded.

He was rejected by the company at first, but he tried again and got accepted.

He was not allowed to enter the company at first, but he succeeded in entering it on his second try.

Although he was previously rejected by the company, he tried again and was accepted.

- '그 회사 입사에 실패하다'는 fail at one's attempt to join the company, be rejected by the company, be not allowed to enter the company로 옮긴다.
- '다시 도전하다'는 try again, on one's second try로 옮긴다.
- '입사하다'는 succeed, get accepted, succeed in entering the company, be accepted로 옮긴다.

(5) Despite the hot weather, the library is full of students.

The library is filled with students though it is very hot.

The library is full of students, even though the weather is hot.

There are lots of students in the library regardless of the hot weather.

- '날씨가 더운데도 불구하고'는 despite the hot weather, though it is very hot, even though the weather is hot, regardless of the hot weather로 옮긴다.
- despite는 명사구 the hot weather를 목적어로 가진 전치사이다.
- '~로 가득 차 있다'는 be full of~, be filled with~, there are lots of~로 옮긴다.

(6) He was invited to the party but he did not go to it, because he had previously made other appointments.

He did not go to the party though he was invited, for he had previously made other engagements.

Even though he received an invitation, he did not go to the party due to other appointments.

He was invited to the party, but he did not go there because of previous engagements.

- '초대장'은 '한 통의 초대장'을 가리킬 때는 an invitation으로 옮긴다.
- '초대장을 받다'는 be invited, receive an invitation으로 옮긴다.
- '선약이 있다'는 have previously made other appointments, have previously made other engagements, due to other appointments, because of previous engagements로 옮긴다.

(7) A common person like me cannot afford a BMW because it is so expensive, though it is a nice car.

A BMW is a good car, but a common person like me cannot afford it.

Although a BMW is very nice, a common person like me cannot afford it because it is too expensive.

A BMW drives well, but it is too expensive for a common person like me to buy.

- '(차가)잘나가다'는 be a nice car, be a good car, be very nice, drive well로 옮긴다.
- '나 같은 서민'은 a common person like me로 표현하며 like는 전치사이고 me는 전치사의 목적어이다.
- '살 수가 없다'는 cannot afford~, is too expensive to buy로 옮긴다.

(8) The student's friends told him to be quiet.

The student's friends asked him to be quiet.

The student's friends asked that he be quiet.

The student was asked to be quiet by his friends.

- '조용히 하라고 요청하다'는 tell~to be quiet, ask~to be quiet, ask that~be quiet, be asked to be quiet으로 옮긴다.
- 셋째 예문처럼 요구를 나타내는 동사 ask 뒤에 오는 that-절에서는 동사가 가정법으로 오므로 be를 쓴다. be 대신 조동사 should 뒤에 동사원형을 둔 should be로 쓸 수도 있다.

(9) They can visit the prisoner once every six months.

They can see the prisoner only once every six months.

The prisoner is allowed to meet his visitors once every six months.

They are allowed to make visits to the prisoner once every six months.

- '6개월에 한 번'은 once every six months로 옮긴다. 양화사 every 뒤는 단수명사가 오지만 시간을 나타내는 minute, hour, day, week, month, year가 올 때는 복수명사가 올 수 있으며 이것을 하나의 단위로 본다.
- '그 죄인을 면회하다'는 visit the prisoner, see the prisoner, the prisoner meets his visitors, make visits to the prisoner로 옮긴다.

(10) I was born in the house that my grandfather built, and spent my childhood there.

I was born in the house built by my grandfather and spent the early years of my life there.

I was born in the house that my grandfather made, and I spent my very early days there.

I was born and raised up in the house that my grandfather made when I was very little.

- '할아버지가 지은 집'은 the house that my grandfather built, the house built by my grandfather, the house that my grandfather made로 옮긴다.
- '거기서 어린 시절을 보내다'는 spend one's childhood there, spend the early years of one's life there, spend one's very early days there, be raised up there when~is very little로 옮긴다.

2. (1) a. You need to be very careful not to be looked down on by others.

b. Special care should be taken if you want to be respected by others.

c. It is necessary that you take special care to be respected by others.

d. If you do not want to be disrespected by others, you need to be extra careful.

- '~의 멸시를 당하다'는 be looked down on by~, be disrespected by~로 옮긴다.
- '~하지 않도록'은 not to do~, if~do not want to do~로 옮긴다.
- '특히 주의하다'는 be very careful, special care should be taken, take special care, be extra careful로 옮긴다. extra는 '특별히'라는 부사이다.

(2) a. As soon as he slapped her face, she slapped him back.

b. He slapped her face and she slapped him back right away.

c. Right when she got slapped on the face by him, she slapped him back.

d. She slapped him back right away when she got slapped on the face by him.

- '~에게 뺨을 맞다'는 get slapped on the face by~로 옮긴다.
- '곧'은 '즉시'의 의미이므로 as soon as~, right away, right when~으로 옮긴다.
- '~의 뺨을 때리다'는 slap one's face로 옮기고, '~도 ~의 뺨을 때리다'는 slap~back으로 옮긴다. back은 '되'를 의미하는 부사이다.

(3) a. His place and job are not known.

b. Both his place and job remain a mystery.

c. It is unknown where he lives and what he does.

d. No one knows where he lives and what he does.

- '그가 어디에 사는지'는 '그의 사는 곳'의 의미로 명사구 his place로 옮기거나 간접의문문 where he lives로 옮긴다.
- '무엇을 하는지'는 '그의 직업이 무엇인지'의 의미로 명사구 his job으로 옮기거나 간접의문문 what he does로 옮긴다.

• 셋째 예문의 it은 가주어이고 간접의문문 where~and what~이 진주어이다.

(4) a. One can always find peace of mind from the country view seen through the car window.

b. Seeing a view of the country landscape through the car window, always makes a person peaceful.

c. The view of the country landscape seen through the car window always makes a person find a peaceful state of mind.

d. I always feel peaceful whenever I see a view of the country landscape through the car window.

• '차창 밖으로'는 '차창을 통해'의 의미로 전치사구 through the car window로 옮긴다.
• '시골풍경'은 the country view, the country landscape로 옮긴다.
• '마음을 평온하게 하다'는 find peace of mind, make~peaceful, make~find a peaceful state of mind, feel peaceful로 옮긴다.

(5) a. She heard him going out, but she stayed in bed.

b. Even when she heard him going out, she remained in bed.

c. He was heard going out. However, she continued to stay in bed.

d. Even though she heard him going out, she did not get out of her bed.

• '외출하는 소리가 들리다'는 hear~going out, be heard going out으로 옮긴다.
• '여전히 침대에 누워 있다'는 stay in bed, remain in bed, continue to stay in bed, not get out of one's bed로 옮긴다.
• even when~은 '~할 때조차도'의 의미로 even은 when-절에 초점을 맞추는 초점부사이다.

## 제15장 법

### Ⅲ. 심화연습

1. 정답 : d

• 이유 : 등위접속사 and에 의해 연결된 세 개의 절이 법의 일관성을 유지하지 않고 있다. 첫 번째 절과 두 번째 절은 동사가 각각 turn과 go로 명령법인 데 반해 세 번째 절은 will go로 직설법으로 되어 있다. 따라서 직설법 will go를 앞의 두 절과 같은 명령법 go로 통일하여 법의 일관성을 유지한다.

2. 정답 : c

• 이유 : 명령, 요구, 주장, 제안, 소망을 나타내는 동사 또는 명사가 that-절을 보어로 가질 때 이 절 내에서는 동사의 가정법이 쓰인다. 따라서 요구를 나타내는 동사 required가 that-절을 보어로 가지고 있으므로 이 절 내의 동사는 직설법 과거 answered가 아니라 가정법 answer가 된다.

3. 정답 : d

• 이유 : 등위접속사 and에 의해 연결된 세 개의 절에서 동사의 법이 일관성을 결여하고 있다. 첫 번째 절은 직설법 과거 made, 두 번째 절은 직설법 현재 puts, 세 번째 절은 직설법 과거 washed이다. 따라서 두 번째 절의 동사를 나머지 두 절의 동사처럼 직설법 과거 put으로 바꾸어 법의 일관성을 유지한다.

4. 정답 : a

• 이유 : 현재의 사실은 직설법 현재시제로 나타낸다. 내년 이맘때가 내가 10년 동안 영어공부를 해 오는 셈이 되는 때라는 것은 현재의 사실이다. 따라서 be동사의 가정법 be는 직설법 현재 is가 되어야 한다.

5. 정답 : b

• 이유 : 담배 cigarette은 셀 수 있는 명사로 일반적으로 수의 개념으로 쓰인다. 예문에서는 마치 셀 수 없는 명사처럼 한정사도 붙이지 않고 복수어미도 붙이지 않아 비문이다. 따라서 담배 한 대는 a cigarette으로 표현한다.

6. 정답 : a

• 이유 : 한국어 문장이 명령문이므로 동사의 명령법을 사용한다. 예문의 주절은 일반적으로 명령문에서 생략되는 주어 you가 나와 있을 뿐만 아니라 be동사가 직설법 현재 are로 되어 있다. 따라서 주절의 주어 you를 생략하고 be동사의 직설법 현재 are를 명령법 be로 바꾼다.

7. 정답 : b

• 이유 : 주절동사가 직설법 과거 was recommended로 되어 있으므로 종속절도 과거의 일을 나타내므로 동사 graduate는 가정법 graduate가 아니라 직설법 과거 graduated가 되어야 한다.

8. 정답 : b

• 이유 : 주절동사 begin이 직설법 과거 began이므로 전체 문장은 과거의 사실을 나타낸다. 따라서 종속절도 주절과 같은 과거의 사실을 나타내므로 be동사의 가정법 be가 아닌 직설법 과거 was가 되어야 한다.

9. 정답 : d

• 이유 : 요구를 나타내는 동사 require는 that-절을 보어로 취할 때 이 절 내에서 동사가 가정법으로 온다. 따라서 동사 submit의 직설법 과거 submitted를 가정법 submit으로 바꾼다.

10. 정답 : d

• 이유 : 그의 친구가 도착한 것이 과거이고 이 때 그는 친구를 한 시간 전부터 기다리고 있던 중이었다. 따라서 한 시간 동안 기다리고 있었던 행위는 과거완료진행시제가 되고 그의 친구가 도착한 것은 단순과거시제가 된다. 따라서 과거완료 had arrived는 단순과거 arrived가 된다.

## Ⅳ. 기본영작

1. I am Chul-Su and my friend is Mary.
I am Chul-Su and my friend is called Mary.
My name is Chul-Su and my friend's name is Mary.
They call me Chul-Su and they call my friend Mary.

• '나는 철수이다'는 I am Chul-Su, My name is Chul-Su, They call me Chul-Su로 옮긴다.

• '내 친구는 메리이다'는 My friend is Mary, My friend is called Mary, My friend's name is Mary, They call my friend Mary로 옮긴다. 동사 call은 '~을 ~라고 부르다'는 의미를 전할 때 목적어와 목적보어를 취한다. call my friend Mary에서 my friend가 목적어이고 Mary가 목적보어이다.

2. Although he has never been to any foreign country, he speaks foreign languages very well.
Even though he has never been abroad, he is good at foreign languages.
He has never been to a foreign country, but he speaks foreign languages very well.
He has never been to a foreign country but speaks foreign languages very fluently.

• '어떤 외국'은 any foreign country, abroad, a foreign country로 옮긴다.

• '외국어를 잘하다'는 speak foreign languages very well, be good at foreign languages, speak foreign languages fluently로 옮긴다. foreign languages는 일반적인 의미의 외국어를 뜻한다.

3. I was pressed by her to do her work.
She pushed me to do her work for her.
She insisted on my doing her work for her.
She insisted that I should do her work for her.

• '그녀 대신에'는 '그녀를 위해'의 의미이므로 for her로 옮긴다.

• '~하기를 주장하다'는 동사 press, push, insist를 사용하여 옮길 수 있으며 주장을 나타내는 insist는 that-절을 보어로 가지면 이 절 내의 동사는 가정법으로 와야 한다. should와 동사원형을 대신 쓰기도 한다.

4. The President ordered the ministers to eradicate inhumane crimes.
The President commanded the ministers to get rid of inhumane crimes completely.

The ministers were ordered to root out inhumane crimes by the President.

The President ordered the ministers to cut out the roots of inhumane crimes.

- '장관들'은 한국어 문장에서 일반적인 의미의 장관이라기보다는 대통령의 '그 장관들'의 의미이므로 정관사를 붙여 the ministers로 옮긴다.
- '반인륜적 범죄' inhumane crime은 셀 수 있는 명사로 한국어 문장이 일반적인 반인륜적 범죄를 가리키는 것으로 보아 inhumane crimes로 옮긴다.
- '~을 뿌리 뽑다'는 eradicate~, get rid of~, root out~, cut out the roots of~로 옮긴다.

5. Make sure to turn the engine off, pull the key out, and lock the car doors when you get out of the car.

   When getting out of the car, turn off the engine, remove the key and lock the doors.

   When getting out of the car, turn the engine off, pull the key out, and lock the car doors.

   When you get out of the car, be sure to turn off the engine, remove the key and lock the doors.

- '차에서 내리다'는 get out of the car로 옮긴다.
- '시동을 끄다'는 turn the engine off, turn off the engine으로 옮긴다.
- '열쇠를 빼다'는 pull the key out, remove the key로 옮긴다.
- '문을 잠그다'는 lock the car doors, lock the doors로 옮긴다.
- 한국어 문장은 명령문으로 동사를 turn, remove, lock처럼 명령법으로 옮긴다.

6. When you return from France next year, I will already be married.

   When you return from France next year, I will already have gotten married.

   When you come back from France next year, I will already have been married.

   By the time you return from France next year, I will have been married.

- '이미 결혼해 있을 것이다'는 미래의 기준시점까지의 행위의 완료를 나타내므로 미래완료시제를 써서 will already have gotten married, will already have been married, will have been married로 옮긴다. 또한 첫째 예문처럼 단순미래시제 will already be married를 써서 미래에 대한 예언이나 예측을 하는 문장으로 옮길 수도 있다.

7. The scholar has been spending five years on the same subject.

   Five years have been spent on the same subject by the scholar.

   The scholar has been doing the same research for the past five years.

   The scholar's research has been centered on the same thing for the past five years.

- '5년 동안 해오고 있다'는 과거부터 현재까지 해오고 있는 중이므로 현재완료진행시제 have been spending, have been doing이나 현재완료수동형 have been spent, have been centered로 옮긴다.
- 주어는 '그 학자' the scholar, '5년' five years, '그 학자의 연구' the scholar's research로 옮긴다.

8. When you called yesterday, I was in the shower.
   I was taking a shower when you called me yesterday.
   Yesterday I got your phone call while I was taking a shower.
   It was while I was taking a shower that I received your phone call yesterday.

- '네가 전화했을 때'는 when you called, when you called~, got your phone call while~, received your phone call로 옮긴다.
- '샤워를 하다'는 be in the shower, take a shower로 옮긴다.
- 넷째 예문은 it와 that 사이의 부사절인 while-절을 강조하는 강조구문이다.

9. In case it snows tomorrow, it will have been snowing for three days straight.
   If we get another snowfall tomorrow, we will be having snow for three consecutive days.
   If it snows tomorrow, it will have been snowing for three days in a row.
   If we see snowfall tomorrow, we are going to see it for three straight days.

- '내일 눈이 오면'은 in case it snows tomorrow, if we get another snowfall tomorrow, if it snows tomorrow, if we see snowfall로 옮긴다.
- '3일 동안 눈이 내리는 셈이 될 것이다'는 미래완료진행시제 will have been snowing으로 옮긴다. 미래진행시제 will be having이나 be going to do를 쓸 수도 있다.

10. When I went to my friend's house, he had already gone out.
    By the time I went to my friend's house, he had already gone out.
    I went to my friend's house and soon found that he had gone out.
    As soon as I arrived at my friend's house, I found that he had gone out.

- '친구의 집'은 my friend's house로 옮긴다.
- '~했을 때'는 when~, by the time~, soon~, as soon as~로 옮긴다.
- '이미 외출하고 없었다'는 과거의 기준시점에서 보아 이미 끝나 있었던 일이므로 과거완료시제를 써서 had already gone out으로 옮긴다.

## V. 심화영작

1. (1) You should be careful not to get sunburned when going outside.
   Be cautious of your skin getting sunburned when going outdoors.
   Take care that your skin does not get sunburned when you go out.
   When going outside, be careful not to let your skin get burned by the sun.

- '야외에 나가다'는 go outside, go outdoors, go out으로 옮긴다.
- '피부가 햇볕에 타다'는 get sunburned, one's skin gets sunburned, one's skin gets burned by the sun으로 옮긴다.

- '~하지 않도록 주의하다'는 be careful not to do~, be cautious of~, take care that~으로 옮긴다.

(2) He is smoking outside after having lunch.
After lunch, he is smoking a cigarette outside.
He is smoking outside after he has finished lunch.
He is smoking a cigarette outside after having lunch.

- '점심식사를 하고'는 '점심식사를 한 후에'의 의미로 after having lunch, after lunch, after~have finished lunch로 옮긴다.
- '밖에서'는 부사 outside로 옮긴다.
- '담배를 한 대 피우고 있다'는 피우는 행위가 현재 일시적으로 진행 중에 있다는 의미이므로 현재진행시제 is smoking으로 옮긴다.

(3) The kid pestered his mother to buy him a toy.
The kid insisted that his mother buy him a toy.
The kid persistently asked his mother to buy him a toy.
The kid was being stubborn about his mother buying him a toy.

- '그 꼬마'는 the kid로 옮긴다.
- '장난감'은 '장난감 하나'의 의미로 보아 a toy로 옮긴다.
- '~하기를 고집하다'는 '~해달라고 조르다'는 의미로 동사 pester 뒤에 목적어와 to-부정사를 써서 옮기거나 동사 insist 뒤에 that-절을 써서 옮길 수도 있고 persistently ask~, be being stubborn about~으로 옮길 수도 있다.

(4) About this time tomorrow I will be lying next to my girlfriend on the beach.
Around this time tomorrow, my girlfriend and I will be lying side by side on the beach.
About this time tomorrow, I will be lying on the beach with my girlfriend.
I will be lying on the beach with my girlfriend around this time tomorrow.

- '내일 이맘때는'은 about this time tomorrow, around this time tomorrow로 옮긴다.
- '나의 여자 친구와 누워 있다'는 lie next to my girlfriend, my girlfriend and I lie side by side, lie with my girlfriend로 옮긴다.
- '누워 있을 것이다'는 미래의 일시적으로 진행 중인 행위이므로 미래진행시제 will be lying으로 옮긴다.

(5) Be cautious not to get mosquito bites and not to eat spoiled food in summer.
In summer, be careful not to get mosquito bites and not to eat spoiled food.
You should be careful not to get mosquito bites and not to eat spoiled food in summer.
In the summer, be careful not to get bitten by mosquitos and not to eat spoiled food.

- '모기에 물리다'는 get mosquito bites, get bitten by mosquitos로 옮긴다.

- '상한 음식을 먹다'는 eat spoiled food로 옮긴다.
- 첫째, 둘째, 넷째 예문은 명령법 be를, 셋째 예문은 당연함이나 의무를 나타내는 조동사 should를 사용하여 작문한 것이다.

(6) The doctor told her to stop both smoking and drinking for her unborn child.

The doctor said to her, "You'd better quit smoking and drinking for the baby inside your womb."

The doctor told her to quit smoking and drinking for the baby inside her womb.

She was told to quit smoking and drinking by the doctor for the baby she was expecting.

- '뱃 속의 아이를 위해'는 for one's unborn child, for the baby inside one's womb, for the baby ~is expecting으로 옮긴다.
- '담배와 술을 끊다'는 stop both smoking and drinking, quit smoking and drinking으로 옮긴다.
- 둘째 예문은 직접화법의 문장으로 옮긴 것이다.

(7) His mother asked him to take the package to his relative's home.

His mother asked him to deliver the package to his relative's house.

His mother requested that he deliver the package to his relative's house.

He was asked to deliver the parcel to his relative's house by his mother.

- '꾸러미' package는 셀 수 있는 명사로 한국어 문장에서는 특정한 꾸러미 하나를 말하므로 the package로 옮긴다.
- '그의 친척집'은 his relative's home, his relative's house로 옮긴다.
- '~하길 요구하다'는 동사 ask, request를 사용해 옮길 수 있으며 셋째 예문의 request 뒤의 that-절에서 동사 deliver는 가정법으로 쓰인 것이다.

(8) When he arrived at the swimming pool, many people were happily swimming.

As soon as he arrived at the swimming pool, he saw lots of people swimming about pleasantly.

Many people were enjoying a swim when he arrived at the swimming pool.

He found a lot of people joyfully swimming about the moment he arrived at the pool.

- '수영장' swimming pool은 화자가 그의 청자도 알고 있다고 보는 수영장을 가리키는 것으로 보아 the swimming pool로 옮긴다.
- '즐겁게 수영을 하고 있었다'는 과거의 일시적으로 진행 중인 행위이므로 과거진행시제로 were happily swimming, were enjoying a swim으로 옮기거나 현재분사를 써서 swimming about pleasantly, joyfully swimming about으로 옮긴다.

(9) He asked that his life be spared, and said that he would remember the favor.

He begged that his life be saved, and added that he would never forget the favor.

"Please spare my life," he asked. Then, he said, "I will always remember this debt of gratitude."

He asked to have his life spared, and said that he would always remember the favor.

- '목숨을 살려주다'는 one's life be spared, one's life be saved, spare one's life, have one's life spared로 옮긴다.
- '~해 달라고 청하다'는 ask that~, beg that~, ~ask, ask to do~로 옮긴다. ask와 beg 뒤의 that-절에서 be는 be동사의 가정법이다.
- '은혜를 잊지 않다'는 remember the favor, never forget the favor, remember this debt of gratitude로 옮긴다.

(10) The commander ordered his subordinates to get the people who stole arms and ammunitions as soon as possible.

The commander demanded that his men catch the criminals who took others' arms and ammunitions as soon as possible.

The commander's order for his subordinates was to get the people who stole arms and ammunitions as soon as possible.

The commander ordered his followers to catch the robbers who took the arms and ammunitions as soon as possible.

- '부하들'은 his subordinates, his men, his followers로 옮긴다.
- '총기탈취범들'은 특정한 여러 명의 총기탈취범을 뜻하므로 정관사를 붙여 the people who stole arms and ammunitions, the criminals who took others' arms and ammunitions, the robbers who took the arms and ammunitions로 옮긴다.
- '~을 잡다'는 동사 get~이나 catch~로 옮긴다.

2. (1) a. His diligence will surely bring him success.

b. His success is sure, because he is industrious.

c. He will certainly succeed because he is diligent.

d. I am sure that he will succeed because of his diligence.

- '그는 부지런하므로'는 his diligence, because he is industrious, because he is diligent, because of his diligence로 옮긴다.
- '반드시'는 surely, be sure, certainly로 옮긴다.
- '성공하다'는 bring~success, one's success is sure, succeed로 옮긴다.

(2) a. Lack of exam time made him fail the exam.

b. Due to lack of exam time, he failed in the exam.

c. He failed the exam because he did not have enough exam time.

d. It was because he was not given enough exam time that he failed the exam.

- '시험시간이 모자라'는 lack of exam time, due to lack of exam time, because~do not have enough exam time, because~is not given enough exam time으로 옮긴다.
- '그 시험에 떨어지다'는 fail the exam, fail in the exam으로 옮긴다.
- 넷째 예문은 부사절인 because-절을 강조하는 it~that~ 강조구문이다.

(3) a. You can feel tired more easily because of extended activity hours, which are the result of the longer daylight.

b. The longer daylight results in extended activity hours, and this can make your body be tired more easily.

c. Your body is apt to get easily tired from the extended activity hours, which result from the longer daylight.

d. The hours of activity are extended because of the longer daylight, and this can subsequently make your body be tired more easily.

- '낮이 길어져'는 the result of the longer daylight, the longer daylight, from the longer daylight, because of the longer daylight로 옮긴다.
- '활동시간이 늘어남에 따라'는 because of extended activity hours, result in extended activity hours, from the extended activity hours, the hours of activity are extended로 옮긴다.

(4) a. I am sure you will excel in English composition if you study it every day just like you have your daily meals.

b. English composition will be mastered if you practice it every day as you eat every day.

c. Your daily practice of English composition just as you eat every day will surely make you be good at it.

d. You will excel in English composition, if you study it every day just as you have meals.

- '매일 식사를 하듯이'는 just like you have your daily meals, as you eat every day, just as you eat every day, just as you have meals로 옮긴다.
- '잘하다'는 excel, be mastered, be good at으로 옮긴다.
- 주어를 '나' I, '영작' English composition, '너의 매일의 영작연습' your daily practice of English composition, '너' you로 두어 옮길 수 있다.

(5) a. His foreign languages are very good, so he has no trouble communicating with foreigners.

b. Because of his good foreign language skills, he has no trouble communicating with foreigners.

c. He is good at foreign languages, so he does not have any trouble communicating with foreigners.

d. Good foreign language skills make it possible for him to communicate with foreigners with no difficulty.

- '외국어' foreign language는 셀 수 있는 명사로, '한 외국어'는 a foreign language이고 일반적인 의미의 외국어는 foreign languages이다.
- '~와 의사소통을 하다'는 communicate with~로 옮긴다.
- '~하는 데 전혀 문제가 없다'는 have no trouble -ing, do not have any trouble -ing, make it possible to do~로 옮긴다.

## 저자 약력

한국외국어대학교 대학원 영어과 박사과정 졸업(문학박사: 영어학전공)
한국외국어대학교 영어과 강사
성공회대학교 영어과 강사

# 기초를 잡아주는 영작문

초 판 1쇄 인쇄 / 2007년 12월 10일
초 판 1쇄 발행 / 2007년 12월 15일

저자 정용권
발행처 형설출판사
서울 종로구 통의동 7-33 · 전화 (02) 738-6052～4 · 팩시밀리 (02) 736-7134
대구광역시 북구 노원 3가 303-1 · 전화 (053) 425-2811～4 · 팩시밀리 (053) 425-7315
발행인 장지익
등록 라-제9호 · 1962년 5월 1일
홈페이지 http://www.hyungseul.co.kr
e-mail hs@hyungseul.co.kr



정가 15,000원

ISBN 978-89-472-3197-8 93740